The QUEEN MOTHER

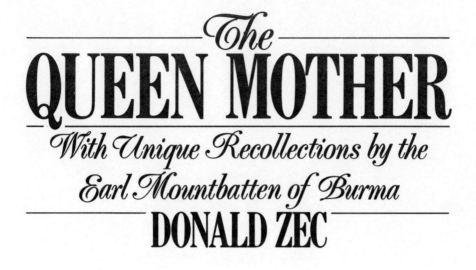

The
QUEEN MOTHER

With Unique Recollections by the
Earl Mountbatten of Burma

DONALD ZEC

SIDGWICK & JACKSON
LONDON

Remembering Leah

First published in Great Britain in 1990 by Sidgwick & Jackson Limited

Copyright © 1990 by Donald Zec

ISBN 0 283 99921 7

Typeset by Rowland Phototypesetting Limited
Bury St Edmunds, Suffolk
Printed by Mackays of Chatham plc, Chatham, Kent
for Sidgwick & Jackson Limited
1 Tavistock Chambers, Bloomsbury Way
London WC1A 2SG

Contents

Contents

Acknowledgments

The Queen Mother's formidable age and substantial life as our most popular royal makes her a subject rarely out of print. But though it is well-tilled soil, no new biography can ignore the valuable explorations of earlier prospectors. These include, of course, the biographies of others whose lives were inextricably linked to the Queen Mother's. All the books I have consulted are listed in the Bibliography and I gladly acknowledge my indebtedness to them. My apologies for any omissions. In addition I wish to thank the following for sharing their reminiscences: Lord Callaghan of Cardiff; Michael Foot MP and Mrs Foot (Jill Craigie); Ruth, Lady Fermoy; Lieutenant-Colonel Sir Martin Gilliat; Lord Home of the Hirsel; Michael Oswald CVO; Mr and Mrs Fulke Walwyn; The Rt. Hon The Lord Wilson of Rievaulx . . . and those others who preferred not to be identified. I am grateful to Len Greener, Picture Editor, and the excellent Library personnel of the *Daily Mirror* for their customary goodwill in making research material and pictures freely available. I am also obliged to the University of Reading Library for their kind assistance regarding the Astor Archive.

Introduction

On Friday, 13 September 1940, King George VI and the Queen, now the Queen Mother, motored from Windsor to London arriving at Buckingham Palace in the middle of an air raid. The day was overcast and it was raining. Upstairs in a small sitting room they could hear over the wail of the sirens the roar of diving aircraft. The windows were open, giving them a royal circle's view of the quadrangle. A single German bomber had detached itself from the formation flying along the Mall towards the Palace. Seconds later, the royal couple saw two bombs fall less than a hundred yards away. They ran into the corridor as four more bombs fell. Large craters disfigured the quadrangle. What had been the Chapel was a shambles of rubble, broken glass and shattered pews. The single item salvaged was the old family Bible which recorded the births, marriages and deaths in the Royal Family over several generations. Its significance, at that precise moment, was not lost on the Queen. Nor was the realization of how close she and the King had been to serious injury if not death. As Churchill would write years later, 'I must confess that at that time neither I nor any of my colleagues were aware of the peril of this particular incident. Had the windows been closed instead of open, the whole of the glass would have splintered into the faces of the King and Queen, causing terrible injuries.' Shortly afterwards when the 'all clear' sounded the Queen went to her study. She wrote two letters. They were addressed to the two princesses Elizabeth and Margaret, and sealed, with instructions that they be opened only on her death. It is not necessary to be a mother to speculate on some of the thoughts the then Queen might have wanted to share with her daughters. The dominant theme, of course, would have been love since this has always been the generating current of their lives, in contrast to the norms of previous royal matchmaking in which pedigree counted for more than passion. And so those two letters were locked away, happily outlived by their author for nearly fifty years. We shall never know their contents. Whatever other queens may have done in the past – or might do in the future – the Queen Mother has never 'gone public' about herself, even less about others close to her. But if we don't know the substance of those two 'moment of truth' letters, we can at least focus on their author.

There has never been a 'royal' who has lived through so much but said so little about the lives she has influenced and the major crises she has defused in her triple role as a wise mother, understanding grannie, and elder statesperson to the entire royal family. Still, not even this apparently shrinking violet of the monarchy can conceal the considerable impact she has made upon her times; or prevent others – I include three former Prime Ministers and the late Earl Mountbatten – from revealing the glint of steel behind the cosy 'Queen Mum' image. And what a dossier! There is one statistic alone which even the most stubborn anti-royalist might find it hard not to cheer.

The Queen Mother will be ninety on 4 August 1990. The occasion will not be lost on the media or the British people, with whom this remarkable lady has shared the longest-running love affair of the century. It has compelled the relevant authorities to think the unthinkable. Secret rehearsals were conducted in June 1988 for the Queen Mother's eventual state funeral. Anticipating a massive display of public mourning, units from the BBC, the Armed Forces and the Metropolitan Police staged – late at night and at dawn – a run-through of the solemn formalities complete with a funeral cortège and gun carriage along the deserted streets of London. Just in case news of that morbid display should catch the Queen Mother at a wrong moment, it was decided to tell her what was going on. She was, according to the intelligence at the time, 'tickled pink'. More, she wanted to know 'how things were going' and were they interested in any suggestions? That alone, you might think, stamps her as a royal 'original'.

For while the Queen, deservedly, is universally admired as a thoroughly professional and dedicated monarch, her mother has achieved a special affinity with millions of ordinary people, and sustained it for more than half a century. She was once called the greatest queen since Cleopatra, which must have amused her. She has also been described as a magnificent actress, a compliment that has a double edge. For it implies a marked contrast between the private woman and the royal 'performance'. Which of course must be partly true. While the everyday rituals of the royal folk may not be soap opera, images have to be sustained and myths perpetuated – the basics of good theatre. What distances the Queen Mother from the rest of the 'cast', however, is that she manifestly enjoys what she is doing right down to the last soft-gloved handshake.

Royals, like other famous people, view celebrity in profoundly different ways. To Arthur Miller, influenced no doubt by the tragedy of his wife, Marilyn Monroe, it is 'just another form of loneliness'. The late Onassis, appropriately for a Greek christened Aristotle, accepted it philosophically: 'If you're going to be raped you might as well lie back and enjoy it.' The late President Kennedy used it brilliantly as a political gambit, but also as a fig leaf behind which he was as flawed as any other restless heterosexual. Her Majesty the Queen cares little for it. She does her job. Yet the work is often more than merely demanding, it can be deadly tedious. Nevertheless she will do everything that is required of her – and more. These varying attitudes have one thing in common – the public knows what is real and what is ritual. And in this respect the Queen Mother carries the Gold Seal of Approval. One admiring Frenchman, at some familiar ceremony, put it well: 'She seems to have discovered an entirely new occupation!' And her enjoyment of it was something the crowd could see, and share. 'Have you noticed,' a guest at Clarence House once said, 'that when the Queen comes into a room everyone stiffens and backs away to the wall, and when the Queen Mother is there, they light up?' (To be fair a reigning monarch is bound to inspire more awe than a superannuated grannie everybody knows as the Queen Mum.)

Unquestionably, then, this serene and unruffled lady is the best-loved 'royal' of them all. But behind that famous smile under the oyster-shell hat there is an awesome will which intimates as well as strangers confront at their peril. (Offenders, as we will hear from an unimpeachable source, are not royally scolded, just rendered temporarily mute by a fleeting glance of exquisitely confided displeasure.) Her formidable strength, like the base of an iceberg, lies beneath the surface, and demands the same prudent navigation. That strength has not merely taken

Her Majesty sublimely through her challenging roles as the daughter-in-law, sister-in-law, wife and mother of four successive monarchs. It carried this sheltered Bruton Street beauty through two World Wars; the destructive fall-out from the Abdication; two episodes of critical surgery; and, more crucially, kept royalty afloat, albeit pitching awhile, during the squally episodes of Princess Margaret's controversial love affairs and ill-fated marriage. Moreover, the fact that the British Monarchy has survived the self-indulgent eccentricities of some of its more extrovert members, remained all of apiece in this age of Spitting Image, 'Naff Off!' and similar diversions, owes much to the unruffled chatelaine of Clarence House. She has, smiling benignly over the shoulder of the Queen, helped to keep the family business not just a going concern, but flourishing. The media, more and more, regard the royal family as a legitimate target for parody, with some involuntary assistance from a couple of the leading players themselves. But when it comes to the Queen Mother, hostilities cease. Intuitively, editors, TV producers, columnists and other marksmen hold their fire when Her Majesty saunters into view. Though most of the royal family have been mercilessly lampooned, the attack stumbles hopelessly in the case of the Queen Mother. To pull it off, the performer must have the courage of his or her convictions. But midway along the road their nerve fails. The target is missed. And for sure, the loyal public has snorted indignantly away. You may poke fun at the Queen's stilted delivery, at Philip's prickly asides to the media, Fergie's St Trinian giggles, and Charles's misanthropic eyebrows. But you can't take on That Smile. As with everything else between the feathered hat and the sensible shoes, it is as impervious to satire as Glamis, the family castle, was to centuries of Scottish winters. For more than sixty years the Queen Mother has enjoyed a kind of diplomatic immunity which perhaps the Queen, and certainly Prince Philip, might envy. But then it is difficult to feel upstaged by an imperial great-grandmother who keeps her own racing ticker-tape machine near the Upper Stairway at Clarence House, and whose butler arrives with the Racing Calendar neatly folded on a silver salver. This intriguing mix of queenship and the sport of kings is clearly reflected in her public image – part Gainsborough Lady, part Pearly Queen, that common touch enhanced by a visibly broken tooth and a handbag that wouldn't look out of place on the back of a supermarket trolley.

'Where do you live?' she once (as Queen) asked a Londoner.

'Back of 'arrods Mum. And where do you live?'

'Oh . . . (pause) . . . back of Gorringes (in those days a store behind Buckingham Palace).'

It takes a special adroitness to chat to jockeys or to the smaller fry at the Royal Households, putting them at their ease yet subtly remaining distanced. Apart, but not aloof. Bagehot's stern dictum on the monarchy that 'they must not let light in on magic' couldn't have envisaged a 'royal' as sure-footed as the mother of the Queen. Sometimes at her Castle of Mey in Scotland she comes in from fishing or tending flowers and sits with the staff watching television. As one of them remarked, 'She doesn't treat us like servants, more like broken-down toffs.' So as we would expect, the visitors' book at Clarence House reflects a wide-ranging list of friends and acquaintances of all types and income levels. (The shrewd among them are alert to her weakness for soft-centred chocolates, snappy dogs, horse-talk and juicy gossip.) 'Dishing the dirt' was the mandatory pastime of the cloche-hatted debs of the twenties. Sixty years on it still brings a gleam to the Queen Mother's eye. The late Daphne du Maurier discovered this on a visit to Balmoral. The Queen Mother asked her what she was writing. The distinguished author hedged a little, then finally admitted that it was a novel about her great-great-grandmother, Mary Anne Clarke, mistress of George III's second son, Frederick, Duke of York. The face of the former Duchess of York 'positively glowed' with mischief. 'Put it all in,' she insisted. 'Don't leave anything out.'

This response is typical of the paradox in the Queen Mother; at times more 'royal' than them all, then head back, leading everyone in the chorus of 'Let's All Go Down the Strand . . . 'ave a banana!' Lady Thelma Furness, the long-suffering but ultimately rejected 'companion' of the Duke of Windsor, recalling an ice-skating session with the then Duchess of York, wrote: 'The lovely face of the Duchess, her superb colouring heightened by the cold, her eyes wrinkled with the sense of fun that was never far below the surface, made a picture I shall never forget. I remember thinking at the time that if ever I had to live in a bungalow in a small town, this is the woman I would most like to have as a next-door neighbour to gossip with while hanging out the washing in our backyards.' (This generous tribute must have a slight sense of guilt behind it. It was Lady Furness who, perhaps naïvely, introduced Wallis Simpson to the frisky Prince of Wales when she herself was heavily involved with him, and in doing so turned the Duchess of York's world on its head.)

So there are these two images: a royal 'goddess' by, say, Cecil Beaton, and a happy garden fence companion straight out of *Coronation Street*. Both equally appealing. Which image you are likely to encounter on any given day depends entirely on the whim of the lady herself. A puzzled governor-general asked her once in East Africa why she preferred to go on long journeys by car, and unaccompanied. 'Because,' Her Majesty smiled, 'that's the only way I can kick my shoes off, put my feet up, and eat as much butterscotch as I want.' You cannot be more reasonable than that. 'Without Fear or Favour' is basic to her scheme of things. Her friendliness towards Lord Callaghan, the former Labour Prime Minister, says more than his anecdotes reveal. As the mother of the Queen to Margaret Thatcher's government, socializing with socialists may not be the 'done thing'. But we all know – or learn – that the 'done thing' for the Queen Mother is what she wants to do. The coolness commentators have referred to between the Queen and Mrs Thatcher will not have escaped the Queen Mother's notice. The Prime Minister's 'we are a grandmother now' must have induced delicious amusement over the great-grannie's five o'clock G and T at Clarence House. Some years earlier, Michael Foot MP, the then Labour Leader, caused a furore (sensationalized by the tabloids) by wearing a kind of storm-proof jacket at the Armistice Day ceremony in Whitehall. The ritual dress for the Cenotaph is a long dark overcoat. It is doubtful whether Mr Foot, who loves tramping the Welsh hills, possesses one. He is not one to follow fashion. And in any event, as a fervent patriot and one of the few outspoken critics of the Munich surrender, he saw no need to wear a 'uniform' to show his respect for the war dead. The nasty campaign in the press astonished him, and hurt his wife, Jill. They had both met the Queen Mother on several occasions, mutually enthusiastic about dogs, flowers, and Constitutional history, probably in that order. Not long after the Cenotaph incident she sought Michael out at a public function. 'I must tell you,' she said, not exactly in a whisper, 'I liked that coat you wore. I thought it was a very nice coat.' She did not add, 'So there!' but her eyes implied it.

To what extent the public's perception of her matches the real individual behind the media image, is the question that has to be answered. All witnesses deserve to be heard, even those whose testimony is, perhaps unavoidably, delivered on bended knee. But it is not difficult to distinguish between the deferential noises of a dutiful palace subordinate, and the genuine article from a time-serving confidant. I expected the Queen Mother's Private Secretary, Sir Martin Gilliatt, to anoint Her Serene Majesty with fairly uncritical admiration. He has been her friend, advisor, troubleshooter, and racing guru for more than a quarter of a century. And yet there was something touchingly authentic in this unsolicited testimonial: 'I have worked for many different bosses but there's never been anybody like her. Never a day that I don't thank the Almighty for my good fortune.'

There has to be another side to the coin, of course. It would be no compliment to her stern Scottish ancestry to suggest that the Queen Mother doesn't have a cutting edge and a powerful disdain for those who offend her, or more crucially, rock the royal boat. There has been no shortage of such high dramas in her seventy adult years. The most significant, perhaps, was her confrontation with Wallis Simpson, the late Duchess of Windsor. That chillingly polite affair is best examined in the context of the events at the time. But even if there'd been no Abdication and the two had met socially, they would not, it is fair to assume, have become soul-mates. There could have been no instant rapport between a twice-divorced American socialite besotted by jewellery and flattering attention, and a rigorously sheltered Scottish aristocrat raised on all the conventional virtues. What she really thought of Wallis Simpson is a question which the Queen Mother is content to leave to the speculation of others. (The Duchess of Windsor, as we will see, showed a little less reticence, choosing her venom with care.) I asked Lord Home, an old friend of the Bowes-Lyon family and of the Queen Mother's, how he thought she found the whole episode. 'Distasteful' was his chosen word.

When news reached her that His Majesty King Edward VIII of Great Britain, Ireland and the British Dominions Beyond the Seas had just been spotted painting his mistress's toenails, the fair Elizabeth delicately bayed the moon. She must have imagined how her late and tyrannical father-in-law, George V, let alone his Lady Bracknell-type consort, Queen Mary, might have reacted to the scene. No intention here to present the Queen Mother – admittedly born when Victoria was still alive and moping – as a prude with all that old dragon's priggish obsessions. All the evidence points to precisely the opposite. Considering her many sadnesses, including a brutally premature bereavement and the assault of serious illnesses, the Queen Mother's soaring fun quotient is close to astonishing. Retracing the steps way back to her emergence as a deb to be reckoned with, is as rewarding as it is revealing. She has a limitless curiosity and a zesty inclination to try any experience short of Commando training or Arctic exploration. She flew through the sound barrier on Concorde at an age when most self-respecting grannies are seated over their petit-point with a blanket on their knees. On her 85th birthday to be precise. Pushing sixty, she was the first member of the royal family to fly around the world. And the first to fly in a helicopter. A glance through the Court Circular of recent months reveals no let-up in the Queen Mother's energy and concern for 'earning her keep'. That is part of her motivation. The rest is an inexhaustible interest in life and living.

She knows a great deal about subjects not strictly demanded in the curriculum vitae of royalty. Long ago a young American film producer, Frederick Zollo, found himself taken along to a Buckingham Palace tea party. The Queen Mother paused to speak to him. They talked about America, Watergate, then went on to discuss films and literature. She asked him what he'd read by John Steinbeck. He said, with some relief, that he had read *The Grapes of Wrath*. 'Of course,' she smiled. 'But not *Cannery Row, Of Mice and Men, East of Eden. . .*?' He mumbled his regrets and was instantly put at his ease by a smile no ice-cap would survive. The conversation continued about American life, the places she had visited. Officials gently tried to steer her away. And found themselves clutching an immovable elbow. 'Just a moment,' she insisted, 'I wish to continue speaking to this handsome young American.' Fifteen years have passed but the memory of that episode, he says with evident admiration, is as vivid, and as sunny, as the day it happened. But then the Queen Mother, a veteran of countless encounters with visiting celebrities at royal premières, well knows the spell she casts upon them. I have witnessed moguls, verbal terrorists to a man, reduced to weak-kneed gush and blushes, face-on to the radiance of Her Majesty. Even Shirley McLaine, that cool articulate opponent of the Establishment, couldn't resist saying publicly after meeting the Queen Mother: 'She has the face of an angel. When I look into those wonderful eyes of hers it gave me such a feeling of peace. . . .'

This then is the dilemma of the Queen Mother's biographers: steering a middle course between unabashed hagiography and, say, the feline taunts of Penelope Mortimer in her book, *Queen Elizabeth: A Life of the Queen Mother*. The problem is compounded by other frustrations. Her Majesty, following protocol, and, to her, a disastrous encounter with a reporter more than sixty-five years ago, gives no interviews. The offending story, as we will see when we come to it, was no more than the trilling excitement of a happy young woman on her engagement. The stern rebuke this brought from the Palace at the time (1923) apparently sealed her lips for ever. (That self-denying ordinance has not extended to the present Duchess of York who following the birth of her first child giggled, 'I can't wait to have another one – and practising is rather fun, isn't it?') Quite harmless of course, and it's doubtful if it disturbed the olive in the Queen Mother's evening cocktail. But there are signs that the new generation of 'royals' – Prince Charles in particular – are restlessly tearing at their straitjackets. On 14 May 1989, in an interview transmitted on American TV, Charles complained of having to plan his life six to nine months ahead. 'I try terribly hard not to set my life in concrete, but that's what happens.' The interviewer, former 'News at Ten' presenter, Selina Scott, asked him if that meant he felt trapped. Charles obligingly took the bait with an instant, 'Oh yes, very much.' He went on: 'I look around and I see so many in far less fortunate positions than I am, and I feel, "Here am I in this position. What can I do to the best of my ability to improve their lot?"' Significantly, the interview will not be screened on British TV. Charles insisted on that. We can understand his reasons. It would embarrass the Queen who has had to bite on that bullet in all her years as the monarch. And it would also perplex the grandmother he respects and adores. Yet I doubt if the Queen Mother has ever felt disadvantaged by royalty's vow of silence. Occasionally she will speak out against hardhearted officialdom and, as the record will show, get a homeless unfortunate re-housed, or maybe a hospital ward kept open.

But mostly, the Queen Mother holds her cards very close to her maternal bosom. As Dorothy Laird, who produced the most fragrantly effusive biography of all, revealed, 'The Queen Mother dislikes all things being known about her at all times and will keep little, inconsequential matters secret even from her own Household.' Her intimates respect this and in the manner of the Mafia's sacred ceremony of 'omerta' would happily fuse the blood of their cut wrists to prove it. What makes the Queen Mother such an intensely fascinating public figure is her genius for survival – on her own terms. Royal families are an increasingly endangered species. Many of them have sunk into oblivion over the years, dismissed as irrelevant, or as expensive anachronisms. The late ex-King Farouk of Egypt read the cards correctly when he told our ambassador in Cairo in 1951: 'Soon there will be only five kings left, the kings of England, Diamonds, Hearts, Spades and Clubs.' A year later, King George VI died. What Farouk said of kings applies equally to queens. Ours, today, could scarcely have had a better role-model than her mother. In a sugar mountain of superlatives attached to the Queen Mother, 'jewel in the crown' is the current favourite. To switch metaphors, there have been several attempts to trap this veteran butterfly under glass, the better to examine the secret of its longevity and the source of its restless energy. But when we think we're getting close, she has soared off into some new and exciting dimension. Robert Lacey, the much-favoured royal biographer, went further than most, describing the woman he called 'the mother of the nation' as being 'sensuous, flirtatious even'. True she was much younger then. Eighty-seven.

Archive material was helpful. Talking to those who know her intimately was obviously essential since, as we've established, the Queen Mother is uncommunicative with the media. I am much obliged to the Turf's most popular double, Fulke and Cathy Walwyn, who train the Queen Mother's horses at their Lambourn, Berkshire stables. Dubbed steeplechasing's First Lady, the Queen Mother will, according to the Walwyns, stand in her mackintosh and wellies with the rain coming down in stair-rods, the wind threatening to lift all five feet two of her over the Members' Stand, just for the thrill of seeing the horses hammering towards the fences. She did so at sixty . . . seventy . . . eighty, and God willing, will do so at ninety. The Walwyns assured me she is not particularly interested in starting prices and doesn't fret when her horse comes nowhere. But when she does have a big win it is cocktail time at Clarence House with everybody who played a part in it invited over to celebrate.

Sir Martin Gilliat, her Private Secretary, spoke to me with the authority and insight of a long-standing friend and racing companion over three decades. I am grateful to him for his comments on the Queen Mother and life at Clarence House.

Ladies-in-waiting are, by definition, bound to speak favourably of those they serve. But five minutes in the cultivated presence of Ruth, Lady Fermoy would convince anyone that she spoke from no particular brief but from her heart. Much wisdom, compassion, and wit are evident in this elegant widow who studied with Cortot in Paris, and now tinkles melodious accompaniment to the Queen Mother's Cole Porter songs at the Castle of Mey. But I owe particular thanks to the late Lord Mountbatten. He knew the Queen Mother when as the young Elizabeth Bowes-Lyon she was strenuously courted by his friend the late King George VI. Lord Louis, as shipmate and personal friend of the Duke of York, was the couple's closest confidant. He observed with delight as his royal chum and Lady Elizabeth fell in love and married. When they were propelled by the Abdication into becoming King and Queen, he watched her with warm admiration mould a faltering stand-in into a star. 'I saw it all happen,' he said. His reflections on those years and after are both intimate and authoritative. But there were ground rules, set out with the clarity and precision we would expect from the distinguished statesman and wartime's Supreme Commander S.E. Asia.

'Now look, I don't mind speaking absolutely freely. All I want is such part of what you write as is based upon what I tell you, you show me first and let me muck it about. For two reasons; I don't always make myself quite clear and secondly, you may misinterpret or misunderstand what I wanted to say. And finally, although I don't mind your quoting me within reason, it doesn't want to involve me too much.' I was happy to oblige him. In navigating the uncertain waters surrounding royalty, having Mountbatten's hand close to the tiller was worth a hundred 'un-named sources close to the Palace'. His final stipulation reveals much humility behind the dashing, gallant sailor image. His wish 'not to involve me too much' was to avoid even the remotest suggestion that he was exploiting his friendship with the Royal Family, particularly the Queen. That notion was inconceivable. As Prince Charles declared in a recent broadcast, 'He was, in essence, the centre of the family.' Despite that, in this exercise at least, Lord Mountbatten preferred to be in the wings rather than centre stage. 'One of the most remarkable ladies of the century', was how he judged the Queen Mother. An assessment which inspired both this book and its title.

1

August 1900 seems to have been as typical a month as any in the idiosyncratic history of the British Empire. The Boxer Rebellion had been crushed at Peking. It rained buckets on Bank Holiday. The Boer War was going so well, a smart ape taught to sound an alarm bell during the Siege of Mafeking was brought triumphantly home under escort to be ceremoniously saluted by senior officers, though a march past was ruled inappropriate. It was subsequently sold at auction for forty-two guineas but it pined for Mafeking and died soon after. Scotland's usually dour broadsheet, the *Forfar Herald*, announced for 'One Night Only' at the town's Reid Hall, Miss Lilly Mowbray's original London Company in 'The Joking Girl' – 'It Starts with a Laugh and Ends With A Yell'. (Small beer compared with the first performance of *Tosca* which Puccini, then only forty-two, had brought to London before fluttering into *Madame Butterfly*.) Not far away at Balmoral, Queen Victoria was taking her last sad look at the distant Grampians before her death one year later. Yet oddly, what the *Forfar Herald* – or any other newspaper at that time – did not record was the happy event which occurred that Saturday, 4 August, at some indeterminate hour, at an unspecified place, with unidentified persons in attendance. The birth, in fact, of Lady Elizabeth Angela Marguerite Bowes-Lyon, ninth child of Lord and Lady Glamis. And here we have a mystery; one of the more intriguing skeletons in the Queen Mother's cupboard.

Until the Queen Mother's eightieth birthday nearly ten years ago, the Bowes-Lyon home at St Paul's Walden Bury, Herts, was officially recognized as the place where she was born. It then emerged, courtesy of a ferreting parishioner, that local records were inaccurate. And the Wedgwood plaque in the twelfth-century church of St Paul's Walden which proclaims that the Queen Mother was born in the parish, perpetuates the error. Her birth certificate, dated even more oddly, 21st September 1900 – four days over the legal limit set for registering a birth – compounds the mystery. We know now that the Queen Mother was born in London, probably at her parents' Grosvenor Gardens apartment. And that's not certain either. One educated guess suggests that our much-travelled Queen Mother might have actually been born in an ambulance. Or not. And since, with this glamorous great-grannie, all statistics are vital, the matter was raised with Clarence House, ('Where precisely was Her Majesty born?' seeming a reasonable enough question at the time). The official response was a classic in polite evasion. 'It really doesn't matter where she was born or whether there were some inaccuracies' a spokesperson drawled, probably over a yawn. The notion being, presumably, that the existence of the Queen Mother was magnificently sufficient in itself.

Well what is clear, nearly ninety years on, is that Claude George, the Lord Glamis, soon to become the 14th Earl of Strathmore, didn't bother either. In fact on 23 August, his newly born only nineteen days old and cooing away in Herts, his lordship was playing cricket in Scotland for the Lord Glamis XI against Strathmore. It was a hot day. Strathmore sent their opponents into bat and grabbed the first three wickets for forty-three runs. But the team rallied, two of the batsmen scoring centuries. Later, Lord Glamis, a dashing forty-five year old, moustache spreading under a puce face and cricket cap, took three Strathmore wickets for twenty-two runs. We can speculate as to why bowling his medium pacers up at Forfar appeared to be a more enticing proposition than being with his wife, the former society beauty Cecilia Cavendish-Bentinck and the daughter he hadn't yet christened. Maybe having sired Violet, Mary, Patrick, John, Alexander, Fergus, Rose, and Michael, the ecstasy of rushing to tickle yet another infant under the chin had worn thin. And yet this baby, born seven years after Michael, was a precious event to him and Cecilia. Her marriage to this handsome ex-Guards officer, heir to the 13th Earl of Strathmore, was more than just ideal casting from the Social Register. Cecilia, like all the Cavendish-Bentinck women, was a highly desirable catch with a flawless skin and chic, satin-smooth style. Even the prominent Bentinck nose, (which tactfully didn't appear in the Queen Mother's genes) seemed to make her even more striking. She was the daughter of the Reverend Charles Cavendish-Bentinck and the great granddaughter of the 3rd Duke of Portland who was once Home Secretary (under Pitt) and twice Prime Minister. But she had more than an impeccable pedigree. She was a very seductive lady. Clearly eight children in eleven years suggests more than an upper-class marriage of convenience. The Strathmores, in fact, not only married for love. Intensely proud – they called themselves a clan rather than a family – all potential suitors, male or female, were judged more on merit than on status. (A future King of England would discover that to his considerable anguish.) The Strathmores were rich landowners who for more than two hundred years lived in austere contentment behind the massive walls of Glamis Castle, and feared no one except God. And they had spilt much blood over the centuries to prove it. One Lord Glamis, and two of his brothers, fell at the battle of Flodden in 1513. A Lord Glamis was killed in a fracas in 1578, while another lost his life in the battle of Sherriffmuir in 1715. Some of their womenfolk, on the other hand, were a shade less heroic. The attractive Lady Janet, widow of the 6th Lord Glamis, was burned as a witch in Edinburgh for allegedly conspiring to procure the death of James V. Glamis Castle was confiscated by the crown. But six years later a court reversed its decision on the ill-fated Janet and the Glamis family were back in favour and residence.

With all that behind him (including a direct blood link to Robert Bruce) Lord Glamis, *circa* 1900, was indifferent to the niceties of English law concerning a birth registration in Hitchin, Herts. He didn't show up at St Paul's Walden until late September bringing the Bowes-Lyon boys with him. They stood awkwardly around in the late summer sunshine, wearing the ill-fitting tweed knickerbockers Scottish aristocrats inflict upon their offspring. On arrival at the Register Office, the embarrassed registrar fined him seven-and-sixpence (47p) for failing to register the birth on time. His lordship studiedly handed over the cash. With 50,000 acres of land, vast fortunes culled from the iron and the coal mines of Durham, he could just about afford this Sassenach imposition. Two days later at the christening the Reverend Tristram Valentine of St Paul's Walden, went weak at the knees at this Scottish invasion led by Lord Glamis. The records show he made an unholy mess writing the names 'Elizabeth Angela Marguerite' on the register and was forced to cross out the mistakes on the baptismal certificate.

With His Lordship smiling wickedly, he fumbled on, forgetting to describe the father as a lord. He corrected the error later with a shaky hand. Finally it was over and the blue-eyed infant was officially documented into history.

All this was a minor blip measured against the checkered history of Glamis and the Bowes-Lyon dynasty. The most notorious skeleton in their cupboard was a slightly-built beauty with long brown hair, named Mary Eleanor Bowes. Born in 1749, she was the daughter of George Bowes, a colliery millionaire and his second wife, whose father was the squire of St Paul's Walden. It was Mary – the Queen Mother's great-great-grandmother – who forged the link with the Lyon family, marrying John Lyon later the 9th Earl of Strathmore. She had five children by her husband, known as 'the beautiful Lord Strathmore' because of his matinee-idol looks. But her highly sexed ladyship, more Chatterley than Strathmore, looked restlessly for new sensations. She had a passionate affair with the brother of the local laird, confessing long after, according to J. Wentworth Day in *The Queen Mother's Family*, 'I received one letter only from him which I burnt to ashes and drank them up for fear of any accident.' When Lord Strathmore died, aboard ship *en route* to Lisbon, the fair Mary Eleanor was pregnant courtesy of a chap named George Grey, described in her *Confessions* as 'a fundamentally dishonest, lazy, amorous, greedy pussycat of a man'. A saint apparently compared with Captain Andrew Stoney, a drunken and belligerent opportunist with whom, subsequently, she fell wildly in love. In his drunken bouts he punched and kicked her. His other diversions included raping nurserymaids and scullery girls. One of the victims recalled a dinner where he threw a dish of hot potatoes at his wife's face and then a glass of wine 'to wash the potatoes off'. She took the brute to court. But together with hired thugs, he abducted her while she was shopping at an ironmongers in Oxford Street. Bleeding and bruised, she was dragged on a gruesome coach-journey North. Police finally caught up with Stoney on the snow-covered moors above Newcastle. He had hoped to filch all her family fortunes. He got nothing despite his ruse of changing his name to Bowes. He was described at the time as 'hypocritical, tyrannic, mean, violent, selfish, jealous and savage' hyperbole being the fashion of the period. He died on 23 January 1810 and was buried in a pauper's vault of St George's, Borough, in south-east London. Lady Strathmore had died ten years earlier, 28 April, 1800. She was buried in Westminster Abbey in her wedding dress. Her eldest son, John Bowes-Lyon, the 10th Earl of Strathmore had his moments too. He had an eyebrow-raising affair with the frisky Lady 'Hussey' Tyrconnel, whose husband, Lord Tyrconnel accepted with a gallant shrug her living with her lover at the Bowes-Lyon mansion near Durham. There was a bizarre finale to the lurid episode. On her death, Strathmore, according to local records:

'Had her face painted like the most brilliant life. He dressed her head himself! And then, having decked her out in all her jewels and covered her with ruffled lace from head to foot, he sent her up to London, causing her to lie in state at every town upon the road, and finally to be buried in Westminster Abbey.'

But almost before the bells ceased tolling, the earl was energetically proposing – unsuccessfully – to his late mistress's daughter. Baulked, he fell for a housemaid, Mary Milner, a gardener's daughter, and lived with her in Chelsea. He settled a sizeable fortune on their son John. Three years later when he was a dying man, he sought to legitimize his son's claim to the earldom by marrying Mary. He was carried, dying, in a sedan chair to St George's Church, Hanover Square, London, and with her expiring lover propped up by friends at the altar, the gardener's daughter became a countess. In the event, their son John, was denied the title due to a vital difference between the English and Scottish laws of succession. The title passed to John Bowes-Lyons' brother who became the 11th Earl of Strathmore. (John, incidentally suffered no acute deprivation at the failed death's-door attempt to make him an earl. He earned a reputed £1,000 a day from his inherited coal interests. He bought racehorses and won the Derby four times. He went to Paris, married a French actress and bought, presumably for her, a theatre. Her predilection, back at the family home at Streatlam Castle, near Durham, was for bathing in a coal-black preparation which left her with long black finger-nails. Why she needed to douse herself like an ink-fish to achieve that effect is nowhere explained.)

It is when we look at the 11th Earl's heir, Thomas, Lord Glamis, that we disclose the darkest corner in the Bowes-Lyon cupboard. Thomas and his wife Charlotte are recorded – in *Burke's Peerage* among other sources – as having their first son on 28 September 1822. But *Debrett's* refers to a son who was born and supposedly died on 18 October 1821. A child, according to some reports, 'born so hideously deformed that his parents decided to record him as dead since he could not possibly inherit the title and estates.' Fact, myth and superstition merge portraying a 'monstrous, hairy freak with spindly limbs dangling from an egg-shaped body'. Expecting him to die, his parents, it is said, had him baptized as a final act of compassion. But according to such evidence allowed to filter through the years, the wretched thing survived. And was incarcerated in a secret cell, ten feet by fifteen, at the end of a long passage which the first Earl of Strathmore had built in 1684. The Queen Mother's grandfather, the 13th Earl knew about the secret cell. So too did his son, the family lawyer and the agent of the estate. What they knew about the piteous creature alleged to have occupied it remained, like the cell itself, sealed within the walls of the castle. Yet consider this strange sequel: in 1880 a workman carrying out repairs at Glamis chiselled open a door revealing a passage. Probing further he froze and, not all that coherently, reported what he saw to the Clerk of Works. Events now moved rapidly. A telegram is sent to London. The Earl hurries as fast as he can to Scotland. The lawyer is roped in from Edinburgh. Both men closely question the workman. By the most benign coincidence, he and his family display a sudden enthusiasm to up and emigrate to Australia – a desire which His Lordship is only too pleased to subsidize. The worker's disappearance abroad was ruled a forbidden subject below stairs. The door was re-sealed. It would take several decades before Rose, Elizabeth's older sister would say in her last years: 'We were never allowed to talk about it. Our parents forbade us ever to mention the matter or ask any questions. My father and grandfather absolutely refused to discuss it.'

Glamis' most celebrated visitor was Shakespeare. He is supposed to have dreamed up the plot for *Macbeth* there. Bonnie Prince Charlie slept there. So did Sir Walter Scott two hundred years ago. He laughed at rumours that the place was haunted by 'Beardie', an apparition who favoured the Blue Room, and 'Jack the Runner', a bugaboo who filtered around all floors. That was before the great man retired for the night in his shadowy, candlelit bedroom beneath the turrets. After that experience he grudgingly conceded; 'I must confess that when I heard door after door shut . . . I began to consider myself as too far from the living and somewhat too near to the dead.' There was a bloodstain on the floor of the room where Malcolm 11 was murdered. It would never wash out. Lady Strathmore, wife to the cricketing earl, had the whole floor boarded up.

The contrast between Glamis Castle, Scottish baronial with French château overtones, and St Paul's Walden Bury, a solid Queen Anne mansion blushing with honeysuckle and magnolia, could not have been more striking. The Hertfordshire garden was caressed into existence by the French landscape artist Le Notre. 'Idyllic' must have been the first English word he acquired. A 'Fairy Wood', lily ponds, and moss-covered statues; a tall oak tree with two ring-doves preening coquettishly beneath – the whole outdoor scene suggested a joint effort by Disney and Barbara Cartland. The mandatory menagerie for the baby Elizabeth, as for all children in the English stately homes of the day, included dogs, tortoises, Persian kittens, and a Shetland pony of her own. Born at the tail end of the Victorian age with its flagrant contrasts between prodigious wealth and Dickensian poverty, the Lady Elizabeth Angela Marguerite would blossom in a world of nannies, governesses, valets, footmen and a chattering of maids. At weekends, selected guests would saunter down for madcap parties and the seasonal shoots. And in the evenings, with the cultivated Lady Strathmore at the piano, there would be singing, charades, and on birthdays a Scottish piper or two to celebrate the cutting of the cake. Forty miles away in London, an eleven-year-old urchin name Charlie Chaplin was living off parochial charity in a Lambeth workhouse. When his mother was discharged from the lunatic asylum – the correct descriptive of the day – she moved with him to a slum dwelling in Kennington between a slaughter house and a pickle factory. (Thirty years on that same Chaplin would join the Duke and Duchess of York and Sir Philip Sassoon for lunch at Eton.) Marie Lloyd, short, plump and suggestive, was the star attraction at the music hall, not overly up-staged by Sir Henry Irving clutching imaginary daggers at the London Lyceum. That heart-bleeding lament 'It's the rich wot 'as the pleasure, it's the poor wot takes the blame' wept alongside the sweet innocence of 'You are my honey . . . honeysuckle . . .'. At the South London Music Hall the Fred Karno Comedy Company were performing in 'Early Birds' while at St Paul's Walden Bury, Lady Strathmore was expecting another child fourteen months after the birth of Elizabeth.

The last of the Bowes-Lyon children, David, was born on

2 May 1902 at St Paul's Walden Bury. Less than two years later, the Earl of Strathmore died and Lord Glamis, Elizabeth's father, became the 14th earl, or more precisely, the 14th Earl of Strathmore and Kinghorne, Viscount Lyon and Baron Glamis, Tannadyce, Sidlaw and Strathdichtie, Baron Bowes of Streatlam Castle, County Durham and Lunedale, County York. Those acquisitions meant more than an extra couple of paragraphs in *Debrett's*. It was a windfall enabling the abundant Strathmores not simply to live in the style to which they were long accustomed. That was merely lavish. They now had enormous material wealth in England and in Scotland to buttress their already daunting independence. They moved to a princely Adam mansion in London's élite St James's Square. But here the conventional 'idle rich' image must be jettisoned. The 14th Earl of Strathmore, a religious man, lived the way he played cricket: a straight bat, loyal, strictly to the rules of the game. Cecilia, his wife, behaved no differently. Described by one admirer as 'a piece of absolute perfection' she was highly accomplished too. Add those delicate features and the fabled Cavendish-Bentinck complexion and the genes that twinkled in the baby Elizabeth's bloodstream were positively gilt-edged. When Cecilia, the new Lady Strathmore, went up to take possession of Glamis castle, she brought in fine Italian and French antiques; changed the funereal drapes to bright English brocades; added some of her own masterpieces to enliven the walls.

Clearly Cecilia Strathmore presided over homes, not establishments. She approached the upbringing of her children with the same preference for substance over aristocratic ritual. She taught Elizabeth to read and pray before a governess could get at her. At bedtime after reading fairy tales, she and the 14th Earl gave her the last cuddle of the night. No surprise then, that the child crawled, walked and talked earlier than most. All the evidence available for that period suggests a petite, hyper-active mini-thoroughbred with long dark hair, displaying just the right balance between sweet obedience and well-bred naughtiness. The following examples will not, I suspect, induce shock. Unimpressed by the arrival of a particular governess she wrote in her diary, 'some governesses are nice, some are *not*'. According to Elizabeth Longford, 'She once, in a moment of childish anger, shredded her new sheets with a pair of scissors. Her mother said, "Oh Elizabeth . . . !" that was all; but said it in

such a reproachful voice that Elizabeth immediately repented.'
Not the end of civilization as we know it, but a fascinating
pointer to how this same Elizabeth, years on, might handle
those who offend her – or hers.

But there were few such tantrums in Elizabeth Angela's
earliest few years. St Paul's Walden Bury, with its fountains and
dreamy yews, the 'Fairy Wood' at the end of an alley of
peach-limes; riding Old Bobs the pony by day, dancing and
singing with Mama at the piano at night – not much to test the
nerves or ripple the surface of the Strathmore tranquillity. At the
age of four she was put in the hands of a French governess, a
Mademoiselle Lang whom she apparently received as to the
manner born with, 'I do hope you will be happy here'. At the age
of five, this happy ninth-in-line was already displaying the
self-assurance of She Who Would Never Be Fazed. Taking her
cue from her mother, she relished playing hostess. Once when
the doorbell clanged at Glamis Castle she rushed to let in the
factor on his weekly call. 'Do come in,' beckoned her little
ladyship grandly. 'I hope you are well, but you will be sorry to
learn that Lord Strathmore has toothache.' Not surprising then
that on meeting Edward VII's grandson, Albert, five years older
than she but a decidedly timorous nipper, that it was she who
took charge and put him at his ease. She gave him the crystal-
lized cherry off her fruit cake. A minor titbit, you might think,
in one thousand years of monarchy. Yet even our most staid
historians refer to that first meeting in orb-and-sceptre language. It took place at a children's party given by the Countess
of Leicester at Montague House, London. The time, Christmas
1905.

No child was ever born under an unluckier star than Albert, the
second son of King George V and Queen Mary. His arrival at
three o'clock in the morning on the 14 December 1895, was bad
on timing and worse on gender. His father, then Duke of York,
noted that the birth coincided with the thirty-fourth anniversary
of the death of the Prince Consort. This event was annually
ringed in black by the widow who mourned him relentlessly,
Queen Victoria, the newly-born's great grandmother. Despite
the irritating fact that not even royalty can precisely date and
time a birth, George considered it was downright tactless for a
'happy event' to occur on a day Victoria set aside for further
spasms of grief. The story is that he was so apprehensive about

her feelings he wired his apologies for the unforgivable lapse. Victoria was 'graciously pleased' at this deep sensitivity, indicating that she was prepared to take a merciful view of the awkward timing. (Fine words, though years later the then duke told friends he was sure Queen Victoria never forgave this 'personal affront'.)

But the luckless infant had another strike against it. He was a boy. His well-organized parents already had one son, David, born fourteen months earlier, and sensibly during Ascot Week. They now wanted a girl. Nature failed to oblige. There was rejoicing in public, much disappointment in private. The father was not amenable to having his hopes dashed, plans thwarted. The second son of Edward VII, he had married Princess Mary of Teck in 1893. Twenty-five years later, as George V, he would change the name of the royal family from Saxe-Coburg to Windsor. But he still clung to some of his old Saxony hang-ups, like having his trousers creased at the sides instead of front and back. Only an analyst could determine what, if anything, this quirk indicated psychologically. But by all accounts he was a cold fish to his sons, particularly to Bertie, who almost from the day he could speak, was literally tongue-tied in the looming presence of his father. The family home, at York Cottage on the Sandringham estate, was scarcely designed to dispel the young boy's gloom. Harold Nicolson remembered it as 'a glum little villa with a leaden pelican gazing dejectedly over a pond. The rooms inside with their fumed oak surrounds and stained glass fanlights are indistinguishable from those of any Surbiton or Upper Norwood home.' Nobody within earshot was likely to hear the sound of children laughing.

Even when a daughter, Princess Mary, was born and became the King's darling, none of the warmth rubbed off on to Bertie. Moreover, he was born left-handed in an era which regarded a 'sinistral' as an oddity, one of Nature's rejects. This view was clearly shared by the parents who engaged a tutor to force the boy to write right-handed. This well-intentioned disciplinarian could not have had the remotest notion of the cerebral havoc he was inflicting on little Bertie. Hour after hour the boy struggled to re-programme the signal box inside his brain but with disastrous results. He became increasingly agitated which intensified his stammer. We can assume that neither the royal couple nor their hired expert were aware of the strong evidence linking stammering with left-handedness. The more Bertie struggled the worse became the muscular seize-up around his larynx. The more he spluttered on his 'p's and 't's, the more comical he appeared to others, particularly to the family. He was already tormented by a sense of 'second son' inferiority. His stammer, and the guilt induced by an impatient father, compounded his misery. And he had knock-knees. A universal favourite for ridicule. A second 'tyrant', Sir Francis Laking Bt, was brought in to straighten them. He put Bertie's legs into splints which had to be worn for several hours each day. If, as some will say, he became difficult to get along with, picture him as a stammering ten year old, with steel-braced legs, laboriously pen-pushing with an unresponding right hand. No basis there for a happy, well-adjusted personality.

Of course Elizabeth, the shining-eyed five year old, was unaware of the boy Bertie's problems as she confronted him at the children's party at Montague House. She arrived with her younger brother David wearing a long blue-and-white party frock, her long curls tied in bows. She took off her velvet wrap and handed it without a trace of shyness to a servant. Poised and deliciously self-confident in her stunning party frock, she was a Cavendish-Bentinck writ small. The Countess of Leicester greeted her, bringing three other children with her. 'Here is another David,' she said, introducing the future Edward VIII, 'and this is his brother Bertie and his sister Mary.' Left alone with Bertie later she detected an obvious shyness, the stammering embarrassment of a born misfit. She felt a surging need to cheer him up. All she had was a slice of cake with glacé cherries embedded in it. She winkled them out and presented them to him. (No small sacrifice from a sweet-toothed child.) Bertie blushed gratefully. He would forget the sugar-coated gesture, but not the dreamily pretty child who made it. She was soon going to have the same effect on others. At seven she made, unknowingly, her first real 'conquest' at another party given at Lansdowne House, London. This time, it was a besotted Lord David Cecil, aged six, whose subsequent recollections soar lyrically over the top: 'I turned and looked and was aware of a small, charming, rosy face around which twined and strayed rings and tendrils of silken hair, and a pair of dewy grey eyes. Her flower-like mouth parted in a grave, enchanting smile, and between the pearly teeth flowed out tones of drowsy melting sweetness that seemed to caress the words they uttered. From that moment my small damp hand clutched at hers and I never left her side. . . . Forgotten were all the pretenders to my heart. Here was the true heroine. She had come. I had seen and she had conquered . . .'.

With her father the Earl of Strathmore busy supervising the family estates, Elizabeth and her brother David were looked after by Clara Knight. A farmer's daughter, she was devoted to the Strathmores who treated her as one of the family. Life for Elizabeth at St Paul's Walden, at St James's Square and up at Glamis, was peaceful, ecstatic almost. The Strathmore sons followed each other to Eton with the inexorable certainty of night following day. As soon as they were old enough they shot the mandatory number of hares, pheasants, and rabbits. When Elizabeth occasionally entered the vast kitchen at the castle, she might find a kitchen maid asleep in a bed set up under the table for catnaps between meals. There was Barson, a valet-cum-butler frequently drunk to the point of spilling food and drink down the decolletes of the lady guests. He was often sacked but always reinstated, though his lordship kept a closer watch on the levels in the decanters. The Queen Mother remembers with wistful pleasure the riding to the village church at Glamis in a horse-drawn carriage, the curlew and the wild duck soaring overhead. The singing around the piano and a special treat, helping her mother with the family sewing. For all their wealth, Countess Strathmore, the clergyman's daughter, regarded thrift as a dominant virtue. Many of Elizabeth's dresses showed signs of careful patching. Rose's cast-offs often ended up in Elizabeth's wardrobe. Once she found herself stitching into history as she helped her mother mend a hole in the counterpane of the bed where Bonnie Prince Charlie had slept.

If Europe was moving towards the Great War, no ripples of it were discerned in Britain's stately homes. Rose, the elder sister and David the younger brother, were closest to Elizabeth during those jelly and blancmange years. Dressing up was the most popular party game. Costumes of all periods were kept in the 'acting box' at Glamis. The cricketing Earl having been as prolific a father as he was a run scorer, the family was large enough to fill several parts. The records shows that putting on a flowing robe and imperiously announcing, 'I am Princess Elizabeth . . .' was this prescient seven year old's favourite role. The yellow-haired David, the imp in the family, played more blood-curdling parts, his shrieks bouncing marvellously off the lofty castle walls. Then they would line up for their candles and like a Shakespearian chorus line, file up the wide staircase to their four-posters in the castle's upper rooms.

When the day arrived for David to be sent away to prep school, Elizabeth pined. She and he, the two last-born, had been styled 'the two Benjamins' by their mother, (Benjamin having been the youngest son of Jacob and Rachel). Now David was gone and attention focused on the other 'Benjamin'. The Countess had firm ideas about education. Elizabeth as a tot had been to a nursery class in London and later spent a couple of terms at Dorothy and Irene Birtwhistle's 'select classes for girls' in South Kensington. But aristocratic conventions apart, the countess decided she wanted more for this versatile child. She was sent to the Froebel-trained Constance Goff school in London's Marylebone High Street. There were dancing classes with the children of other gentlefolk at Madame d'Egville's academy in Knightsbridge. Piano lessons at the Mathilde Verne school in the Cromwell road. The Countess achieved her objectives. Elizabeth was maturing attractively towards her teens. All the other girls envied her looks and self-assurance. Most of the small boys fell in love with her. And no wonder. With her soft features, flirty eyes, and swirling talent on the dance floor, she had all the dreamy promise of the born heart-stealer.

She was determined too. There was always going to be more to this Elizabeth than dutifully following the guns up at Glamis; being groomed solely for social ritual; the mute terror of being 'presented' and the ultimate goal – a safe betrothal to a well-heeled 'eligible' with a string of directorships plus a genial sense of his own superiority. The great excitement for this eleven year old and her brother David was to visit her maternal grandmother, Mrs Caroline Scott who lived in a fine Medici mansion, the Villa Caponi, on the outskirts of Florence. This meant an overnight journey on the Rome express, ecstasy even to these well-indulged youngsters. Their escort was a spinster aunt Violet who took them sightseeing around Florence's fine squares, boulevards, and the picturesque Ponte Vecchio offering the Palazzo Vecchio at one end and the Pitti Palace at the other. It was in this year, 1911, that they returned home to learn that their brother Alexander had died from an illness that was never explained. Their eldest sister, Violet had died of a fever at the age of eleven, seven years before Elizabeth was born.

In her thirteenth year Elizabeth was put in the care of a governess, a sturdy fraulein named Kathy Kuebler. As highly trained as a Sandhurst drill sergeant, and no less formidable, Miss Kuebler none the less had her own special charm and doted on Elizabeth, and David too when he was home at school holidays. He remembers her, albeit with evident affection, 'shaking the foundations of Glamis Castle with her Teutonic tread!' But this Wagnerian image did the good fraulein an injustice. She was a fine teacher and by the time Elizabeth was twelve she was conversing easily with her in German. Fraulein Kuebler taught the children history, (unaware that two years later, 1914, the script would be violently and tragically re-written). Nor was there anything Teutonic in her recollections of her years with Elizabeth: 'at thirteen she had a small delicate figure, a sensitive, somewhat pale little face, dark hair and very beautiful violet-blue eyes; she was far more mature than her years warranted.'

Some of the credit for Elizabeth's early maturity must go to the Earl of Strathmore. He didn't share the chauvinistic rituals of his class which banished females, especially thirteen year olds, from serious, more important company. He insisted Elizabeth should share dinner and the conversation with his guests which on one unique occasion had four ex-Viceroys of India seated round the table. Frequently, then, the atmosphere would be stiff with imperialistic overtones. While Elizabeth, prettily dressed and coiffeured, daintily forked her food, talk flowed about the state of the Navy, Free Trade, the Empire, but most crucially, England's cricketing chances against Australia. Lord Rosebery, the statesman and fabled racehorse owner, was a frequent visitor and might just have been the one to kindle the ardent young listener's interest in the turf. It was he who, according to Helen Cathcart, 'was apt to observe that it was a symptom of the modern British monarchy that every word of the King's was as treasured in England as if it were God's . . .' Whether he meant this as a compliment or a criticism, isn't clear. It hardly mattered then since the young Elizabeth was still some distance away from 'royal circles'. What pleased her though at the time was when Fraulein Kuebler was occasionally invited to dinner. 'The German governess,' says Helen Cathcart, 'was sometimes drawn into the conversation. With aristocratic decorum their noble lords would put her at her ease by talking of their studies and friendships in her native land. This pleased Elizabeth so much she squeezed the governess's hand under the table.' The fact that their noble lords were just possibly being crassly patronizing, was neither here nor there. That secret little hand-squeeze reflected well on the young girl at the table, indicating a kindly spirit and an instinctive empathy with an 'outsider'.

But the said 'aristocratic decorum', at least in relation to Germans in general, was soon to lapse. At breakfast, on 29 June 1914, the good fraulein noticed Lord Strathmore reading the *Morning Post* and tugging moodily at his drooping moustaches. 'This means war,' he said. Fraulein Kuebler rose from the table and went to her room. She sensed that her days with the Strathmores but particularly with Elizabeth, were ending. A month or so later she became an enemy alien overnight. She went home to Germany ostensibly for a family celebration, but didn't return. On Tuesday, 4 August 1914, her fourteenth birthday, Elizabeth awoke in her room at St James's Square, to breakfast in bed and a pile of telegrams and lavish gifts from her family, friends and admirers. She had just passed her Oxford Local exam with distinction. The Strathmore's reward for that and her birthday treat was a box at the Coliseum then styled the 'Palace of Entertainment'. On the bill were Lipinsky's Dog Comedians, jugglers Moran and Wise, and a Russian ballerina, Fedorovna. As they watched their birthday girl laughing and wildly applauding the acts, the Earl and Lady Strathmore knew that the euphoria would be brief. Elizabeth's childhood and the peaceful years were finished. By the time the curtain fell Army reservists were assembling in their barracks. Mobilization was speeding up. The Great War had begun.

2

Within a week of the declaration of war Lord and Lady Strathmore closed No. 20, St James's Square and took the family up to Glamis. The first glimpse of this Forfarshire stronghold with its Hans Andersen turrets over massive battlements, pink-tinted in the evening sunset, placed this already remote castle even further from reality. No indication then of how their lives were about to change. Nothing was happening in that first week of the Great War to touch the emotions of the young Lady Elizabeth Bowes-Lyon in the afterglow of her fourteenth birthday.

Not that she was specially privileged or sheltered from events. At the beginning few, least of all the government of the day, had any notion of the catastrophic blood-letting in store. The pervading mood was that war was the state's problem. For the unsuspecting population it was, in Churchill's phrase at the time, 'Business as Usual'. There was no conscription. No register of manpower and resources. Everybody expected the war would be over in months if not weeks. The troops marched cheerfully to their embarkation points, singing 'It's A Long Way To Tipperary' convinced that after firing a couple of shots in anger they'd be home for Christmas. The notion that they might be marching towards Armageddon did not enter their heads as they whistled and sang their way to slaughter. In the first week of war at least, England, and the Strathmores, felt secure, contented, with just a frisson of excitement as the British Expeditionary Force sailed away. So there was more pride than fear in Elizabeth's emotions as the Bowes-Lyon brothers quickly exchanged cricket flannels for khaki and joined the battle. Patrick, in his thirtieth year and a reservist in the Black Watch, was immediately called up. Jock, aged twenty-eight, and Fergus twenty-four, joined the same regiment but were posted to different battalions. Michael enlisted in the Royal Scots Guards. Even if they had not all been schooled at Eton where patriotism is taken for granted, the Bowes-Lyon men would scarcely have dragged their feet. They were typical of scores of titled families encrusted in the landscape who galloped out to fight the war. As Penelope Mortimer noted: 'The Glamis neighbours – the Dalhousies, Southesks, Butes, Monymusks, Douglases and Stuarts – became sonless overnight.' We can suppose that to the innocent fourteen year old caught up in the Bowes-Lyon men's eagerness to get to the Front, the mood was more thrilling than threatening. There were sessions with tailors to measure the brothers' uniforms; polished revolver holsters lying around on the Jacobean tables; advice from Boer war veterans on the estates on how to stay alive under fire; last-minute letters to write; wills jauntily drawn up; wordless handshakes between a proud Lord Strathmore and his sons – and a little romantic business to be taken care of by Jock and Fergus.

War tends to prod wavering sweethearts into leaping in droves towards the altar. The phenomenon was true of the 1914–18 war. It would repeat itself in 1939–45. Fear of death not only concentrates the mind wonderfully. It can be a powerful stimulus to romance, not to mention its alleged aphrodisiac potential. The familiar war-bride scene, the fierce embrace inside the church followed by a tearful parting as the train or troopship moves out of sight, was reenacted thousands of times early in the First World War. Jock and Fergus Bowes-Lyon characteristically led from the front. After lightning engagements both married within a week of each other.

On 17 September, Fergus married Lady Christian Dawson-Damer, daughter of the Earl of Portarlington. Seven days later, Jock took as his bride an attractive and much-hyphenated girl, by name, Fenella Hepburn-Stuart-Forbes-Trefussis. (The explanation for this bizarre sausage-link of titles is that since the line was created in 1299 there had been a wholesale acquisition of different families many insisting on their names remaining in the credits.) As the brothers said their goodbyes, there were hugs and kisses from Elizabeth who then quietly slipped away to pray for their safety with her mother, in the chapel at Glamis. Within months, Michael, soon after his twenty-first birthday, was also a soldier in France. The tide of events rapidly swept away the *Boys' Magazine* jingoism which had lingered for a while after the declaration of war. The first shots were fired near Mons on 22 August 1914. It was not a success and the British generals ordered a retreat. As she read newspaper reports of the first casualties – 1,600 – (trivial compared to the holocaust to come) Elizabeth, like everyone else at home, fought against thinking the worst. She took her lead from her father. He set the ground rules for the Strathmore approach to the war. God would look after the brothers in France, the family would do its stuff at home.

Rose, Elizabeth's elder sister, enrolled as a nurse and went to London for her training. Glamis Castle, for centuries a sleeping fortress in a peaceful landscape, awakened to find itself mobilized. Grouse shoots, picnics, fun and Highland games were fine. But this castle, its walls fifteen-feet thick, was constructed more for deadly argument than for pleasure. When they were children, Elizabeth and David used to climb laboriously up the stone steps and chuck pails of water from the ramparts 'repelling invaders'. Now at fourteen she would play a more serious role. Ailing and beyond war service, Lord Strathmore did the next best thing; he put Glamis Castle at the disposal of the military. It took in the over-flow of wounded, shell-shocked soldiers from the Royal Infirmary at Dundee. The long and lofty banqueting hall was cleared to make way for rows of iron bedsteads lined up against the dark, oak-panelled walls. Family portraits, brooding down over an unchanging audience of earls, duchesses, and the odd royal, now gazed at soldiers in army-issue pyjamas, heads bandaged or limbs in plaster, while a fourteen-year-old Bowes-Lyon in a white blouse and long black skirt chatted and smiled from bed to bed. The kitchen menus switched tactfully from Cordon Bleu to standard rations. But it was more a home than a hospital. The Countess and her daughter Elizabeth were no token hostesses retiring to their private boudoirs once the lower-orders had been watered and fed. Elizabeth, her beloved brothers in the firing line in France, suppressed her constant fears with the intensity of her duties. Years afterwards the Glamis intake of soldiers would recall the peace of it all; the recurring nightmares of the trenches fading as a lone piper circled the castle in the Scottish twilight.

With Rose away, Elizabeth rolled up her sleeves to become ADC to Lady Strathmore. Those who were there tell a tale of a petite little power-house, bustling round the Castle, thrilled at being needed. (An attractive and blooming teenager, to find herself with a captive and admiring audience of forty or so fighting men, must have been quite a confidence-booster.) And so she threw herself into the prime activities for the womenfolk of Glamis – 'knitting, knitting, and knitting'. Scarves, mittens, socks – bundles of them were stacked on shelves in the library or in parcels on the billiards table. Elizabeth had been taught to sew by the Countess and now that skill was useful, stitching shirts for the local battalion of the 5th Black Watch. All the ingredients here for sweet nostalgia; her industrious ladyship bent over her needle as wounded soldiers down below sang 'It's a Long Long Trail A-Winding . . .'. When she wasn't sewing shirts or knitting socks, the Countess had her crumpling up sack-loads of tissue paper to fill Glamis's custom-made sleeping bags. As the Queen Mother herself recalled: 'my chief occupation was crumpling the tissue paper until it was so soft it wouldn't crackle when put into the linings of the sleeping bags.'

That's not all the soldiers remember about her. She knew all of them by their Christian names; took their photos and sent the snaps home to their families. She wrote letters to mothers and sweethearts for those unable to use their hands. She played whist with them, dominoes, cribbage – not exactly the leisure activities of the upper classes, but what she didn't know, she learned. She ran errands for them, buying their packets of Gold Flake or Navy Cut tobacco. No soldier's birthday went uncelebrated either. She bought gifts of fountain pens, books, cigarettes, sang and played 'Happy Birthday' on the Countess's concert piano. By now, her role as a kind of assistant chatelaine of the castle, encouraged her to adopt a more sophisticated appearance. She wore her hair in a bun, and brushed a soft fringe down over her forehead which became her favourite hair-style over the years. One appreciative patient soared into prose:

'She had the loveliest eyes, expressive and eloquent eyes, and a very taking way of knitting her forehead when speaking . . . for all her fifteen years she was very womanly, kind-hearted and sympathetic.'

The worse the news was from France, the more thrilled Elizabeth was to receive letters. These were always cheerful, reflecting the *dolce vita* of the British officer class, *circa* 1915. Their understatement could not hide the truth that the war would not be over that Christmas or the next. No one spoke any more of 'Business as Usual'. Elizabeth was safe at Glamis and it is likely that she felt a tremor of guilt. In April 1915 London was bombarded from the air by a German Zeppelin. On 7 May, the *Lusitania* was sunk without warning by a German submarine. Over a thousand passengers and crew lost their lives. There were violent anti-German riots in London's East End. Elizabeth thought of Fraulein Kuebler, but now saw her in the uncomfortable light of 'the enemy'. She had learned a great deal from this conscientious teacher, and missed her. One morning the postman handed her a letter addressed in the fraulein's familiar handwriting. She wrote that she was a nurse serving in a reserve hospital near the family home at Erlangen. And wished Elizabeth and the Strathmores well. It could not have been an easy letter to write. Elizabeth never heard from her again. She was now fifteen, with an English governess, Miss Boynard, a hearty, sports-oriented tutor who put playing good tennis on a par with translating from the Greek.

There was great excitement at the Castle in September 1915. Fergus was coming home on leave to spend his first wedding anniversary with his wife at Glamis and to see for the first time their two-month-old daughter. The occasion glowed with all the tear-streaked features of a soldier's homecoming from the war. Fergus looked cheerful enough as he strode past the curtseying housemaids, his eyes widening at this transformed castle full of bandaged soldiers and reeking of surgical spirit. But the familiar battle pallor and the shadows under his eyes, did not go unnoticed by the Strathmores. At night, Elizabeth sat at his knee as he told stories, rose-tinting the truth about the carnage in France. He returned there a week later. The timing was unfortunate. It was that day, 25 September 1915, the combined British and French forces decided to attack the Germans entrenched around a village called Loos. The German divisions were protected by barbed wire and a murderous spread of machine guns. The attack initially succeeded, but then faltered. British casualties were an appalling 48,267. Captain Fergus Bowes-Lyon was one of them. He had left Glamis late on the Friday night, had barely unpacked his valise when he was dead, killed in action on his first day back in France. He was twenty-six. It was Rose – now back home as a qualified Sister – who received the telegram at the castle doors. She showed it to Elizabeth then ran with it to their mother. Elizabeth burst into tears and hugged Lady Strathmore who was momentarily silent, with the fleeting thought perhaps that with the escalating deaths of other Scottish soldiers there was no reason why her family should be spared. But then the tragedy struck home. She collapsed. A Bowes-Lyon son would have his name carved in the memorial granite at Forfar.

Bad news travels fast. Glamis Castle subsided into a respectful silence. No gramophone, no piano. The men huddled together in the make-shift ward, sensing the measure of the Strathmore's loss. Only a week or so before Captain Fergus had been joking with them, exchanging experiences of the action in France. Yet his death was nothing special of course. They had lost too many comrades just as abruptly to see anything unique in the Bowes-Lyon loss. But here at Glamis her ladyship and especially the busy little daughter, had made them feel close to, if not part of the family. They reacted accordingly. They all signed a letter of condolence, and respectfully kept the noise down. In her bedroom at night, Elizabeth might just have heard the faint sob-song of a mouth organ floating up from the ward, but nothing more. On the Sunday following the news of his death, the villagers crowded into the parish church of Glamis to join the Strathmores in mourning the death of their son. The Reverend J. Stirton preached a sermon in which he quoted from John 14: 'I will not leave you comfortless . . .'

Fergus's death demanded more of Elizabeth and her sister Rose, than grief. Their mother remained inconsolable. At private chapel in the castle, wearing little lace caps on their heads, they prayed for Fergus's salvation, but just as fiercely for his three brothers still in the firing line. The prayers did nothing to diminish the shock to Lady Strathmore. She stayed in her room, virtually raising the drawbridge and leaving the affairs of the castle to her daughters. In the event, it was Elizabeth alone who ran Glamis. Lord Strathmore was busy with the farms feeding the war effort; the Countess was too ill to cope. Then on 24 May 1916, Rose went off to marry Commander William Spence Leveson-Gower, at St James's, Piccadilly, London. A big event for Rose's sixteen-year-old sister, dressed like the other bridesmaids in a froth of white chiffon topped by a Dutch bonnet. The motif of this wartime affair was dominantly naval because of the bridegroom's command. The wedding cake flew the Royal Ensign, and presumably rum was available for the few not weaned on champagne. It was a blissful day – the air raids on London had tactfully ceased for a while – and Elizabeth was blushingly aware of the admiring glances from the young naval officers among the guests. Whether she caught Rose's tossed bouquet isn't recorded. But now in her mid-teens, she must have had her share of romantic day-dreaming, sketching out in her imaginings the man she herself might one day marry. What is certain, at that time, is that her ideal was unlikely to have resembled the young naval lieutenant, Albert, son of King George V, who had just rejoined his ship the *Collingwood*.

Bertie was not having an easy war. Or an easy life for that matter. Having survived his 'shifted sinistral' period (whereby the King had ruled that his left-handed son must switch to his right); having finally jettisoned the steel braces which had straightened his knock-knees, and overcome some chronic intestinal problems in between, Bertie happily escaped to the Navy. Happy, not because he was obsessed with a passion to command a ship and order guns to fire. In fact, the early indications were he disliked the sea and was frequently seasick. But these matters are relative. He was having a tougher time with his despot of a father, George V. Neither this dour monarch nor Queen Mary had the remotest notion of how to communicate with their children, least of all with this hapless younger brother of the idol, the Prince of Wales. Their eldest daughter, the Princess Royal, was usually referred to as 'poor Princess Mary' but the sympathy was for her not for the King and Queen. What else could she and Bertie have expected of a father who, when Lord Derby accused him of being too tough on his children, scowled, 'My father was frightened of his father; I was frightened of my father; and I am damn well going to see to it that my children are frightened of me!' After that, the Battle of Jutland, 31 May 1916, must have come as a welcome diversion to Bertie. True the action barely lasted ten minutes. But with the order 'Prepare for Action!', Bertie rushed to his position at Turret A on the *Collingwood* and remained there until the engagement was over. Official intelligence at the time declared that the young sub-lieutenant performed well under fire. He was one of the officers Admiral Sir John Jellicoe commended in his dispatch to the Admiralty. Bertie was promoted to full lieutenant that same night. The experience raised his morale dramatically. He acquired the self-confidence that had been all but crushed by myopic upbringing. The letter he wrote to his brother the Prince of Wales after the famous sea battle, underscores the transformation: 'When I was on top of the turret I never felt any fear of shells or anything else. It seems curious but all sense of danger and everything else goes except the one longing to deal death in every possible way to the enemy.'

Scarcely the language of a lame duck. Jutland had catapulted Prince Albert into manhood. Another tragic telegram from the battlefield and a serious fire at Glamis Castle, would prove just as salutory to the woman who would one day become his queen.

The fire occurred on a Saturday night in September 1916. Most of the soldier-patients who were not bed cases were at the local cinema in Forfar. From the window of her room high above the courtyard, Elizabeth saw smoke and bursts of flame rising nearly a hundred feet above the central keep. She called the Dundee and Forfar fire brigades, organized a chain of servants, ghillies, gardeners and estate workers to throw buckets of water on to the flames. Lord Strathmore was out shooting, her brother David and their mother appeared just as the roof tank burst in the heat, the water flooding down the stone stairway. Soon part of the top floor was in flames including centuries-old oak beams. Maids panicked inside the castle. Cattle stampeded outside. The brigades' fire hoses weren't long enough to stretch from the nearby river Dean so the villagers joined in the bucket-chain. No lives were threatened but some valuable paintings and a few items of antique furniture might have been incinerated. Elizabeth lined up thirty villagers to pass the portraits and the furniture to safety. In the event no Landseer or lance-corporal was lost. Glamis Castle was good for another five hundred years or more. True, no great heroism was involved though the Forfar papers were lyrical about the way Her smoke-streaked Ladyship instantly took command of the situation. Fraulein Kuebler would have been pleased at this example of the leadership and self-reliance she had always impressed upon Elizabeth. The future would test those qualities to the limit.

The fire was followed by a brief interlude of normality which for Elizabeth – war notwithstanding – imposed no intolerable hardship. With Glamis, St Paul's Walden Bury, and 20 St James's Square to move between, she was kept busy with Red Cross functions, trips to visit David at Eton, and the occasional dance in London. Suitably chaperoned, milady would be brought home at night by a yawning coachman atop the Strathmore's brougham. Occasionally some of the family retainers would disappear as conscription was finally brought in. It helped replace the enormous losses on the Western Front. But it played havoc with the social imperatives of the rich. Life without butlers, valets and the like was certainly irksome. As Lady Cynthia Asquith, a friend of the Bowes-Lyons', lamented afterwards; 'The plight of the average Lady was piteous. There are only two housemaids so we can only have breakfast and tea in.'

But life went on, and up at Glamis it was hospital business as usual once workmen had cleared the debris from the upper floors, and put a new water tank in the roof. Lady Strathmore appeared to be slowly recovering from the loss of her son Fergus. The other brothers Patrick, Jock and Michael were never out of Elizabeth's thoughts and always in the family prayers. The one unexpressed fear was that another of the brothers might be killed. Then, less than two years after Fergus's death, that dreaded notification arrived from the War Office. Michael was reported killed in action. Predictably, Lady Strathmore's anguish was hard to bear, harder still for Elizabeth whose own grief had to be stifled as she comforted her distraught mother. The eventual outcome was both happy and bizarre. This account of one Bowes-Lyon's prescience has never been refuted. Informed at Eton of his brother's death in action, David refused to believe it. He didn't care about the War Office telegram, he just *knew* Michael was alive. On his way home to help console his parents he was taken to lunch in London by a family friend. This gentleman was displeased that David was not wearing a black tie or dark suit. 'But Michael is not dead,' he insisted. 'I've seen him twice. He's in a big house surrounded by fir trees. I think he is very ill, his head is tied up in a cloth. I know he is alive.' Adolescent fantasies or not, three months later the War Office corrected their error. Michael Bowes-Lyon was alive; a prisoner in Germany after being shot in the head. To give this joyful tale the ultimate heroic twist, it appears that Michael could have been repatriated in an exchange via Holland but surrendered the chance to a fellow officer more seriously wounded. Pride was now added to the Strathmores' rapture. Their son Michael had survived and had done so with a fair show of gallantry.

Whatever skeletons may have skulked in cupboards centuries before, the Bowes-Lyons acquitted themselves handsomely in the Great War. The fact that officers died in a ratio to other ranks of three to one indicated a distinct tendency to lead from the front. This courage was in the Strathmore bloodline sustained by the booster-shots of Eton. They were typical of the breed. While the young officers strolled off to war, their tweedy or *Vogue*-cover wives raised funds, ran troop canteens, rolled bandages, or marched in McAfee brogues in the uniform of their choice. Lady Elizabeth Bowes-Lyon was no exception. Her brothers, Fergus tragically, had carved the bench-mark. She was determined to be as patriotic a Bowes-Lyon as they. She joined the Girl Guides, the Strathmore connection creating her deputy District Commissioner of Glamis and Eassie. When Princess Mary came to Forfar to inspect the Guides significant smiles passed between her and Elizabeth. They had met before at select little parties in and outside the palace. The hostess for many of these meetings was Mabell, Lady Airlie, lady-in-waiting to Queen Mary whose flat in Ashley Gardens, London, was 'open house' to Elizabeth, Princess Mary, the young Prince of Wales, and of course, Bertie if he happened to be passing by. 'Mabell, Lady Airlie,' wrote Helen Cathcart, 'eased the wheels of royal friendship and even royal romance more than she knew.' But those wheels were not yet for turning as Elizabeth saw out the last year of the war.

She pitched into the fund-raising events of the Angus (Forfar) Red Cross. If this meant helping to run local dances, it was a cross she might just be able to bear. At seventeen – slim, zesty and mad about dancing – she was never going to be a shrinking violet on the dance floor. At regimental functions, young officers watched and grew hot under their tunic collars as this delicious, dark-haired nymph virtually swept her partners around the floor. What amazed them was her apparently in-exhaustible energy. And even now in her ninetieth year, she is still erect on her feet at Ascot or Epsom while mere seventy year olds, male and female, are visibly wilting on their shooting sticks. The source of that energy – 'miraculous' is the favoured descriptive – must go back to those early Bowes-Lyons, brawny defenders carved out of the granite of the Highlands. But this Bowes-Lyon has added an unflagging endurance beautifully concealed beneath the alabaster surface. Which was fine for the young Elizabeth as she danced her partners to their knees. But it was when she was out walking the Scottish hills, a diminutive Boadicea in tartan skirt and brogues, that her awesome energy was revealed. One such victim was Lord Home, a long-standing friend of the Bowes-Lyons who smiled ruefully as he recalled the long marches with Elizabeth. 'She loved walking over the hills and could out-walk the guns, the keepers and the beaters. I had to walk further to get to those hills because I lived in the lowlands so I was pretty tired before we started. But she could walk all day and then dance right into the night. I'm not far off ninety myself, so we started level, but she could go on walking long after I'd virtually given up.' Lord Home also attributed the Queen Mother's astonishing staying power to the 'Scottish blood which flows strongly through her veins'. But as a friend of David's at Eton and a frequent guest at Glamis, he saw other influences at work. 'She was almost the youngest of a very large family. So she had to take the rough and tumble with all those countless brothers and sisters. But she gave as good as she got! She moved around the tenant farmers on the estates talking to them about their animals, the crops, their dogs and the farm life. I think if you lived in that part of Scotland you can't avoid being to a certain extent a philosopher, competing with the elements, understanding the animals and the rhythms of life. I think this laid the foundation of her ease of manner with a whole lot of different people.' Lord Home remembers Elizabeth's 'fairy-like quality, and being exceedingly light on her feet. Once we were all staying down at St Paul's Walden Bury at some Red Cross fête or something. Everybody was dead beat. She ought to have been. The clock struck midnight and we were all going off to bed when suddenly she said, "Wouldn't it be fun to have a square dance?" So we square-danced on the hard stone flags for two more hours . . .' Even then what milady wanted, milady got.

Besides the round-the-clock energy Elizabeth was developing a composure and serenity which suggested an alert maturity way beyond her years. The childhood dancing classes, the piano lessons, the play-acting at Glamis, above all the Countess's style, had given Elizabeth poise and self-confidence. This, together with the volatile Bowes-Lyon spirit had made her a female no man could confront with ease. Sparkling to be sure, but potentially intimidating too, perhaps, with that look of cool appraisal occasionally eclipsing the renowned Bowes-Lyon charm. Any recuperating soldier who even thought of making a pass at Her Ladyship (let alone actually making a move) was demurely but devastatingly rebuffed.

Altogether 1,500 servicemen were cared for at Glamis castle during the First World War. None of them left without a special goodbye to this dark-fringed teenager who had written their letters, fetched their Woodbines, soothingly persuaded the amputees and the shell-shock cases that their lives still had meaning. Elizabeth kept an autograph book in which soldiers wrote their farewell messages. One of them, W. H. Harrup of the Eighth Seaforths, was not just appreciative; he revealed all the signs of an incubating clairvoyant. His inscription, as Ann Morrow records, reads: '12th September, 1917. For Lady Elizabeth. May the owner of this book be hung, drawn and quartered. Yes, hung in diamonds, drawn in a coach and four, and quartered in the best house in the land.' He deserves a medal for guesswork if not for gallantry.

By the time Elizabeth celebrated her eighteenth birthday, in 1918, the war was exhausting itself towards its close. Her 'tour of duty' at Glamis was coming to an end too. At eleven a.m. on 11 November when the Armistice officially came into force, Forfar, like the rest of the United Kingdom, wept, sang and cheered. Bonfires were lit, the orange glare silhouetting the dark outline of the castle. Funny hats and costumes were dug out of the castle's prop box as the Strathmores and their patients caught the prevailing ecstasy with a sing song, a few tears mingling with the cheers. Everybody rushed on to the streets. Elizabeth watched as the villagers danced to the Scottish pipers. Lady Strathmore wept, thinking of Fergus but grateful that three of her sons at least, would soon be coming home. (Eventually all did.) Londoners were a shade less restrained than the people of Forfar. As A. J. P. Taylor noted with the historian's respect for detail: 'Omnibuses were seized, and people in strange garments caroused on the open upper deck. Total strangers copulated in doorways and on the pavements. They were asserting the triumph of life over death . . .' But there were plenty of other ways to let off steam. To celebrate the end of the war and Elizabeth's 'coming out' Lady Strathmore gave a dance for her. At the back of the Countess's mind, of course, was that at eighteen, her daughter had to be groomed for marriage. There were problems. War had decimated the 'eligible bachelor' market. The catalogue of well-born, well-heeled, well-connected young men was necessarily curtailed. The dance offered the dual opportunity for Elizabeth to put her dainty toe into adult society and the Countess to survey the field.

On the day of the dance, Elizabeth awoke with a fever and a high temperature. But she insisted that the dance go ahead. Elizabeth Longford may have been correct in asserting that 'characteristically she [Elizabeth] insisted on holding the dance so as not to disappoint her friends'. An equally persuasive notion is that nothing short of the mercury actually exploding out of the thermometer would have kept Her Ladyship away. It was a dazzling success. She was 'launched'. Lady Buxton, a valued

Strathmore confidante, wrote to a friend, 'Elizabeth Lyon is out now and Cecilia has had a dance for her. How many hearts Elizabeth will break!'

And whose in particular?

3

War was over. The Strathmore sons, Michael belatedly, were home. All had been wounded but were being nursed back to health and a kind of peace of mind. All three had left England with the perky self-assurance instilled on the playing fields of Eton. All returned with the gaunt reticence inflicted by the battlefields of France. Elizabeth was 'out' and as a vital and high-spirited nineteen year old was ready for the incandescent birth of the 1920s. But there was still some unfinished business for her up at Glamis. The soldiers' needs and problems didn't cease with the signing of the Armistice. Some had no homes to return to. Few had jobs. Elizabeth found work and living quarters for many of them on the estates, badgered her friends in London and at St Paul's Walden to do the same for some of the others. And then it was back to the not especially harsh realities of London's fashionable society. Ascot, Goodwood, the weekend parties at St Paul's Walden, grouse-shooting and tramps across the hills of Forfar – it was all fun, but socially incestuous. The same people, the same faces, the same unremitting small talk around those familiar London mansions or country estates.

Stuck with that routine Elizabeth, a striking brunette with a shrewd self-awareness, made the best of it. And clearly with considerable success. Whether she 'took London by storm' as some biographers claim (throwing in as a bonus 'all the men were at her feet') is arguable. What isn't contested anywhere is that those clear blue eyes and rose-pink features under the brushed fringe and floppy hat, made her an instant favourite on every hostess's guest list. The favourite word for this Bowes-Lyon beauty was 'radiant'. (It pulsates like a bleeping satellite out of all the material on the Queen Mother.) Lady Airlie developed the theme, adding 'gaiety, kindness and sincerity' making her 'irresistible to men'. Well she was clearly irresistible to the late 'Chips' Channon, politician and merciless diarist (father of Paul Channon MP) who saw her as, 'well-bred, kind, gentle and slack . . . always charming, always gay, pleasant and smiling, mildly flirtatious in a very proper romantic old-fashioned Valentine sort of way . . . She makes every man feel chivalrous and gallant towards her.' He was, he confessed years after, 'even a little in love with her'.

Surprising if he'd not been. Every red-blooded, well, blue-blooded male presented to her was knocked back on his jodhpurs. Elizabeth Longford tells of one 'besotted young man who tried to advance his suit with surprising roughness. After a night-long hunt ball, he made the remaining hours of sleep hideous by cracking his hunting whip under her window.' The English nobility's equivalent of the woosome troubador. Nothing was more calculated (borrowing from Barbara Cartland) 'to make the senses reel' than a 'gentle, well-bred, creature of surpassing beauty doing her 'mildly flirtatious' best. One adoring character is quoted as proclaiming, 'I was madly in love with her. Everything at Glamis was beautiful, perfect. Being there was like living in a Van Dyck picture. Time, and the junketing world stood still. But the magic gripped us all. I fell madly in love. They all did.'

We will speculate on who this trembling beau – not to mention 'they all' – might have been. But in this area, as in every aspect of her private life thereafter, Elizabeth Bowes-Lyon has been charmingly tight-lipped. The high-born, or more specifically those who don't need the money, rarely go into the 'kiss and tell' market. Royalty never. Moreover those who glide in and out of 'royal circles' instinctively (if not by royal command) tend to be even more secretive than those they serve. But there is compelling circumstantial evidence which points intriguingly towards some behind-the-scenes jousting for Elizabeth's hand. Cue the handsome and carelessly courageous young major, James Stuart, later Viscount Stuart of Findhorn PC, CH, MVO, MC.

The son of the 17th Earl of Moray, Jamie Stuart was a neighbour of the Strathmores. He had gone to Eton too which gave him points with the Bowes-Lyon brothers and in turn steered him into contact with Elizabeth. Like Patrick, Jock and

Fergus, he was in the 1914 war as swiftly as he could get there. He rose to the rank of Brigade Major, winning an MC and bar for the sort of insolent heroics schoolboys – and James Bond fans – relish. The occasion for this piece of derring-do was the initial attack at the Battle of the Somme, on 1 July 1916. Thirteen British divisions went 'over the top' in wave after wave. The German machine gunners eagerly accepted the gift and mowed the Tommies down in their thousands. The attack failed. Nineteen thousand were killed, with fifty-seven thousand casualties in all. With those odds, and his rashness, Major Stuart ought to have been one of them. We can picture the scene from his own throwaway reference to it in his autobiography *Within the Fringe*. 'My success during those nights on solitary patrol was to capture and bring in single-handed one German prisoner. Like me, he was alone, and he was lost in No-Man's-Land. I was unarmed as usual, because I couldn't be bothered carrying arms. . . .' An attitude guaranteed to win an MC.

It also made him – in the terminology of the day – 'a maddeningly attractive' idol at those weekend parties where slinky flappers, long cigarette holders between vermilion lips, danced to the latest craze. An authentic war hero, low handicap golfer, good looking and a great dancer – and heir to an earldom into the bargain – Jamie Stuart was clearly in a class of his own. A degree in law made him almost too good to be true. Bemedalled in his service blues, a touch of arrogance on his rugged Scottish features, it is unlikely any unattached female 'of the class' – which must have included Elizabeth Bowes-Lyon – wouldn't have rated him the catch of the county if not the country. Being a first-class shot he must have bagged more game than anyone else. Elizabeth, who disliked the crack of the guns, found the piles of dead birds repugnant, but she would supposedly have stifled those reactions in his presence. A frequent visitor to Glamis, with all the social adroitness of the born playboy, he must have been seeded Number One in the general speculation on possible suitors for Lady Elizabeth. Aristocratic matchmakers rated her the most exciting girl in the running.

She had established her royal connections through her friendship with Princess Mary, begun in the Girl Guides. Stuart had become friendly with Prince Albert at Cambridge University. According to him Bertie 'was not an easy man to know or handle and I cannot pretend that I ever became a close friend;

indeed I do not know of any very close friends he had, except Louis Greig.'

Surgeon-Lieutenant Louis Greig was assistant medical officer at the Royal Naval College when he first befriended the awkward and stammering young prince. Their friendship developed after Bertie had been invalided out of the Navy following an operation in 1917 for a duodenal ulcer. A year later they were in the RAF together where Prince Albert, now a qualified fighter pilot, became a Squadron Leader. Whatever his official role with the young prince, Greig's self-confessed mission in life was 'to put steel in him'. (In the event, the steel was there, albeit beneath deep-rooted, stammering inhibitions.) But at the time, Greig clearly had a task on his hands and saw in the dashing, extrovert James Stuart a useful ADC. All three were together in Brussels for Belgium's victory celebrations when war ended in 1918. By all accounts, the footloose threesome danced and tippled their way around the capital's exclusive night-spots, now feverishly back in business. Stuart tells of taking a couple of pipers to the 'Merry Grill' where all three leaped into a Highland Fling on the dance floor. Their final duties in the early hours was to return Bertie to the Royal Palace in reasonable shape. No further revelations are made by Stuart. But we can assume that 'putting steel in Bertie' did not exclude normal heterosexual indulgences; virgin queens have been known but not their equivalent in princes.

For James Stuart, the turning point was being appointed as Albert's first Equerry. It is – or was then – a dismally paid job loosely defined as 'an officer attendant upon the British sovereign'. Stuart moved into Buckingham Palace and received £450 a year. 'I was given breakfast and lunch any day I chose.' In return, he was, one suspects, a royal gofer, confidant, fixer, trouble-shooter and court jester who could handle his master's occasional bouts of bad temper. Albert's chronic illnesses and speech difficulty, the sense of inadequacy induced by his frosty father, and an elder brother who condescendingly referred to him as 'poor old Bertie', inevitably made him short-fused, prone to depression. Jamie knew how to cope. Around the time of his appointment – May 1920 – Elizabeth Bowes-Lyon was also in London. It was a fact which wouldn't have displeased her friend the equerry incarcerated in an upper floor of the palace. She was twenty and according to Lady Airlie 'very unlike the cocktail drinking, chain-smoking girls who came to be regarded as typical of the nineteen twenties.' She wasn't Dresden china either; no frigid ladyship in coy chiffons blushing at the risqué party talk. She was developing a smooth, controlled persona which distanced her from the bright young things of the day. Poised, discerning, yet teasingly irresistible when the moment – if not the man – was right.

All the evidence suggests that such a moment arrived on 20 May 1920 at a May Ball given by Lord and Lady Farquhar at their home at 7 Grosvenor Square, London. Since that lavish spree would one day have historic consequences, Lord Farquhar should be given his due. He had been Master of the King's Household to Edward VII. A surprising choice since he appears to have been a galloping eccentric. According to Douglas Liversedge he made preposterous claims to enormous wealth. In his will which must have caused discreet guffaws at Whites and similar haunts, he made sizeable bequests to various members of the royal family. Solicitors hunting for funds to support this largesse, found none. He was not only broke. He left considerable debts. But society forgave him. Taking into consideration, perhaps, That Ball he gave in Grosvenor Square.

Elizabeth, of course, was invited. And so was Bertie, which automatically included his equerry who would probably have been invited anyway. We know that Elizabeth looked 'absolutely stunning'. We know too that she foxtrotted with the masterly hero of the Somme. And that their evident enjoyment was closely scrutinized by Prince Albert, soon to be made Duke of York. From then on, accounts of what happened differ. One version has the prince saying to his equerry 'That's a lovely girl you have been dancing with. Who is she?' Unlikely since we know that he had met her before through her friend, his sister Princess Mary. And having met Elizabeth Bowes-Lyon he was not likely to have forgotten her. (We can discount their childhood encounter when she gave Bertie the sugared cherry off her cake. Neither of them remembered it.) Minor discrepancies apart, the fact is that Bertie having expressed an interest in the girl, his faithful equerry got the message and discreetly withdrew. Bertie, who was as good a dancer as he was a first-class tennis player, politely invited Elizabeth to join him on the floor. Her Ladyship graciously consented. How often they danced together is not recorded. What is clear, however, is that Bertie was royally bowled over by the experience. One look into those playful eyes and Albert Frederick Arthur George, second son to

George V, was as dazed as the day he was in the Battle of Jutland. For him at least – to relocate the lyric – a nightingale sang in Grosvenor Square.

But not, apparently, for Elizabeth Bowes-Lyon. If the prince glowed all the way back to the palace the euphoria was scarcely shared either by his equerry or the radiant daughter at NO. 20, St James's Square. No reflection on Bertie. The Lady Elizabeth was never going to be the type to be swept off her feet. Like Glamis Castle, rushing the defences would be futile if not fatal. 'One knew instinctively,' Lady Airlie observed, 'that she was a girl who would find real happiness only in marriage and mother-hood. A born homemaker.' Bertie would happily have settled for that. But at twenty, Elizabeth, not long discharged from hospital duty at the Castle, had a lot of catching up to do. Moreover, Lady Strathmore was now increasingly infirm. Elizabeth was called more and more to play hostess to the Castle's visitors. Frustrating to Bertie who was experiencing all the familiar pangs and mood-changes of the unrequited lover. Not that he read the symptoms at the time. He told his friends long after that he had fallen in love that evening although he did not realize it until later. What he did realize was that he found an irresistible urge to see more of Glamis. And if not Glamis, St Paul's Walden would be fine. Failing that, St James's Square. The criterion in all cases being the presence of this ravishing Bowes-Lyon. He had in fact seen her up at Glamis in September 1920. His sister, the Princess Mary, was on a visit to Scotland staying with Lady Airlie. The Strathmores observed the courtesies and invited the Duke to stay with them at Glamis. Any notion that they viewed him as a possible suitor at the time can be rejected. Robert Sencourt, a New Zealander on the General Staff at Delhi claims that when he asked Lord Strathmore what hopes he had for his heirs, he replied: 'Well if there is one thing I have determined for my children, it is that they shall never have any sort of post about the Court.' (Helen Cathcart adds an arcane footnote to that quote: 'Background circumstances unknown to Sencourt make this story highly suspect.')

Nevertheless the Strathmores were known to have taken a frosty view of the Prince of Wales's antics and the exploitation of his playboy image. Bertie, by contrast, was safe, sanitized, and pulled no princely rank at Glamis. At the evening dance at the Castle, a bright moon dutifully agleam over the ramparts, the couple took the floor. The records show that Lady Elizabeth wore a 'rose brocade Vandyck dress with pearls in her hair'. He'd already run a head of steam on the long journey up from London. Now they were dancing together. He returned home to Buckingham Palace where both Queen Mary and George V detected all the familiar signs. At subsequent encounters with Elizabeth Bertie transmitted unmistakeable signals but received no responses in kind. He persisted and was demurely kept at arm's length. A sweet rebuff no doubt. He was after all a prince of the realm, while her good nature required she let him down gently. She liked him, of course, but on that night at least, he was just one of the men she danced with; another of them being his equerry James Stuart. Which brings us to that unknown admirer who claimed he was 'madly in love with her . . .'. The unnamed gallant for whom, 'time and the gossiping world stood still'. The trouble is, the gossiping world having been thus immobilized, we possess few hints as to who that character was. But it's not difficult to be persuaded that he was Bertie's equerry, the Hon. James Stuart. And here an intriguing sub-plot brings key supporting players into the arena.

Whether she was aware or not of the newly created Duke of York's feverish interest in her, Elizabeth gaily carried on her life as a desirably unattached socialite. In October 1920 she went back to Glamis for the 'shoot'. A group picture in that month's *Tatler* of the aristocrats present – milords Strathmore, Glamis and Elphinstone standing behind their seated womenfolk – is fascinating. Was it coincidence or Strathmore strategy that the two furthest apart are Lady Elizabeth Bowes-Lyon and the Hon. James Stuart, MC? A separate shot of him, tweedy, pipe-smoking, roguish smile under the sporting cap, resembled the archetypal Mills and Boon heart-throb. One might have wondered what on earth he was doing alongside the grim, fossilized gentry but for the fact that Elizabeth Bowes-Lyon was in the front row, right. Since the Duke of York wasn't in the party, Stuart was there as a close friend, not as an equerry. But in a strong field of admirers he was certainly one of the favourites. Who were the other rivals for Elizabeth's hand against whom the young Duke of York would have to fight his corner? Helen Cathcart elegantly traps these gadflies under glass: 'Within her light-hearted social scan there were now young Guards officers, young men from *The Times* and the publishing world, tyro diplomats and junior stock brokers, banking and accountancy types perhaps indirectly linked with her father's presidency of the Scottish Widows Fund, his fellow directors on North British Assurance or even his role as a deputy Governor of the Royal Bank of Scotland.' Not a pauper amongst them. Any one picked at random could have been guaranteed to have kept Elizabeth Bowes-Lyon in the style to which she had been born – and intended to remain. But as Cathcart concludes, 'her admirers, though numerous were kept comfortably at bay'.

At bay, perhaps. Comfortably, less so. Lady Buxton's 'how many hearts Elizabeth will break!' was good thinking. She had watched her kittenish young friend in action on many dance floors; and seen her partners reel away decidedly unsettled. The fact that Elizabeth's fierce old puritan of a father Lord Strathmore insisted she be chaperoned everywhere, merely raised the temperature. And the stakes. The uncomfortable Duke of York must have envied his elder brother's rakish ease with women, notably married women. But David, to put it crudely, was usually pushing at an open door. A royal stud, he was in the hunt for playthings not home-makers. He had danced several times with Elizabeth Bowes-Lyon and gossip fleetingly hinted at a possible engagement. Fat chance. The Prince of Wales's known and unknown peccadilloes may have amused and excited the twittering daughters of the nobility, but would have cut no ice with Elizabeth Bowes-Lyon. His pouch-eyed good looks and skill on the dance floor -- he was mad about New Orleans jazz – entranced the Mayfair 'eligibles'. But Elizabeth, recognizing the nature of the beast, responded coolly. Fifteen years on she would congratulate herself on her discernment. They couldn't have been more different. For the Prince of Wales, self-indulgence was practically an art form. His sensual appetites matched those of his grandfather, that ram of a monarch Edward VII. His image abroad, particularly in America, displeased his father. A New York magazine ran a competition for the 'best love letter to the Prince of Wales'. *Vanity Fair* speculated mercilessly on the number of ladies he'd kissed, blondes he'd dated, gallons of champagne he'd drunk, horses he'd fallen off, marriage proposals he'd received, concluding with 'Hats off to the indestructible Dancing Drinking Tumbling Kissing Walking Talking and Sleeping – but not Marrying – idol of the British Empire'. An image that would have the Countess of Strathmore reaching for her smelling salts. Lady Donaldson's character reading was more terse: 'At the end he had three interests – golf, gardening, and money . . . and the greatest of these was money.'

Nothing there to turn the head of Elizabeth Bowes-Lyon, raised as she was on all the virtues, with Chastity and Thrift way ahead of the field. So he was no problem to her, though he was to the King and Queen. They badly wanted him married off, and having been advised that the country would not tolerate him marrying a foreigner were ready to settle for a bride from the British aristocracy. And that went for Bertie too. Queen Mary told her lady-in-waiting: 'I have discovered that he is very much attracted to Lady Elizabeth Bowes-Lyon. He's always talking about her. She seems a charming girl but I don't know her very well.' That blandly innocent 'I have discovered . . .' is a hoot considering the wily old Queen knew all about the couple's meetings – the dates, the places, even the arrival and departure times. She was pleased at the notion of Elizabeth Bowes-Lyon as a prospective daughter-in-law. George V felt the same way, telling Bertie with his usual confidence-sapping tactlessness, 'You'll be a lucky fellow if she'll have you!'

Bertie was convinced that he could overcome all of Elizabeth's doubts about him. But while he was blithely singing her praises to his mother, Elizabeth was voicing her reluctance and uncertainties to Queen Mary's lady-in-waiting. She had doubts about her feelings. She wasn't sure that he was the man she wanted to marry. Above all she wasn't totally sold on the idea of dangling from the puppet-strings of the monarchy. Those are the favourite explanations for Elizabeth's initial rejection of the Duke of York's first proposal of marriage in the spring. Most are probably accurate. But we cannot discount other possibilities: that she simply wasn't in love with him at the time; or that with his hang-ups, his speech impediment and burdening insecurities he fell somewhat short of the paragon of her dreams. If this is what she thought she certainly told no one. She was as friendly as ever and danced with him again in the summer of 1921 at a Royal Air Force Ball at London's Ritz Hotel. She also danced with his equerry James Stuart. The last waltz, as it turned out for the handsome Guards Officer. When the night was over, Bertie, now hell-bent on marrying Elizabeth, must have experienced a pang of jealousy. But Elizabeth remained as delicately unyielding as ever. In short, she was driving the Duke mad.

We know precisely how the poor chap felt from the memoirs of J. C. Davidson, a friend and influential Conservative politician. 'I had not been in the Duke's presence more than a few minutes before I realized that he was not only worried but genuinely unhappy. He seemed to have reached a crisis in his life and wanted someone to whom he could unburden himself. He told me that sometimes the discipline of the formality of the Court proved irksome . . . Then out it came. He declared he was desperately in love, but that he was in despair for it seemed quite certain that he had lost the only woman he would ever marry.' Davidson soothed him, citing his own experience of having first been rejected. But the Duke wasn't convinced. 'He replied that his case was different. The King's son cannot propose to the girl he loves since custom requires that he must not place himself in the position of being refused.' (The idea that anybody would dare turn down his son was equally unthinkable to George V – a male-chauvinist monarch who believed a royal consort, like any other wife, was commanded, not wooed.)

'Worse still, I gathered an emissary had already been sent to ascertain whether the girl was prepared to marry him, and that it had failed. The question was, what was he to do? He could not live without her, and certainly he would never marry anyone else.'

Davidson made it clear to the Duke that 'In this Year of Grace, 1922, no high-spirited girl of character was likely to accept a proposal made second hand. If she was as fond of him as he thought, he must propose to her himself. . . .' This heart-to-heart discussion – instigated by Bertie's friend, Louis Grieg – took place at Dunkirk where the Duke laid the foundation stone at the War Memorial there commemorating British Officers and seamen who had fallen in the First World War. The Duke returned to England at grouse-shooting time, determined to make a final assault on the Castle. The fair damsel beneath the turrets would have been amused and flattered had she known of the eager band of courtiers, friends, hostesses and well-wishers massing in support of the duke.

Mrs Ronald Greville, daughter of a whisky millionaire who married his cook, was the pushiest of them all. Adoringly awe-struck within curtseying distance of royalty, she loved playing Cupid and claimed credit for the introductions which led to the marriage of Lord Louis Mountbatten to Edwina Ashley (in Delhi, 1922). Mrs Greville, Maggie to her friends, was well equipped for her role. She was stupendously wealthy and owned Polesden Lacey, a magnificent retreat in Surrey to which she invited prospective couples to size each other up over jasmine tea. Not ordinary couples. No mileage, socially, in that. Royalty was her territory or at the very least, selected candidates on the fringe. Like all rich, presumptuous hostesses she was loved by some, detested by others. But nobody denied that she had impeccable connections in high places. Queen Mary, who privately might have found Maggie too brash by half, acknowledged that as a matchmaker she was in a class of her own. And Her Majesty had some royal sons to get off her hands, Bertie most urgently.

So Maggie did her stuff, inviting the duke and Elizabeth to tea, theatre parties and dinner, with other guests merely there as ballast. In between times, Lady Airlie, Queen Mary's lady-in-waiting and strongest ally, threw her London pad and Scottish castle into the pot as backup locations. Elizabeth, who knew perfectly well what all these manoeuvres were about, maintained her look of wide-eyed innocence. Flitting elusively from place to place with amusing friends and dancing partners was not exactly roughing it. And being pursued by the King's son who she knew was mad about her, put her at the pinnacle of society's marriage market. But then a good time was being had by all in the exclusive echelons to which she belonged. The twenties had not roared in as they had in post-war New York. They giggled rather than shrieked into London to the symbolic hit tune of the day, 'Let's Do It!' Bobbed-haired debs and bright young things frolicked awkwardly into the new dance craze. Crimson nails fingering a diamond bracelet over a long black glove; thin shoulder strap dropped over a stark white arm with maybe the odd monocle brazenly screwed into a heavily mascara-ed eye; and the ultimate – a De Reszke cigarette in a long holder held between Clara Bow lips; Lautrec could have sketched another thousand canvases.

Elizabeth danced to Ambrose at the Embassy Club. At Ciros she might have seen the Prince of Wales with maybe Mrs Freda Dudley Ward on his arm. Or it might have been Thelma, Lady Furness, sister of Gloria Vanderbilt. Soon the Prince and his brother the Duke of York would have the Charleston and the Black Bottom to master. They would both become expert at it. No one would ever accuse them of slacking on the job. But good dancer though he was Bertie was still finding it hard to manoeuvre Elizabeth towards the altar. The Countess of Strathmore backed Elizabeth's decision to turn him down, but tactfully wrote to Mabell Airlie, 'I do hope he will find a nice wife who will make him happy' adding shrewdly, 'he is a man who will be made or marred by his wife.'

Those well-intentioned sentiments merely added to the Duke's irritation and depression. His black moods were being gossiped about, and noticed by the press. It was too much for Queen Mary. Her lady-in-waiting and Maggie Greville having failed to influence the reluctant Strathmore girl, she would have to take a hand. Leading a posse of palace flunkeys and bringing Princess Mary along for the ride, she glinted her way up to Scotland. Base camp for the final assault was Lady Airlie's Cortachy Castle. The official reason: she needed a holiday. The truth: to have a final inspection of this girl everybody was talking about and confirm what she suspected, that this was the one for Bertie. (The notion that Elizabeth might have other ideas didn't enter her imperial thinking. Like George V, she believed firmly that Dukes choose, their chosen submit.) Glamis being notified of her presence in Scotland, the invitation to Her Majesty was sent forthwith. Fortuitously, her visit coincided with a sudden bout of illness which took Lady Strathmore to her bed. Elizabeth was left to act as hostess, guide, mistress of the Castle. Facing each other across the tea cups, they small-talked delicately about the Castle's history, the tapestries, the paintings, and the Countess's beloved flower garden. All Elizabeth's governesses would have beamed to see the way she deftly handled her intimidating majesty. Queen Mary, by all accounts, gave her young hostess the full raised-lorgnette treatment. What she received in return was the disarming smile of a young Bowes-Lyon in total control of self and situation. The royal matchmaker – a Dolly Levi turned Lady Bracknell – was impressed and enchanted. Elizabeth may not have been 'of the blood royal'. Much better than that. She was *'plus royaliste que le roi.'* Queen Mary asked that her good wishes be delivered to Lady Strathmore, noted with satisfaction Elizabeth's superbly executed curtsy, and left, her plans decided even before she stepped into her carriage. She told her intimates later that 'this was the one girl who could make Bertie happy'. She hastily added that of course she wouldn't interfere on the grounds that 'mothers should never meddle in their children's love-affairs'. Nor, perhaps, should they. But this mother couldn't wait. She would meddle in them all the way to the Abbey. Not that she thought it would be easy. But whatever it took, this lovely, vital creature would one day be the Duchess of York.

In fact it took another year. Twelve more months of urgent wooing, of further rumour and gossip. But there was now a noticeable softening in Elizabeth's resistance. The more she saw of the Duke, the more she perceived qualities that she liked. Here familiarity was working in Bertie's favour. Society writers were beginning to clock their frequent meetings. One of them wrote in Cassell's *Magazine*: 'If you take the visits recently paid by the Duke of York and Princess Mary you will see how the names of the same friends appear again and again at different houses. When the Duke of York stayed with Lord Strathmore at Glamis in October the daughter of the house, Lady Elizabeth Bowes-Lyon, a friend of Princess Mary was naturally there . . . In September when the Queen and Princess Mary visited Lady Dalhousie at Brechin Castle, Lady Elizabeth Bowes-Lyon was of the party . . .'

No coincidence. All part of Queen Mary's strategy to bring Elizabeth closer to the centre of royal circles. The Queen, who hated being photographed, made an exception at Brechin Castle, posing in a group with Elizabeth in the foreground. A booster-shot in the 'royalization' of Elizabeth was making her a bridesmaid at the wedding of Princess Mary to Viscount Lascelles on 28 February 1922. This lugubrious peer, fifteen years older than his timorous bride had at least one advantage: pots of money (three million pounds in 1922 would multiply prodigiously today). The age difference, and the bridegroom's lacklustre personality scarcely indicated a love-match. Elizabeth, one of seven bridesmaids, looked stunning in a silver dress, a diadem of silver rose leaves, and a 1920s touch, a silver rose worn at the hip clipped to a blue lover's knot. (Lady Airlie recalled Elizabeth 'looking very lovely in her white and silver dress. The Duke of York was deeply in love with her and I was trying to persuade her to marry him . . .') All very romantic but it didn't show in Elizabeth's face on the official wedding photograph. For once the Bowes-Lyon flair for registering a holding-pattern smile regardless, deserted her. 'Sullen . . . pensive . . . anxious . . .' are just a few of the descriptives grimacing out of several biographies. But when it comes to explaining it, then it's anybody's guess. One notion was that this example of royalty pulling out all the stops – the crowds, the processions, the grinding ceremonials and the mind-numbing rituals – clued Elizabeth into what marrying royalty would mean. More likely that she was just thinking of the Duke of York; of his touching, driven devotion, backed by a scramble of hyperactive match-makers. She had plenty to think about, and it showed, even from where she stood in the back row. Curiously, she is missing from the later official painting of the royal group. The reason given at the time was that there was insufficient room on the canvas.

Elizabeth was glad when it was all over and delighted when one of the other bridesmaids, Diamond Hardinge, invited her to Paris where Lord Hardinge was ambassador. We don't know too much about Diamond except that she must have been a St Trinian's look-alike and a scream in the dormitory. A friend, Cynthia Gladwyn, noted that Diamond 'had perfected the knack of cracking her jaw with a loud report; it amused her to do so in public places such as the theatre . . .' No dull days at the British Embassy with a hostess like that. And few dull evenings either. Elizabeth 'did' Paris, swept around by a succession of Embassy attachés, one of whom fell in love with her and later proposed. A couple of others that summer also chanced their arm. And received the same gentle turn down. She returned to London – the Strathmores were now living at 17 Bruton Street, WI – and was back in the re-shuffling pack of society. She must have begun to miss Bertie. In September 1922 he was back at the Castle, certainly by her wish. This was crunch time for the Duke. A brilliant County Ball, Forfar's aristocratic night of the year, was the ideal location. Add the champagne, the dancing, the moonlight over the Grampians – he could almost see the drawbridge descending. He arrived at Forfar's Masonic Hall at nine o'clock and strode in eagerly to loud applause. The music had just begun and as the *Forfar Herald* reported, 'the Duke looking well in his tartan kilt immediately entered into the zest of the Highland Reel, his partner being Lady Elizabeth Bowes-Lyon who presented a dainty picture in her simple mid-Victorian gown of fuschia hyatenne taffeta . . .' More applause for the kilted, jilted lover, and his sparkling partner as they leapt around the floor. The Dowager Countess of Airlie watched intently with the faint smile of the hopeful matchmaker. A Raffles at large among the guests could have escaped with a trunkload of jewellery. The newspaper, dutifully reporting the glistening hardware on heads, ears, throats, necklines and wrists, filled three broadsheet columns. 'The Countess (of Airlie) wore a magnificent diamond tiara and ropes of gorgeous pearls . . .' 'Baroness Bentinck looked well in jade satin veiled with black net, the sequinned bodice of her gown being ornamented with diamonds . . . ' 'Lady Dorothy Hope Morley of Camperdown had chosen apricot satin. On her hair was a diamond bandeau, and in her corsage, pearl ornaments . . .' A tiara and collar of diamonds for Mrs Bouch. Diamond stars, a tiara of diamonds and pearls for Mrs Colin Neish. The list, and the wealth was stupefying. It is unlikely that those mentioned would have glanced at the left-hand column in the paper which announced, 'On 2nd October 1922, there shall be a reduction in the war wage now paid to railway shopmen employed on the North British and Caledonian Railway Companies of ten shillings per week.'

The assembled guests which included the usual crowd, Prince Paul of Serbia, Chips Channon, Lady Doris Gordon Lennox . . . the familiar friends at court, had a notable absentee. The Hon. James Stuart. If his presence had been needed by His Royal Highness, he would have been there. It was obvious the handsome, debonair Jamie was not required, not on the night that the Duke, according to the latest count, intended proposing for the third time. Elizabeth again said 'No' but Bertie caught signs of wavering. Was she at last coming round in his favour? If so, a sequence of curious events speeded the process. On Friday, 5 January 1923, the *Daily News* published a bombshell of a story:

SCOTTISH BRIDE FOR PRINCE OF WALES
Heir to the Throne to Wed Peer's Daughter.
An Official Announcement Imminent.
Happy Choice.
One of the Closest Friends of Princess Mary.
The formal announcement of the engagement of the
Prince of Wales to a young Scottish lady of noble birth
will be made within the next two or three months. The
future Queen of England is the daughter of a well-known
Scottish peer who is the owner of castles both north and
south of the Tweed. A happy feature of the engagement is
that the girl of the Prince's choice is one of the closest
friends of his sister, Princess Mary.

Elizabeth, disingenuously unnamed in the announcement, was shocked. The story unleashed thoughts which so far had not surfaced in the gossip surrounding Bertie and herself. Elizabeth and David . . . the idea may have been unthinkable, but one person, Lady Donaldson, had thought it, observing that 'in her old age, Elizabeth wistfully remembered that "David had been such fun".' Well, he had been fun. Having a good time came more naturally to him than kingship. And when the corks were popping and the band playing, he left his rivals standing. But as a husband? And, of all people, to Elizabeth Bowes-Lyon? Admittedly, he was a heavily-backed favourite. Arrogant, unpredictable and dangerous behind that winning smile he approached his golf, his hunting and his love-affairs with equal violence. That was part of his attraction and he was never short of partners.

But Elizabeth's criteria for a husband went far beyond trophies and stud value. Her attitudes delineated by a friend in the early 1920s indicated a marked distaste for the prince's sexual galivanting. Dennis Judd, a biographer of George VI, quotes this friend as saying: 'Her circle wasn't more moral in a "pious" way. It just never occurred to us that unmarried people should go to bed together. It was unthinkable, especially within our own group of very good friends. With the Prince of Wales we knew it was always married ladies. But Prince Bertie's circle were all "gals", nice "gals", that was the difference between the two men. The basis of their lives was completely different, and Prince Bertie would never have suggested that he might go to bed with anyone. Holding hands in a boat, *that* was courting.'

No one would ever doubt Elizabeth's pristine attitude to life, love and pre-marital sex; a life pure, godly, expletives deleted. And Bertie? Well, he would have drawn a fine distinction between courting the woman he hoped to marry and bedding willing partners when the urge took him. Or them. But unlike his brother David's chaotic liaisons, Bertie's affairs were discreet, hit-and-run efforts. Clandestine transactions, no tears, no fuss, with the equerry taking care of the flowers.

But this activity detracted nothing from Bertie's chivalrous attitude to women in general and Elizabeth in particular. He was prepared to hold her hand in a boat until the tide ran out. And that message was at last getting through to Elizabeth. Bertie sensed it and grew more self-assured each day. It showed and encouraged Elizabeth to re-assess him, and his proposal. The story forecasting her engagement to the Prince of Wales boosted Bertie's chances further. She resented being caught up in a situation which she couldn't control.

That resentment was shared by the Palace where George and

Mary must have pushed the 'action' buttons with a vengeance. The Prince of Wales immediately authorized a denial: 'A few days ago the *Daily News* announced the forthcoming engagement of the Prince of Wales to an Italian Princess. Today the same journal states on what is claimed to be unquestionable authority that the formal announcement of His Royal Highness's engagement to a daughter of a Scottish peer will be made within the next few months. We are officially authorized to say that this report is as devoid of foundation as was the previous. . . .'

Whatever else the Prince of Wales may have said to Elizabeth about the rumours we know that he advised her that 'You had better take him and go in the end to Buck House.' (The idea of the Prince of Wales giving marital advice to Elizabeth Bowes-Lyon is not unfunny.) His official denial was immediately effective. It killed off speculation and interestingly put more steel in Bertie. The decks were cleared for action. All possible distractions, if not rivals, had disappeared. Well almost. There was still the Hon. James Stuart to reckon with. It might be useful if this good-looking, ex-Guards captain were out of the picture.

The circumstances of the fairly abrupt departure of Stuart abroad around that time are cautiously hinted at – and certainly not in the more reverential biographies. But we can sense some matriarchal manoeuvring behind closed doors. Stuart himself refers to it in a few lines in his autobiography, *Within the Fringe*. It is useful to read them – and in between them. 'I had no ideas about my future except that I did not intend to – nor could I afford to – remain a courtier all my life. One day . . . I was offered the opportunity to go into the oil business as a learner . . . in America. So early in the New Year of 1922 I set off for the unknown which turned out to be the oilfields of Oklahoma.' A long way from Tipperary. Even further from 17 Bruton St. We know that the offer came from Sir Sidney Greville who had cleared it with Lord Cowdray (whose family company was linked to the Oklahoma interests). But were they nudged, and if so, by whom? No doubts in the mind of Richard Hough who asserts in *Born Royal*: 'Queen Mary discovered through one of her ladies-in-waiting that Elizabeth was very much in love with the Duke of York's equerry and would accept a proposal of marriage. Through court officials and business contacts, Mary arranged for Stuart to be replaced as Bertie's equerry and sent to the oilfields of Oklahoma. . . .' Ernest King also attributes

Stuart's hasty departure to the manipulations of Queen Mary in *The Green Baize Door*.

True or not, James Stuart swiftly found himself in Rodgers and Hammerstein territory, without the girl. In the first week of January, Elizabeth went to tea with Lady Airlie in London. The conversation turned to the Countess's own marriage to a cavalry officer. It was a life she hated at first, but grew to enjoy. It was a broad hint which concentrated Elizabeth's mind wonderfully. Maybe she was asking or expecting too much. There was a lot of residual goodness in Bertie, and no one would ever love her more. Food for thought as she returned to Bruton St.

Nothing so pensive about Bertie. Stuart was gone. David was out of the picture. On Saturday, 13 January 1923, invited by the Strathmores, he drove down to St Paul's Walden. On the Sunday morning when the family filed into the local parish church there were huddled whispers in the pews when it was noticed that the prince and the daughter of the house were absent. The service was delayed but finally got under way when it was obvious that the couple had gone for a stroll in the 'Fairy Wood', scene of Elizabeth's early childhood years. It was the Duke's choice of venue, and a smart move. Nostalgia, the planets and the Fairy Wood were all working for Bertie. For the fourth time, he asked her to marry him. Laughing mischievously, she is said to have responded, 'If you are going to keep this up for ever, I might as well say "Yes" now!' He was twenty-seven, she, twenty-two. Bertie's torment was over. So were the tranquil years for Elizabeth.

4

We can imagine the general jubilation as Elizabeth brought Bertie back from the woods to say they were engaged. The Duke had dutifully followed convention earlier by asking the Earl for Elizabeth's hand and receiving the necessary blessing. No walk-over, considering Lord Strathmore's known reluctance to have his family hanging on the coat-tails of royalty. His prejudice had largely been inspired by the Prince of Wales's chequered reputation. Bertie's, by contrast, was as transparently saintly as the stained-glass windows at Glamis. In any event, he had promised the Strathmores he would do everything he could to make their beloved Elizabeth happy. They were so convinced they didn't inquire as to his prospects. Meanwhile at York Cottage, Sandringham, King George V and Queen Mary were waiting for a coded message agreed between them and Bertie before he left. If the answer was 'yes' he would telegraph them accordingly. If 'no' . . . that contingency was not discussed. When the telegram did arrive it contained the three words agreed: 'All Right, Bertie.'

King George apparently growled his approval. Allegedly hating the idea of having typical twenties-style daughters-in-law, he softened in regard to Elizabeth. She placated him the way honey sweetens a grizzly. He loved having her around him. On the few occasions they had met she refused to be intimidated, the standard reaction of the females at court. In fact, as she wrote to the royal physician, Lord Dawson of Penn, 'I was never afraid of him. He was always ready to listen and give advice on one's own silly little affairs. And when he was in the mood he could be deliciously funny too.' He was obsessive about punctuality, and once when Elizabeth kept him waiting for dinner 'he couldn't bring himself to give her a wigging' (noted J. Wheeler-Bennett). 'You are not late my dear, I think we must have sat down two minutes early.' If the long-suffering butler had overheard it, it was a miracle he didn't drop a tray of china. George was particularly delighted by Bertie's good fortune. Originally, he saw David as the young lion in the family, born to add glory to the Windsor line. More and more he was adjusting that opinion. One day he would declare that Bertie had more guts than 'all of 'em'. Queen Mary, her role as chief conspirator over, contentedly returned to her petit-point.

Saying 'goodbye' to Elizabeth at St Paul's Walden was tough on the euphoric Duke of York. He had proposed four times; now that the adorable creature had said 'yes' he would have liked to have hung around to enjoy his victory awhile. But protocol demanded that he return to Sandringham and formally tell the King. Bertie and Louis Greig arrived at Sandringham grinning like two fourth-formers who'd triumphantly raided the tuck-shop. The official announcement followed swiftly: 'The Duke of York attended by Wing Commander Louis Greig has arrived at York Cottage. It is with the greatest pleasure that the King and Queen announce the betrothal of their beloved son, the Duke of York to the Lady Elizabeth Bowes-Lyon, daughter of the Earl and Countess of Strathmore to which union the King has gladly given his consent.'

There were other formalities involved. A special meeting of the Privy Council was called on February 14 so that the King could sign a document giving his consent under the Royal Marriages Act of 1772.★

Bertie drove down to London from Sandringham in a daze. His letters to the two prime manipulators behind the scenes – Queen Mary and Lady Airlie – reflect his ecstasy. To his mother he wrote: 'I know I am very lucky to have won her at last.' To the adroit Countess of Airlie: 'How can I thank you enough for your charming letter about the wonderful happening in my life which has come to pass, and my dream which has at last been realised. It seems marvellous to me to know that my darling

★ Under this Act, no descendant of George II other than the issue of princesses who have married into foreign families may lawfully marry without the consent of the sovereign signified under the Great Seal and declared in Council. Once over twenty-five however, the descendants may marry without the sovereign's consent provided Parliament raises no objection. It would have significant implications in the future.

Elizabeth will one day be my wife. I owe so much to you, and can only bless you for all that you did.' His 'darling Elizabeth' was equally grateful. Lady Airlie's role in her and the Duke's life – and its ultimate repercussions – are worth at least a footnote to the record of those times.

As the Duke drove into London, telegrams of congratulations were piling up at the Strathmore home in Bruton Street and at the Palace. At Glamis, estate workers buzzed at the news, with one old grannie telling a reporter, 'It's what I expected. I kent that the Duke wasna comin' down here for nothin'! She will mak' a guid wife.' The engagement would be short. The wedding was set for Thursday, April 26 1923 at Westminster Abbey.

It is interesting to compare today's media coverage of royalty and the press reaction to Elizabeth's engagement in January 1923. Charles, the present Prince of Wales, and his fiancée Diana were put through the wringer on their engagement and forced to endure an unsavoury mixture of bitchiness and cloying sycophancy. Sixty-seven years earlier, newspapers – the word 'media' had not reared its head – far from criticizing royal fiancées, swamped them under a Niagara of gush. When it was announced that Elizabeth's engagement ring would be a sapphire, no newspaper left this stone unturned, and that week, jewellers across the country reported a run on sapphires. Caught up in all the excitement, Elizabeth was also caught on the hop. Having told a friend earlier, 'the cat is now completely out of the bag and there is no possibility of stuffing him back' she did something no Royal had done before, nor she since – she gave an interview. The result was scarcely earth-shattering as interviews go: 'It's all very embarrassing,' said Lady Elizabeth with a captivating smile, 'I've never been in such demand before and it takes a little while to get used to it. I shan't see the Duke of York all day because he's out hunting. But I expect he will slip around for a little while later this evening – I hope so, at any rate. You ask me about my plans but I can't you see, because there aren't any yet . . .' and so on. Bland, predictable, harmless. But if Elizabeth grimaced on reading the stuff the following day it was nothing compared with the rage of King George and the Queen. The very idea of a royal bride-to-be inviting the mob to glimpse her private life was outrageous. An equerry was rushed to Bruton Street sternly instructing Lady Elizabeth that no further interviews be given. That self-denying ordinance has – bar a couple of emollient exceptions – been strictly observed ever since. (The newly formed British Broadcasting Corporation had asked to broadcast the service by 'wireless' but were refused. The Archbishop of Canterbury vetoed the idea because 'the Service might be received by persons in Public Houses with their hats on'.)

And so the presents shimmered in from all over the world. Diamonds, gold, jewellery and precious silks were sent by a variety of distant sultans and princelings eager to demonstrate their loyalty to the crown; ostrich feathers from South Africa; exotic gifts from India; fertility charms from Borneo; while from home, an oak chest from the Pattenmakers filled with two dozen pairs of galoshes and wellingtons (for her Ladyship's trudgings in the rain); 1,000 gold-eyed needles from the Livery Company of Needlemakers; tartans from Scotland; and tiaras from Mayfair. And of course a sunken-galleon's haul of baubles from the King and Queen and the Strathmores including antique diamond necklaces, bracelets and brooches. All that, plus a fair tonnage of silver, requiring, according to a wry Prince of Wales, 'a very, very large vault'.

No discreet Harrods' or Fortnums' 'lists' in those days, at least not for royal brides. You dropped careful hints in public. 'The couple expressed a preference for gifts suitable for furnishing their new home,' records Helen Cathcart. 'These ranged from a magnificent writing table (the King) to a grand piano and a wardrobe with a superfluity of oriental lacquered cabinets. But happiest of all in the bride's eyes, was the unequalled necklace of diamonds and pearls from the Duke of York, and in his eyes her own gift to him of a dress watch-chain of pearls and platinum.'

Three thousand guests were invited including a token intake of thirty 'factory boys' to mark the Duke of York's enthusiasm for the youth movement. All were suitably scrubbed and kitted out with appropriate gear for the Abbey. As the band-wagon quickened its pace towards the Abbey, Elizabeth saw her privacy receding all along the line. What she had feared in secret was being played out in public. She was news everywhere, and every day. Everything about her, her pedigree, bloodlines, fads and favourite things was of interest. The public's appetite for the minutiae of royalty was apparently insatiable. Otherwise how would we have known that Mr Bull, a veteran clerk in the Archbishop of Canterbury's Faculty Office, spent three days engrossing the yard-square marriage parchment using 'twenty quill pens of varying thicknesses'. There were other rituals. On 17 March, Elizabeth and the Duke went up to a 'royal' bakery in Edinburgh to cast their eyes over a plaster model of their four-tiered, nine-foot high wedding cake. Then on to a factory called the 'Blighty Works', a sad euphemism for the training of ex-servicemen short of a limb or two. Photographed in a feathered velvet hat, Elizabeth Bowes-Lyon appears singularly taut and unsmiling for a twenty-two year old only a month away from the altar. Stands were being erected in the Mall: troops were rehearsing; there were interminable fittings for her wedding dress of deep ivory toning with the old lace loaned by Queen Mary; there was a run-through ceremony with the Duke and the six bridesmaids. It was bedlam compared with the peace and quiet of Glamis Castle. And all this simply as the wife of a duke. No thought then of what it might be like to be a Queen.

Reading *The Times* on the morning of 26 April might have been instructive: 'The virtues of womanhood are not necessarily measured by the degree of publicity they receive. And if the Duke of York has not chosen his bride from among those who hitherto have been brought prominently into public notice, the nation will follow with the readier appreciation and sympathy the many beneficent duties which she will now be called upon to perform.

'The English public is properly and proudly a little jealous about its Royal Family. In the public mind Lady Elizabeth Bowes-Lyon is probably all the more welcome an addition to the Royal Family because the public knows practically nothing about her.' The paper follows that patronizing preamble by filling in some details: 'She is small, dark, and piquante. She is a very keen and accomplished dancer. She is good at lawn tennis. She does not hunt much yet, but hopes to do so more in the future. . . . Many a thread of turmoil and strife is gathered up in the girl of 23 who today becomes Duchess of York. But thus all the better does she represent her country. . . .'

Hardly a barrel of fun in prospect. And if Elizabeth read those lines with some misgivings, a shorter item in the same paper a day earlier would also have set her thoughts jangling. She had known that James Stuart had quietly slipped back from America. The oilfields of Oklahoma had served their purpose. Yet the announcement in *The Times* must have surprised her:

Lady Rachel Cavendish.
Engagement to Captain Stuart.
We announce this morning on another page the engagement of Captain the Hon. James Stuart, youngest son of
Lord and Lady Moray, and Lady Rachel Cavendish,
fourth daughter of the Duke and Duchess of Devonshire.
Lady Rachel Cavendish, who was 21 last January, was one
of Princess Mary's bridesmaids. Captain Stuart . . . served
in the European War from 1914 to 1917; was mentioned in
dispatches and received the MC in 1917 with Bar in the
same year. . . . For some time he was Equerry-in-Waiting
to the Duke of York. . . .

Two women, one at Buckingham Palace, the other at 17 Bruton
Street, would have read the news with contrasting thoughts.

Wedding Day . . . and the early morning sky, as with any
other April, was cold, blustery and showery. But by 11 a.m. the
sun came out to shine on the ermine-cloaked bride leaving
Bruton Street, and on the silver breast-plates and gilded scab-
bards bobbing along the route. The ceremony was beautiful.
Lady Strathmore wept. Everybody marvelled at Elizabeth's
exquisite complexion and colouring. The Prince of Wales, as
best man, wore the Cheshire cat grin of the contented bachelor.
He had sacrificed his younger brother to holy matrimony.
Bertie, in the uniform of a Group Captain of the Royal Air Force
waited, a nerve in his jaw twitching apprehensively. Delay. One
of the clerics in the bride's procession had fainted and was
reverentially carried off into the cloisters. Then the tell-tale
gasps as the bridal procession moved up the aisle. The
Archbishop of York intoned: 'You dear bride, in your Scottish
home, have grown up from childhood among country folk and
friendship with them has been your native air. So have you both
been fitted for your place in the people's life, and your separate
lives are now, till death, made one. You cannot resolve that your
wedded life will be happy, but you can and will resolve that it
shall be noble. . . .'

He underestimated the bride. Elizabeth was dedicated to
something more crucial than happiness and nobility. And central to it was the man she had just married, His Royal Highness
the Duke of York. She remembered her mother's words: 'He is a
man who will be made or marred by his wife.' The King and
Queen understood the challenge. But she knew the extent of it.

She glanced at him, his strong face handsomely profiled in the scarlet and gold coach, the escorting cavalry clattering along-side. It was great for a woman to be loved by a good-looking prince. To be *needed* by him, as she knew she would be, must have added a touch of tenderness to her feelings. One day it would be said that he was only half a king without her.

Her journey to the Abbey had been decidedly low key – an ordinary State landau with a simple escort of four mounted police. The basic transport for a lesser-rank bride. But the ceremony over, she entered the gates of Buckingham Palace as the Duchess of York with an escort of Life Guards, ahead of the King, Queen and the rest of the royal family; Baldwin, Churchill, Asquith and other parliamentary giants came behind them. She was no longer, in *Debrett's* precise terms, a commoner. The marriage: the mandatory appearance on the balcony for the Wembley Stadium roars; even the eight-course wedding breakfast confirmed her royal elevation, including as it did *Consommé à la Windsor, Suprême de saumon Reine Mary, Cotelettes d'agneau Prince Albert, Chapons à la Strathmore*, and of course, *Fraises Duchesse Elizabeth*.

On marrying Prince Albert, she was now – as the *London Gazette* officially confirmed – Her Royal Highness the Duchess of York with the status of a princess. But in several ways she would always be a Bowes-Lyon. Some of the guests at the ceremony had noticed that as she entered the Abbey she placed her wedding bouquet of white roses on the Tomb of the Unknown Warrior. It had not been part of the 'arrangements'.

It is a fair assumption that the gesture was in remembrance of her brother Fergus. She must have felt his absence more poignantly that day. There were more white roses in the special bridal saloon on their honeymoon train at Waterloo. White heather, white carnations and lilies of the valley continued the vestal motif. Elizabeth Longford saw great significance in the small, off-the-face hat the Duchess wore as part of her beige and grey going-away outfit. 'It was symbolic of her life-long resolve to maintain her "place in the people's life". She would let them see her clearly, and would herself look them in the face.'

It could also have been that with the forecast reading wet and windy a larger hat might not have stayed the course. At every station along the route, crowds packed the platforms hoping to get a sight of the bride. The happy Elizabeth obliged with a non-stop, thirty-five-minute smile from Waterloo to Bookham.

On to their honeymoon then, to Polesden Lacey, Surrey, 'placed at their disposal' by Mrs Greville. Rich to the point where she'd ceased counting, landing the prince and the new princess in her home was the society coup of a lifetime. Imagine the bliss of this millionaire landlady. Later the famous Sitwells were far from complimentary about her. It might be unkind to quote them, or to name the lady who claimed she would rather have an open sewer in her drawing room than Maggie Greville. Maggie, who had taken a lot of stick from other assorted highbrows – jealousy cannot be ruled out – couldn't have cared less. So what if her butlers were known to be tipsy at times, furtively wine-tasting between cellar and table; who cares if the Regency mansion, with its gold leaf on the walls and frisky cherubs on the ceiling, was a victory for extravagance over taste? The fact was, HRH Prince Albert, son of King George V, and his bride were under her roof for a honeymoon of wine and roses, (both adoringly selected by her). She would happily dine out on that for the rest of her life. To be fair to the colourful Maggie, she amply demonstrated that her adoration of royalty went way beyond aristocratic pretensions. She died in 1942 leaving Elizabeth some valuable Marie Antoinette jewels, £20,000 to her younger daughter Margaret, and the mansion to the National Trust. As for Elizabeth and Bertie, honeymoons being what they are, it's unlikely they noticed the decor or the drunken butlers.

The English part of the honeymoon over, the Duke and Duchess made for Glamis to complete it in Scotland. With its fairy-tale turrets and moonlight over the mountains, the castle promised a storybook finale. It was a near disaster. The weather was bad and Elizabeth caught whooping cough. The ancient four-poster bed, with silken screens on which Lady Strathmore had affectionately embroidered her children's names, was designed for conjugal bliss. But whooping cough was scarcely the appropriate sound-track. No matter. The royal couple returned to London still wrapped in the euphoria of their marriage. On 7 June they moved into White Lodge in Richmond Park which had originally been built as a hunting lodge by George II. It was a two-hundred-year-old edifice bequeathed to Queen Mary by her parents the Duke and Duchess of Teck. Both had died there, and the Prince of Wales had been born there. These sentimental imperatives compelled the newlyweds to accept Queen Mary's offer. But the ancient central heating had long croaked to a standstill. The furnishings were heavy and severely formal, and because of the Teck connection, had Teutonic overtones. Elizabeth, who loved life and colour, did what her versatile mother, the Countess, would have done – immediately rejuvenated the place. The vanloads of wedding presents helped. The Strathmore style completed the transformation. But when Elizabeth looked out of the huge windows at weekends she knew that whatever she did she could never like White Lodge.

Charabancs, coaches, cars packed with holidaymakers and day-trippers besieged the place. Raised to love privacy with a passion, to be the focus of hundreds of Bank Holiday and Sunday sightseers was a joyless prospect for the new Duchess of York. But she accepted it as part of the royal contract she had entered into. The fine print was now emerging. Even before the honeymoon was officially over she had become President of the Scottish Women's Hospital Association. Then suddenly a whole flurry of assorted duties were dumped into her lap. A death in the family, two days after she and Bertie had moved into White Lodge, was the reason for it. The deceased was Princess Schleswig-Holstein-Sonderberg-Augustenburg, 'Lenchen' to her intimates, the third daughter of Queen Victoria. Though she was no great favourite of Queen Mary's, the Court dutifully went into mourning. Elizabeth and Bertie observed all the rituals but when these were over, the Duchess found that all the charities, societies, hospitals, and associations that Lenchen had presided over were now her responsibility. All that and an infinity of foundation stones just waiting for a tap from a silver trowel. We need not follow her through all these engagements to know that she did what was required of her admirably. The fact that she is still doing so nearly seventy years later – and always with a smile – is therefore no surprise. From Day One Elizabeth demonstrated that she could make the leap from being a Bowes-Lyon to a royal princess. The discipline and sense of duty was second nature to her.

But what about the larger challenge, marrying King George V's unpredictable second son, Bertie? Outside the two principal characters themselves, no one was better placed to answer that question than the late Earl Mountbatten of Burma whose distinguished career was cruelly extinguished on 27 August 1979. A lifelong intimate of the royal family, Queen Victoria had held him at his christening. One of his oldest friends, the Prince of Wales, was best man at his wedding. And his was the shoulder almost every royal from the monarch downwards leaned on during larger or lesser crises. As Philip Ziegler noted in his brilliant biography of one of Britain's greatest men: 'His loyalty to the (royal) family was unwavering. He often urged the Queen towards a course of action. "Why don't you say such-and-such to the Prime Minister?" or "I should refuse to see so-and-so". Prince Philip wanted to shoot on the day after Churchill's death; Mountbatten thought it undesirable. Prince Philip was unconvinced. "Well *I* won't anyway," said Mountbatten and in the end the shoot was cancelled.'

Since both Bertie and Elizabeth had frequently consulted him, no one could have a greater insight into the dilemmas their marriage posed – particularly for Elizabeth. Mountbatten was not the sort of man who would invite anyone down to his beautiful home at Broadlands in Hampshire in order to talk about himself even though as the charismatic Supreme Commander South East Asia during the Second World War, the last Viceroy and first Governor-General at the transfer of power in India, and First Sea Lord during the Suez crisis he would not be short of material. The personally inscribed portraits of every member of the Royal Family confirmed 'Dickie's' place in their affections. An astute man, short on patience but with a fusillading patriotism, Mountbatten positively glowed when talking about the Queen and her family. Our interview, on that particular August day 1976 was to talk about the Queen Mother. But Mountbatten insisted on a brief detour to comment on recent adverse comments in the media concerning her daughter the Queen. He had no particular objection to the well-known anti-royalist obsessions of Willie Hamilton MP. But he resented ill-informed criticism, notably about the Queen's prodigious wealth. 'Though she may personally be the richest woman in the world,' he declared, 'her wealth consists of the treasures acquired by her ancestors from the Stuarts onwards. All the Van Dykes, the Reubens, the Reynolds – that collection of pictures is worth many millions. But what is the good of that to the Queen? She can't sell them. She can't give them away. And even if she could she wouldn't dream of it. Yes, she can say 'these are all my pictures'. But in fact she holds them in trust for the nation.

'She was the first Sovereign to have installed an art gallery inside the Palace, in the chapel that was destroyed by bombs. It is open to the public and contains all her finest works of art. There are even more priceless paintings such as the Holbeins at Windsor. King George V started a stamp collection which is worth untold millions. It is the finest stamp collection in the world. The Queen carries on with it. It is not hers. It belongs to Britain.' That salvo delivered, Mountbatten sailed back on course. This is how his reflections on the Queen Mother began.

'King George VI was one of the nicest people – in the best sense of that word – I have ever known. I was tremendously fond of him, really devoted to him. I knew him originally much better than his brother [the Prince of Wales] because he was in the Grand Fleet – in the *Collingwood* when I was in the *Lion*. Then he was in the *Malaya* when I was in the *Queen Elizabeth* and I saw a lot of him. We went to Cambridge together, I under the Naval scheme. He had a house at Southacre and I used to spend a great deal of time with him.

'Now he was completely over-shadowed by his elder brother who he absolutely worshipped. Most people in the country have no idea of the charisma of the Prince of Wales. It was magical. I was mad about him. We all were. It wasn't just the women who were mad about him – they were, sexually, but men too thought he was the most attractive he-man they'd ever seen. He had a knock-about charm, very go-ahead, full of dash, a bit of an extrovert while his second brother, who suffered from being the younger one, and who had this appalling stammer, was completely over-shadowed by him. Having an absolutely brilliant elder brother, the younger one being shy and reserved, was obviously in for trouble. So although they were very fond of each other the relationship was one of tremendous admiration on the one hand and a certain benevolent condescension on the other.

'So that was the state of affairs when he became engaged to Elizabeth Bowes-Lyon. We all knew her socially. She was a very good-looking, sweet, young debutante with whom we all danced. She was almost exactly my age – some two months younger – I was born on the 25th June and she on the 4th August in the same year. That's why we often speak of ourselves as twins. The Prince of Wales said, "Well, this is the best he's ever had." The one thing we both wanted him to have was a wife who'd look after him, make him proud of himself, give him confidence – and this is what she turned out to be. Look – what was she taking on? She was taking on a man who was never likely to be King. She never thought she'd be a Queen. Yet she really brought him out in a way that is difficult to believe. I saw it happen. He leant on her in the most astonishing way. When he went around with his elder brother he definitely was second fiddle. But when he went around with Elizabeth she pushed him forward, into first place. When they first met, Edward was twenty-nine and going to bed with lots of beautiful women, and flirting around. For a long while I thought he might marry Princess Marina. Just imagine – if he had married her, he'd have had children and the whole York family would have been out on a limb the way the Gloucesters are now. For Bertie to pick her at all was fairly dashing because it was not very often done. Secondly, with other Royal families still existing in 1923, she obviously was regarded as not being a member of the "Trade Union". Elizabeth had a very difficult row to hoe and I'll tell you why.

'Up to 1914, the royal families of Europe of which, from memory there were thirty-five distinct ones – were a Trade Union, a closed shop. You had to marry within that circle so that male or female, they might be what the Germans call *"ebenbürtig"*, which means of even birth. The real point is this – the Roman Catholics rarely inter-marry. It's true my first cousin, Princess Ina of Battenberg married King Alphonso of Spain but that's one of the rare cases of someone who was prepared to take the Roman Catholic religion. Now if you had a morganatic marriage, that would pass. (Where a "royal" could marry someone of lesser rank but she would not share his status and their children would have no rights of succession. The marriage of George IV when Prince of Wales, to Mrs Fitzherbert, is the best-known example.) What happened to my family was that Prince Alexander of Hess, my father's father, married this lady-in-waiting of his sister. His sister was the Czarona of Russia who became the Czarina. He was flung out of the Russian army where he was a general. He was stripped of his Russian decorations and sent home. The Grand Duke of Hess would do nothing for his wife. It was five years before they made her a Princess – and even then not a Royal Highness. So we could see in our family what it meant to have a morganatic marriage. But in England, the country did not know morganatic marriages – we do not normally have them. Elizabeth Bowes-Lyon was the first one to break in. This is not a question of the aristocracy. This was a fact of royal blood – blue blood. The Bowes-Lyons were not royal. Not in the closed shop. But Elizabeth rose above all that. She proved she was more royal than the royals.' (When tea was brought in, the former Supreme Commander SE Asia displayed a weakness for jam-filled sponge cake. Half-way through a serious dissertation on the Royal Marriages Act of 1772, his eye lingered on the last remaining slice of cake on the silver stand. He paused in mid-lecture to ask suddenly, 'Do you want that piece of cake?' 'No, thank you.' 'In that case, I may as well have it,' he said briskly. 'Now – let's go on.')

He contrasted the Bertie with whom he was at Cambridge and in the Navy, and the man who became the Duke of York and married Elizabeth Bowes-Lyon. The memories brought a smile to his face. 'In the old days, if I would discuss something with him, or if I wanted him to do something or give me a view, he would probably have bashed straight in and said "Yes, I think you should do this or that". Not any more. The moment he was married whenever I discussed anything with him he used to say, "Well that's very interesting. I have an appointment to keep. Can you come and see me tomorrow, or I'll ring you up tonight." I knew exactly what that meant. He wanted to talk it over with Elizabeth. The answer nearly always came out exactly as it would have anyway, but he just wanted to work it off on her.'

Mountbatten confirmed the general impression of King George V as a stern, hard-to-live-with father. 'The relationship with the King and his sons was not a happy one. Even Queen Mary, bless her heart, was so loyal to King George V she was never a warm mother. The only love and warmth George had in life he found in Elizabeth Bowes-Lyon.'

Prince Bertie was to find much more besides as he and Elizabeth began a marriage which would rarely be out of the spotlight. She was learning that everything she did, wore, ate, or said was in the public domain. An irritant to a person like her who cherished privacy, but it went with the job and she accepted it. Family tragedy was something else. On 10 July of that year, a nephew, Angus Patrick Bowes-Lyon was found dead in his car in a Surrey lane. He had killed himself, at the age of twenty-three. The son of Elizabeth's elder brother Patrick, he had joined the Grenadier Guards and at nineteen was posted to France, but returned soon after as the Armistice was signed. He resigned his commission and went into the City. He fell in love with a Major-General's daughter and gave her a ring. Two months later she wrote a letter breaking off the engagement. He was heartbroken. He brooded over it, then one night after dinner at a London hotel, he drove, still in a dinner jacket and silk hat, to a quiet lane near Ripley. He had a double-barrelled shotgun with him and some time in the early hours ended his life. His father left the inquest in tears. It was a chilling episode occurring so soon after the bells had rung at Westminster Abbey. Less than a year later, another skeleton in the Bowes-Lyon cupboard made a bizarre public appearance. Unlike previous revelations, this throbbed with human interest and might have made a respectable motion picture in the *Anastasia* mode.

The scenario concerned a girl who worked in an Aberdeen shop, named Connie Bain. The sign outside the shop, in the Kittybrewster district of the town announced, 'J. Smith, Newsagent, Hairdresser, & Shaving Saloon' though Connie was mainly concerned with selling spearmint toffee, butterscotch and gobstoppers to the local urchins. A pretty nineteen year old with deep blue eyes and the unique Bowes-Lyon peaches-and-cream complexion, Connie Bain read the account of the royal marriage with special interest. Special in the sense that she believed she had legitimate claims to be considered a member of the Bowes-Lyon family and therewith a kind of kinship with royalty. Naturally if this claim were pressed legally, the shock-waves from Aberdeen to Buckingham Palace would be high on the Richter Scale. The fact that her guardian was known as Bain the Bookmaker along Elmfield Avenue where she lived, added an exquisite frisson to the general embarrassment.

The basis of her claim centred on one of the lustier Bowes-Lyons named Hubert, second cousin to the Duchess of York. It seemed that at the age of twenty, Hubert Ernest Bowes-Lyon, grandson of the 13th Earl of Strathmore, had a love affair with an eighteen-year-old girl named Mary Smeaton. He, then known simply as Hubert Lyon, was an officer in the Black Watch. They had met at a dance in the Egyptian Rooms, Edinburgh, and had fallen instantly, passionately, in love. Since he was an officer and a Bowes-Lyon it was taken for granted that he would be gallant and discreet. This he certainly was. He was determined to marry her but events went a little off-schedule, Mary giving birth to a daughter, Connie, a month before the wedding. Scandal stared poor Hubert in the face. Virtue and chastity being the twin pillars of the Bowes-Lyon prestige, the situation was fraught. A christening preceding a wedding would not sit too well in the 'Social and Personal' pages of the *Tatler* or *The Times*. With the adroitness for which the aristocracy of those days was famous, the controversial new-born was swiftly put in the care of foster-parents. Good, caring, promise-we-won't-say-a-word guardians. They, for unspecified reasons, later handed the child over to another couple. It was from these two that Connie took the name Bain. Meanwhile, Hubert and Mary were married and two fine sons were born. Everything pointed to a very happy future. Unfortunately what they had overlooked in their scurry to avoid scandal, was that under Scottish law their subsequent marriage automatically legitimized Connie Bain. Not that this would ever have emerged had Connie not decided nearly twenty years later, to announce her existence. No question of personal gain was involved; no deep-rooted resentment. Just a desire to give herself an identity; roots that went a little deeper than the Powis Terrace sweetshop in Aberdeen. Elizabeth Bowes-Lyon had raised the family name to royal status. All Connie wanted was her right to shine, if only for a moment, in Elizabeth's reflected glory.

So Connie went to the Court of Session in Edinburgh to establish that she was the 'legitimate, eldest, lawful child of Hubert Ernest Bowes-Lyon, grandson of the 13th Earl of Strathmore and Kinghorne and the late Miss Mary Agnes Hay Smeaton.' In the witness box she gave her name as Connie Bain. But the soft voice and the composure was pure Bowes-Lyon. The evidence of her birth and link with the Bowes-Lyon bloodline was indisputable. Judgement was given in her favour. She could have turned the situation to her considerable advantage. We could well understand the Palace – let alone the Duchess of York – wanting to throw a blanket over the whole affair. In fact Connie Bain, or Constance Lyon as she now prefers to be known, relieved them of all anxiety. With Strathmore dignity she dropped out of sight. In June 1933, she married a tobacco planter in Nyasaland, enjoying a leisurely life with servants, a spacious bungalow, and social status. Not exactly Glamis, or White Lodge, but close. It would be intriguing to know how Elizabeth felt about Connie. A grudging admiration perhaps? Sympathy for sure. They had at least one thing in common; wasn't her own identity on the line?

5

In at the deep end. Any notion that the King might have given the royal couple time for the Duchess to adjust to her new role, was brusquely dispelled. He threw the book, or more specifically, the Royal Calendar at them. Elizabeth's feet barely touched the ground in a marathon of unveiling, planting, visiting, endowing, handshaking all over the country. If she wasn't required at some Court function then she and the Duke would be detailed to open, say, a new factory and appear ecstatic at the sight of a rivet gun or three-speed drill. A few months of this and Elizabeth's initial reluctance to sacrifice the Bowes-Lyon peace for the Windsor band-wagon, was fully vindicated. Back in London after a lacklustre round of engagements in the north of England, she was tired and needed a break. For a while it looked as though this might happen when in September she and the Duke joined her sister Rose at Holwick Hall, a Strathmore home in Yorkshire. On arrival the Duke was handed a telegram from the King, 'The better I know and the more I see of your dear little wife, the more charming I think she is and everyone falls in love with her. . . .'

A cynic, concluding that the old rascal had something up his sleeve, would have holed in one. Elizabeth had barely unpacked her toothbrush, the Duke his hot water-bottle (a minor indulgence) when a telegram arrived ordering the Duke of York to the Balkans. Like it or not, he and the Duchess were to act as godparents to the first-born son of King Alexander of Yugoslavia to be christened on 21 October in Belgrade. The following day they would attend the wedding of King Alexander's cousin, Prince Paul, to Princess Olga of Greece, elder sister of Princess Marina. The Yorks would be there representing the King and

Queen. The christening assignment was manoeuvred by Lord Curzon, the Foreign Minister, who told the King that the Yorks' presence was 'desirable'. Bertie, according to onlookers, was 'white with rage' complaining angrily, 'Curzon should be drowned for giving me such short notice!' A sentiment shared by Elizabeth who would not then have listed the Balkans as an area she was yearning to visit.

In the event, the christening emerged as rich black comedy. When all the guests – a blue-blooded *mélange* of kings, queens, archdukes and duchesses – checked into the newly refurbished palace, they discovered that the plumbing was kaput. There was no hot water. The cold water was not a viable alternative since at full flush it unaccountably became clouded with cement. This proved a hazard for at least a couple of Yugoslavia's ruling Karageorgevitch Dynasty whose dentures might have ossified at a crucial moment in the ceremony. A small risk as it turned out, compared with the near-catastrophe that followed. The venerable Patriarch enlisted to christen the Crown Prince had a pure heart but not a safe pair of hands. He dropped the baby into the font. Elizabeth's cornflower blue eyes widened in horror as she saw the infant sink to the bottom, tell-tale bubbles rising to the surface. Panic. A kind of paralysis froze the Patriarch rigid. Bertie, whose reflexes had been honed at the Battle of Jutland, reached in and brought the spluttering, future King Peter of Yugoslavia to the surface. The atmosphere was heavy with incense and a hint of emergency smelling-salts. Bertie, the godfather, then carried the half-drowned child three times round the altar. The little prince's face was roughly the same colour as his blood. But he was screaming his head off which all agreed was better than lying speechless at the bottom of the font. Everybody rushed to congratulate the godfather. Bertie smilingly shrugged it off. It was, after all, the sort of service any future king might render to another.

After that drama, the wedding between Prince Paul and Princess Olga was an anticlimax although the Duke wrote to the King that 'everybody was enchanted with Elizabeth'. They returned to England to another wedding, linking the Crown Prince of Sweden to Lady Louise Mountbatten, Earl Mountbatten's sister. Somewhere in the proceedings, a wriggling two-year-old boy was held up for Elizabeth's inspection. His four sisters were all bridesmaids at the wedding. He would grow up to be Prince Philip.

Back in the royal routine, Bertie was alerted that in the following year, 1925, he would be required to open the British Empire Exhibition at Wembley. With an innocence that did not deceive the King, Bertie wondered whether he should prepare himself for the event by seeing something of the Empire 'on the ground' – like a safari in Kenya for instance. For once his father showed he could be human and agreed to the trip. (One biographer has suggested that the King might just have been 'a little in love with Elizabeth himself'. The safari was as much a gift to her as to his son.) So away sailed the Duke and Duchess, just before Christmas 1924, to Nairobi. It was ostensibly to get a 'feel' of the dark continent, but mostly to shorten abruptly the lives of a vast tonnage of splendid animals. In those distant colonial days, royal visits were rare. Once government officials and the white settlers heard that the Duke and Duchess were actually coming, they went into near delirium. From the London *Daily Express*:

'The Duke and Duchess will be busy in the entrancing task of gathering together their outfits for their trip. It was no sooner given out that this journey was to take place than catalogues from sporting outfitters and gun-makers poured in on the Duke. He said he'd been offered enough gadgets to exterminate every kind of game between Mombasa and the headwaters of the Nile.' (A rough carcass-count at the end of the mayhem suggested he hadn't failed by much.) The *East African Standard* headlined their departure with: 'Duke and Duchess On Their Way'. Aware that the diminutive princess would soon be among them, the settlers' wives began to practise their curtsies, and shake out their garden party chiffons. Two stanzas from an eve-of-arrival poem, hugely headlined in the *East African Standard*, are an indicator:

To the Duchess of York
(On her visit to Kenya and Uganda)

This is the women's greeting. Oh!
Duchess young and fair!
Our thoughts throng out to meet
you on the rich, sunladen air.
Young and dainty and gracious!
Gathering love as you go.
This is the woman's message, it is

right that you should know.
You fashion the roof of Empire
with strands that shall not fail;
We give our lives to the making–
child-woman and Duchess, hail!

Had the Duchess's gentle gaze wandered to another page, she might have heaved at an item about an African who killed his son and was interrupted trying to eat the evidence.

Furlongs of red carpet unrolled along the red African dust; the safari train, ablaze with carnations and chrysanthemums; cut glass and silverware on spotless white cloths; three chefs and en-suite baths to each bedroom – the proud official, who had set out to give the royal travellers a 'mini-Savoy on wheels', hadn't missed a trick. There were some ticklish scrimmages behind the scenes. One example neatly illustrates an aspect of salad-day colonialism. The problem concerned the placing of the European children and the Indian children around the Pavilion where the Duke and Duchess would be greeted. A Nairobi paper reported: 'Mr Austin explained that after talking the matter over with representatives of the Indian community it had been decided that the European schoolchildren would be ranged on the left side of the pavilion and the Indian schoolchildren on the right. His Excellency thought "God Save the King" might be a little more suitable than "Land of Hope and Glory" when both sections of the community could join in. Mr Abdul Wahid ventured the suggestion that both communities could sing "Land of Hope and Glory" in their native language. He did not think it would spoil the song at all. But the Mayor thought it might spoil the harmony. [No mention of African children whose Swahili version of "Land of Hope and Glory" might have given the combined English and Urdu effort interesting overtones.] Mr Wooton pointed out that possibly the European children could sing and the Indian children remain silent.' This suggestion was rejected. So the whites and the Asians sang 'Land of Hope and Glory' simultaneously in their own tongues. Hyenas might have sounded better but at least an 'incident' was avoided.

So in custom-made safari outfits, hers cream silk topped by a fetching pith helmet, the Duke and Duchess of York embarked on six happy weeks of royal handshakes and 'white hunter' carnage. Having done her fair share of deer stalking up at Glamis and followed the guns in the 'season' Elizabeth was no fumbling amateur in the bush. Between them, the royal pair bagged rhinos, steinbuk, water hogs, buffalo, oryx, dik-dik, Grant gazelle and jackal. It is doubtful whether the Duchess scored instant 'kills' with every shot from her .275 Rigby rifle; even more questionable that as a known animal lover she would have enjoyed seeing the stricken beasts quivering into oblivion. But this was 1924. She, and the world, have a vastly different attitude today.

Meanwhile reports drifted back from the bush that Bertie had been charged by a rhino. This resulted in him being denounced publicly on two counts; the first for risking his life facing a charging rhino; the second for doing so on a Sunday. He snapped back that in fact he hadn't been charged by a rhino and that in any event, the beast would not have known it was a Sunday.

Nit-picking aside, Bertie and Elizabeth fell in love with Africa. They photographed battalions of elephants on the move. They stood at the source of the White Nile at the Ripon Falls. In Khartoum, thousands turned out to sing and cheer. And there were those memorable Technicoloured sunsets; the animals padding silently around the salt licks by moonlight; the exotic dancing of the native men and women. In any event, in August of that year, 1925, it was revealed that the Duchess was expecting her first child. And it was Princess Alice, Countess Alice of Athlone who, congratulating Queen Mary, wrote: 'Kenya is famous for having that effect on people, I hear!'

Elizabeth, of course, was ecstatic. Born of a large and loving family the idea of being a mother thrilled her. And being a royal mother with a full complement of servants, nannies, nursemaids and the rest, it would certainly be no hardship. Bertie, on the other hand, had already faced a more threatening ordeal. He made his first major public speech at the second season of the British Empire Exhibition at Wembley. Among the royal exhibits were Queen Mary's famously magnificent doll's house, a reproduction of the Niagara Falls, and an effigy of the Prince of Wales sculpted in butter. Given the choice, one suspects Bertie would rather have been the effigy than up there on the royal dais. He had privately rehearsed the speech and was terrified. Only he and Elizabeth could hear him stammer then. But up there, in front of the microphones, he knew that the impediment would be amplified to maximum decibels. Thus inhibited, disaster was predicted and achieved. Every faltering 'p' and 't' spluttered out of the wide array of Tannoys like buckshot. There were painful pauses during which officials uneasily shifted their weight on their feet. King George, whose presence was about as helpful as banderillas to a bull, stared moodily at his hands. Elizabeth smiled reassuringly but felt every pang of Bertie's agony.

Birth pangs were shortly to become another preoccupation. Queen Mary and the Countess of Strathmore reacted to the happy news of Elizabeth's pregnancy in the age-old fashion of prospective grandmothers. Since Queen Mary had had her first child at White Lodge she could see no reason why Elizabeth shouldn't have her baby there too. The Countess of Strathmore, who shared her daughter's healthy dislike of the place, offered her home 17 Bruton Street instead. There were immediate advantages. It was close to the Harley Street practice of the obstetrician Sir Henry Simpson. Moreover, for constitutional reasons the Home Secretary (then Sir William Joynson-Hicks) had to be on hand at the place and time of the birth. (This to prevent, as had happened on one notorious occasion, another infant being substituted for the real one.) The Countess had her way and a suite at Bruton Street was prepared for the birth. In the event, Lady Strathmore's decision was a wise one. Sir Henry Simpson decided that the baby would have to be delivered by Caesarean section. On 20 April, Simpson's medical team which included Walter Jagger, Consultant at the Samaritan Hospital for Women, moved into the house. So did Joynson-Hicks, nicknamed 'Jix'. If he frowned his way in to his appointed place it was understandable. Hanging around for hours outside a bedroom door merely to match a newly delivered infant with its mother, was not his idea of an average day in the life of a Cabinet Minister. He had more important things on his mind. Industrial turbulence was moving ominously towards a national crisis. He did not know it then, but the General Strike was less than a fortnight away. And here he was outside the Duchess's bedroom door, playing Witness for the Constitution.

At 2.40 a.m. on Wednesday, 21 April 1926, a baby girl entered the world, feet first, and was named Elizabeth. 'Jix' duly confirmed that the pink and bawling infant was the rightful issue of the Duchess of York then grumbled back to the Home Office for a catnap before preparing the country for strife. At 4 a.m. the news of the birth was telephoned to the King and Queen. The general view of the privileged onlookers was that the baby had fair hair, a lovely complexion, large, dark-lashed blue eyes and tiny ears set close to a well-shaped head. (This last would not, one day, be said of her son.) Meanwhile Bertie who'd kept a vigil with the Home Secretary, was exhausted but 'over the moon'. As he wrote to his mother, 'You don't know what tremendous joy it is to Elizabeth and me to have our little girl. We always wanted a child to make our happiness complete. And now that it has at last happened it seems so wonderful and strange. I am so proud of Elizabeth after all she has gone through. . . .'

The Duchess and the Duke now went through the ritual of choosing a name for their daughter. It was more complicated than usual as formal approval was required from the King, a convention originated by Queen Victoria. Bertie informed the King that they'd decided on Elizabeth Alexandra Mary (giving the child the same initials EAM as her mother, Elizabeth Angela Marguerite). The King raised no objection and on 29 May 1926, in the private chapel at Buckingham Palace, with a bottle of Jordan water sent from the Holy Land, the baby was christened. The father, hero of the ill-fated christening in Belgrade, kept action stations alongside the font. The godparents were the King and Queen, Princess Mary, the Duke of Connaught, Lady Elphinstone and Lord Strathmore. As a special gift, Lady Elphinstone agreed to let Elizabeth have her nanny, 'Alah' Knight. The newspaper coverage of the birth while friendly was reasonably muted. On the face of it the child was third in succession to the throne. But the Prince of Wales, though embroiled in his affair with Mrs Freda Dudley Ward, could one day marry in which case his heirs would take precedence. And it suited the Duchess. Having had her royal baptism of fire she'd have been happy to see the Prince of Wales marry and his wife take on some of the family chores. But that prospect, if it ever existed, was a long way off.

The General Strike had begun and with two million workers out, the gentry, the debs and the bright young things manned the food lorries and the buses, with the residents of Bruton Street rallying to the call. Mayfair was not going to be found wanting. The infant Elizabeth gurgled happily in her crib while not far away, mounted police with truncheons set about subduing rioting strikers. Miraculously, considering the scale of the confrontation, no one was killed. The strike, begun by the miners, failed in its objectives. The baby Elizabeth, one day as

Queen, would see history, in part, repeat itself, with the miners again the losers.

Elizabeth and the Duke now faced a major Royal Tour which would take in Australia, New Zealand, the West Indies, Malta and Gibraltar. They were due to sail out on the *Renown* on the 6 January 1927. They would be away for nearly six months, a long time for Elizabeth to be separated from her child. The baby was barely two months old when the King received a suggestion from the Prime Minister of Australia, Stanley Bruce, that the Duke and Duchess come over on a visit. It could be timed for the opening ceremony of the new legislative buildings in Canberra. Bruce's enthusiasm for the idea was based on the excellent press the royal couple had in Australia. He thought it would help boost Commonwealth relations and trade. He remembered the near-hysteria blown up by the Prince of Wales's visit in 1920. A return visit was proposed but David was in no mood to go there again. In fact he was in no mood for anything much. He was fed up with being tagged 'The Empire's best salesman' just for flashing his matinée-idol smile around the world. He was not merely tired of his Golden Boy image. He could no longer deliver on it. His royal charm was wearing thin in public. 'Let Bertie have the limelight now' seems to have been the message to his father. So the King invited Elizabeth and Bertie over to lunch and put Bruce's idea to them. Elizabeth's mind turned back to the Wembley ordeal. The Duke had similar thoughts. Except that now the stakes would be much higher. He would have to make far more speeches to far more people, in far-flung places.

The notion of stammering his way around the world depressed him. He couldn't risk another fiasco. But Elizabeth was determined that he should accept the challenge. It is doubtful if she was thinking solely of the success of the tour. More likely that she saw the trip as a way of helping the man she loved confront a long-running nightmare in his life. Elizabeth suggested further treatment. Bertie reminded her that he had already seen several specialists. She begged him to 'give it one more try', mentioning an Australian who had had remarkable results with other sufferers.

Lionel Logue, despite his Harley Street address had no recognized medical qualifications. A former engineer he had acquired a wide reputation as a faith healer and as a speech consultant. He moved to London and was almost instantly successful. Those specialists the hapless prince had previously consulted may have regarded Logue as a quack. True they had failed, but they were convinced that the fashionable, but unqualified therapist wouldn't do any better. There were to be several signposts in Prince Albert's uphill climb to confidence and self-assurance. The day Elizabeth persuaded him to see Logue in Harley Street must count as one of the most significant. Inhibited by all the previous failures, he could not have pressed the doorbell with much hope. It must have showed too when he and the Duchess were ushered in. As Logue remembered it: 'He entered my consulting room at three o'clock in the afternoon, a slim, quiet man, with tired eyes and all the symptoms of a man upon whom an habitual speech defect had begun to set the sign. When he left at five o'clock, you could see there was once more hope in his heart.'

The Duke also had Elizabeth in his corner. For although in that one and a half hours Logue outlined the treatment required it was clear that the crucial input had to be from the Duke himself. And from Day One, Elizabeth coached and encouraged him with a mixture of tenderness and tenacity. The treatment involved relaxation, correct breath control, and more co-ordination between his larynx and his diaphragm. But the miracle ingredient, to Bertie at least, was the face-to-face persistence of Elizabeth who mouthed every troublesome word with him. As the late Earl Mountbatten indicated: it played a part not merely in the making of a man, but eventually of a king.

Albert saw Logue almost every day before they sailed from Portsmouth on 6 January on the *Renown*. And every day there was a small but significant improvement. Away from Harley Street he practised his exercises with Elizabeth, working on the speeches he would have to make on the other side of the world.

Parting from the baby Elizabeth was heartache for the young mother. Nanny held the baby up for Bertie to kiss and the infant hung on to the buttons of his naval tunic. And wouldn't let go. Naturally, but illogically, the mother saw this as a reluctance by the nine-month-old Elizabeth to let her father sail away. Her mother shed tears. Bertie instructed the chauffeur who'd collected them at Bruton Street to drive around some back streets to give Elizabeth time to dry her eyes. Mothers may weep in public, but not royal mothers. They would not see their child again until June.

It may have seemed odd to Elizabeth that their eight-week

journey to New Zealand, and then Australia, should have been on board a battleship. A passenger liner would have been more to their liking but George V decided that a battle cruiser would display more muscle and prestige. Elizabeth was no great sailor and as the dreadnought rolled through the Bay of Biscay she kept to her cabin. There would be 30,000 miles of this before she arrived back home. But it was worth it. New Zealand was ecstatic. The women there, and subsequently in Australia, copied Elizabeth's clothes' style. Thousands of 'duchess hats' – turned-up brims with a feather on the side – appeared everywhere. 'The beautiful little Duchess', as she was tagged delighted the crowds, and had the media eating out of her white-gloved hand.

Students of the Queen Mother's famous public persona and skilful walkabouts, would find these first encounters with the masses in 1927 instructive. It was when facing the Auckland crowds that she originated what has now become a brilliant stratagem – making eye contact with just one or two people instead of a vague catch-all glance to no one in particular. Homing in on one individual achieves an intimacy which the crowd swiftly senses. All those people – we calculate in thousands – who have enjoyed, over the years, this selective treatment fervently agree that 'she makes you feel that you're the one person she wants to talk to'. Which is what was said about her more than sixty years ago on the other side of the globe. (One well-known communist activist in Auckland had been forced by his wife to take her and their children to see the Duchess. One of the children waved. Two yards away the Duchess smiled, then as the bemused Bolshevik exclaimed afterwards, 'I'm blessed if she didn't wave back and smile right into my face. I'll never say a word against them again. I've done with communism for good and all!'

Elizabeth went trout fishing on Lake Taupo and went out for bigger stuff in the Bay of Islands. Was it pure coincidence or adroit stage management that one face she recognized in the crowd turned out to be a soldier she had nursed at Glamis? It scarcely mattered. The crowd loved it. And her.

Wherever they went toys by the hundredweight were pressed on them by officials and total strangers. Dolls, teddy bears, fur rabbits and koalas were stuffed into crates for taking home. Meanwhile the Duke was getting increasingly confident at public speaking. Every morning before an important speech, the Duchess would put him through the tortuous tongue athletics devised by Logue: 'Let's go gathering healthy heather with the gay brigade of grand dragoons' is one example which had the Duke and Duchess falling about. (There might be difficulties reciting that exercise today.) But the regime paid off. When he unlocked the doors of Australia's Parliament in Canberra with a golden key, the Duke made one of his best speeches ever. The Duchess, fetchingly turned out in fur-trimmed chiffon, smiled at him through the ordeal, thrilled by the success he made of it.

No longer in the shadow of his more glamorous brother, the Duke was relaxed and confident. Discovering that he could actually stand up before a crowd of fifty thousand and string whole sentences together without stumbling, vastly increased his self-assurance. And after each challenge had been overcome he blessed the fact he'd met and married Elizabeth. What pleased him even more was the way enthusiastic crowds turned out to cheer her.

Clearly, being thrust on to the world stage demanded a kind of performance from the Duchess. It required the calculated development of a role; and the artifice that makes it appear as spontaneously genuine as Fergie's freckled smile. Those who have asserted that Elizabeth is 'royalty's greatest actress ever', imply no lack of sincerity. They simply recognize an essential element of show business in the modern monarchy. But in this sense, Buckingham Palace would always have the edge on the Victoria Palace. Where royalty is concerned, all seats are taken and there are queues outside. Every actress, and that includes this talented Strathmore, would find that irresistible. She has now perfected the role to the point where no other actress need apply. Over the years that public image has been so beautifully crafted, it enables her to shelter behind it, to be what she always has been, an exceedingly private person. It is true, as events will underscore, that there is a touch of steel beneath the gossamer surface. Or as Ann Morrow wrote, 'polished marble beneath the cream'. Without that strength, her life, her husband, her family and the monarchy would have been the poorer.

It was while she was on the *Renown* that Elizabeth received a message telling her that her close friend, and bridesmaid, Diamond Hardinge had died. Memories flooded back of the fun she and the irrepressible Diamond had enjoyed in Paris, London, and at Glamis. Now here she was on a purpose-built battleship, being groomed for a life of protocol and rigid Court procedures. The faceless mandarins of the Royal Household intimated that as she had now entered the rarified atmosphere of the Court, the Duchess's early relationships might have to be carefully scrutinized. But determinedly loyal, Elizabeth was not prepared to jettison old friends as she stepped up into tiara territory. But there is some evidence that shadowy figures behind the throne moved in to ensure that old acquaintances were soon forgotten. Helen Hardinge, the wife of King George V's private secretary, observed more in sorrow than in anger: 'Before long, however, my happiness about this engagement was slightly marred by one or two of the older members of Queen Mary's entourage who said that it was thought wise that Lady Elizabeth should not see "too much of her old friends after her marriage". By friends, they meant people like me and my sister-in-law Diamond. The older ladies were afraid that we would not treat her with enough dignity. . . .'

That may be what the 'older ladies' thought. But there is abundant evidence to show that this lofty view was not shared by the Duchess.

It was an energy-draining tour. What sweetened it were the letters and photographs which gave Elizabeth progress reports on the baby. The *Renown* would have logged many dramatic signals in its history. The news that Elizabeth Alexandra Mary had cut four teeth, did not feature in the Captain's report. What was mentioned, though, was the fire in the ship's boiler-room midway on the journey home. Sailing without escort in the Indian Ocean, a thousand miles from the nearest landfall, flames shot up from the ship's boilers. They spread uncomfortably close to the main oil tanks. The Duke went below to see if his naval experience could help in the fire-fighting and evacuations. The ship was full of smoke and all passengers and personnel were alerted to prepare for the worst. Captain Sullivan admitted afterwards that he was close to ordering 'Abandon Ship'. He asked the Duchess: 'Did you ever realize, Ma'am, that at one time it was pretty bad?' 'Yes, I did,' she smiled. 'Every hour someone came to tell me that there was nothing to worry about so I knew there was real trouble.'

At last on 25 June, the *Renown* reached Gibraltar. Only a day or two now before Elizabeth would be reunited with the infant everyone would call Lilibet. Both were unaware that the news of the spectacular success of the Tour had preceded them. The newspapers, with scarcely a dissenting voice, chorused such cliché headlines as 'Unqualified Success' and 'Took the Duchess To Their Hearts'. The result was that on arrival at Buckingham Palace a large crowd pressed against the railings. Neither the police nor the Palace guards had anticipated it. And when the ever-smiling Duchess appeared on the balcony holding her daughter in her arms, there was a burst of cheering and hand-clapping.

We can be sure King George and Queen Mary exchanged satisfied glances. Elizabeth as the Duchess of York had been a great piece of casting. Her Antipodean debut had been a triumph and had received rave notices. They must have wondered, with David a decidedly disgruntled heir, whether – if it ever became necessary – she could take on a starring role.

6

Even as far back as her marriage to the Duke of York, many key figures of the Court underestimated Elizabeth at their peril. Most notable of these was the Prince of Wales. He'd given condescending, elder brother approval to Bertie's marriage. But privately, he probably considered the match too tame, too saccharin by half, compared with the dangerous liaisons which featured famously in his love-life. The long-running affairs with Freda Dudley Ward, wife of a Liberal MP, and the American, Thelma, Lady Furness, had the excitement and whiff of scandal essential to his playboy persona. Gossip was as important a 'fix' for him as the five o'clock martini. By contrast, the Duchess of York with her pristine image was OK for the stammering Bertie, but not his style. A pouch-eyed prince of the night, he liked to be seen around the West End clubs with famous sportsmen, preferably with their wives with whom he would flirt on cue. He performed his royal duties by day. But he drew his adrenal stimulation from the exclusive night haunts where he was king more than prince.

The Embassy Club was the Buckingham Palace of night clubs. Its decor had been inspired by the Palm Court of the *Lusitania*, and its most seductive hostess, Miss 'Queenie' Thompson, would later be known as Merle Oberon. There was 'Quags' ('Quaglinos') and the 'Kit Kat'. Ambrose or Lew Stone to dance to; and selected entertainers like those black singers at the piano, Layton and Johnston, who the Prince would occasionally bring back to York House in the early hours with whoever might have been round his neck at the time. (His reputation as a royal stallion may have been based more on fantasy than fact. It is known that on one transatlantic crossing to New York, a woman seen leaving his cabin was said to have told a friend, 'He wasn't much good, but it isn't every night that one sleeps with the future King of England.')

But that kind of prowess – or lack of it – was of no concern to King George V. What mattered was whether the future King of England would measure up to more crucial challenges. He was beginning to have doubts, and his eldest son and heir was aware of it. Suddenly 'dear old Bertie' had entered the royal equation. Even the Prince of Wales had to acknowledge the remarkable change in his younger brother.

In place of the shy, petulant stammerer, was a more self-reliant, articulate prince, happily married to the most desirable creature in Court circles. She had made Bertie strong. The King doted on her, and frequently confided in her. The public loved her too. Reluctant though David was to admit it, Elizabeth, the Duchess of York, was a force to be reckoned with. Had he misread that artless smile; assumed there was nothing beneath the charm except more of it? If so he was not the first to make that mistake. Or the last.

Poets, pundits, and prime ministers have all testified to the clever brain humming away behind those disarming smiling eyes. The late Harold Nicolson, an astute politician and diarist, knew a sharp mind when he encountered one. He had met the Duchess and the Duke in Berlin in 1929. They had stayed at the British Embassy there after attending the wedding of the Crown Prince of Norway to Princess Martha of Sweden in Oslo. Nicolson, who was chargé d'affaires at the embassy, took them to lunch at the nearby Golf Club. They talked about his books. What struck Nicolson immediately was not just that she had read *Some People* but could talk so perceptively about it. She was clever. As he wrote to his wife, Vita Sackville-West, 'She and Cyril Connolly are the only two people who have spoken intelligently about the "landscape" element in *Some People*. She said to me, "You choose your colours so carefully; that bit about the Palace in Madrid was done in grey and chalk-white; the Constantinople bits in blue and green; the desert bits in blue and orange."' This incisive appreciation of his work in particular and literature in general, impressed Nicolson, as it had impressed the late Osbert Sitwell. Asked at a press conference in Hollywood in January 1951 whether it was true that he advised Elizabeth on what to read, 'I was able truthfully to reply that, if anything, it was the other way round' and that this 'singularly

Preceding page: Lady Elizabeth Bowes-Lyon and her brother David as small children. (Simon Bowes-Lyon)

Left: Glamis Castle, Scottish home of the Strathmores. (Camera Press)

Below: Lord and Lady Strathmore with their children at St Paul's Walden Bury. Back row, from left to right – Fergus, John, the 14th Earl of Strathmore, Mary, Patrick, Alexander; front row, from left to right – Rose, Lady Strathmore with David on her lap, Elizabeth and Michael. (Popperfoto)

Above: Lady Elizabeth Bowes-Lyon age nine, on her pony at St Paul's Walden Bury. (Syndication International Ltd)

Right: Dressing up was the most popular party game at Glamis. Lady Elizabeth Bowes-Lyon age nine and her brother David age seven. (Syndication International Ltd)

Above: Lady Elizabeth Bowes-Lyon in 1923, the year she became engaged to the Duke of York. (Press Portrait Bureau)

Opposite page: The Duke and Duchess of York on their wedding day, 23 April 1923. Photograph by Bassano. (Camera Press)

Above: Lady Elizabeth Bowes-Lyon leaving Bruton Street for Westminster Abbey. (Camera Press)

Left: The Duke and Duchess of York leaving for their honeymoon at Polesden Lacey. Photograph by I.L.N. (Camera Press)

Opposite page: The Duke and Duchess of York talking on the rustic stairway at Polesden Lacey during their honeymoon. (Popperphoto)

Left: The Duchess of York holding Princess Elizabeth aged eight months. Photograph by Marcus Adams. (Camera Press)

Below: The York family in 1931. The Duke and Duchess of York, Princess Elizabeth aged five and Princess Margaret Rose aged ten months. Photograph by Marcus Adams. (Camera Press)

well-read lady, advised me!' (But for the absurdities of protocol, far stricter in those days, we'd have known how bright the Duchess was. As a newcomer, however, with King George V still on the throne, she was required to be seen, not heard.)

How long the King would remain on the throne was suddenly in people's minds when in October 1928 he developed a serious lung infection. The Prince of Wales, on safari in Africa with Thelma Furness, was cabled to return to England immediately. The King was gravely ill. Bertie relieved the tension by telling his brother of a story going the rounds: 'The reason for your rushing home is that in the event of anything happening to Papa I am going to grab the throne in your absence!! Just like the Middle Ages. . . .'

But Papa wasn't ready to make his exit. Though he had acute septicaemia, was weaker and breathing badly, he survived a lung operation and in February 1929 went to Bognor to convalesce. The Yorks were away at that Oslo wedding, and the King had the three-year-old Lilibet to himself. The joy the frail old monarch found in his grandchild was touching and a rare experience for him. Everything about this family pleased him. David, on the other hand was a mess. He said to Lady Airlie, Queen Mary's lady-in-waiting, 'I pray to God that my eldest son will never marry and have children, and that nothing will come between Bertie and Lilibet and the throne!' Not a thought that would have thrilled the Yorks. The Duchess, feeling herself already restricted, much of her privacy gone, would have been undazzled at the thought. Bertie, despite his new-found confidence and more assured speech, would have been terrified by the idea. He was prepared to accept his role as the royal 'stand-in', obediently deputizing for the King, or for David when golf, girls, or other priorities beckoned. And in any event, the problem was unlikely to arise. David could have the glittering prizes. He had Elizabeth and never ceased congratulating himself on his good luck. His devotion to her was an obsession.

Hooked to the generating current of her strong personality, Bertie detested being separated from her. In January 1930 they were due to visit Rome for the marriage of Umberto the Crown Prince of Italy and Princess Marie-Jose of Belgium in Rome. The Yorks weren't being sent there for fun. As usual, George V saw some political mileage in the event though few could read his byzantine thoughts. (Perhaps because the marriage ostensibly reconciled differences between the Italian Crown,

Mussolini and the Vatican, the King decided the Empire ought to be present at the nuptials.) Also, with Bertie and Elizabeth away he could enjoy little Lilibet the more. But to his annoyance and Bertie's despair the Duchess went down with bronchitis. The Duke had to go to Rome alone. He loathed the idea and left England in a foul mood.

It worsened once he arrived in Rome. Somebody had boxed up (from the Duke's standpoint) the placings at the ceremony. He was placed lower in the royal pecking order than an ex-King of Afghanistan. The fact that this amiable character had once been a guest at Windsor cut no ice with the Duke. He felt upstaged. 'Dammit, nobody's ever heard of the feller!' is what he might have thought. The fact that the inoffensive chap was coloured is what he might have noticed. There was a further slight. The Duke was presented with the Grand Cross of San Maurizio e Lazzare instead of the more prestigious Ordine dell'Annunziata which is on a level with the British Order of the Garter. David had been given that one and by protocol no two members of the same family could hold the honour. Second fiddle again!

The Duke fumed back to England ready to give Elizabeth a blow-by-blow account of his humiliation. She stopped him in mid-bleat. Smiling her ecstatic, giveaway smile she told him she was expecting another baby. Storm over. He was going to be a father again. Suddenly the Ordine dell'Annunziata looked very small beer indeed. He whinnied around Elizabeth's boudoir like a contented stallion. Whatever else David was achieving with his gals, he was not producing heirs. The proud Bertie was not just preening with confidence. He was making children with the prime thoroughbred in the pack, (later to be described as 'the most successful sex-symbol British royalty has ever known'). And only a week ago he had been fretting because a superannuated potentate had been placed ahead of him at some kind of Ruritanian wedding. It was said that he never forgot that slight. More likely it faded from his mind on his first night home with Elizabeth.

Both thought she might have a son this time, boys predominating in the two families. It was not something that concerned Elizabeth unduly. What she had made up her mind about was that the child would be born at Glamis. A subtle switch of emphasis was occurring in her relationship with George and Mary. Before, Mary had tried to dictate where Lilibet would be born, the young mother respectfully suggesting alternatives. This time Elizabeth informed her surprised in-laws that she had chosen Glamis. It was her father's house. In insisting on it she was asserting her Scottishness as much as her own independence. No stamping of her pretty four-and-a-half-sized foot. Just a hint of the 'marble beneath the cream'. It was sufficient. The King and Queen were graciously pleased to recognize when they were beaten. All the evidence suggests that Elizabeth's mother, the Countess of Strathmore, played a strong supporting role in the decision. By choosing Glamis, Elizabeth was not merely staking out territorial independence. She was gently letting the Palace know that she was a wife first, daughter-in-law second. Something else was happening to the Yorks which didn't entirely displease the King. He recognized that in bringing out the steel in Bertie, Elizabeth was shrewdly fashioning him into the kind of man she herself would ultimately depend upon.

Royal births are rarely without drama. The birth of Elizabeth's second child at Glamis was no exception. First, doctors, nurses, and a gleaming range of surgical equipment had to be transported up to the castle. Harley Street was represented by gynaecologist Neon Reynolds and his team. Sir Henry Simpson stood by in case a caesarean section was again required. Meanwhile the Home Secretary, J. R. Clynes, had to down tools and go with the Ceremonial Secretary at the Home Office, a Mr Harry Boyd, to prove once again that the new infant had been umbilically linked to its mother. On the last occasion Elizabeth had quipped, 'If there's going to be a man standing outside my door I hope it's somebody I know!' She learned not to joke with pin-striped minds. Apparently, Mr Boyd, a nervous official mummified in red tape, thought that Elizabeth's decision to have the child at Glamis might create the impression that the affair was going to be conducted in 'an irregular, hole-in-the-corner way'. Nevertheless Mr Boyd took with him to Glamis historical evidence of an attempt to switch an ordinary newborn with the royal one. He showed the Duchess a page in an ancient book which included a passage heavily underscored in red ink concerning the birth of James II's son and how a substitute had been brought in concealed in a warming pan. Apparently he showed the same item to the Strathmores, Lady Airlie and anybody else on hand. Lady Airlie perfectly describes the episode, and Harry Boyd, 'a small, anxious-looking man, meticulously neat in his dress and movements, who had spent many years of his life in China'. (A beautiful put-down which Evelyn Waugh could not have bettered.)

'Originally it had been suggested that he and the Home Secretary might book into a hotel in Perth and that two sleepers be reserved for them on every night train from London until the event was over. But the implications horrified him. "Just imagine," he said, "if the birth should occur in the early hours of the morning and the Home Secretary could not get to Glamis in time!" In his agitation he sprang out of his chair and paced up and down my sitting room. "This child will be in direct succession to the throne and if its birth is not properly witnessed its legal right might be questioned. It has happened before in history!"' Mr Boyd then produced that book for Lady Airlie to prove his point. She probably humoured him with another cup of China tea.

So the idea of the round-the-clock sleeping berths was dropped and Lady Airlie invited the Home Secretary and the agitated Mr Boyd to stay at Cortachy Castle. The birth was expected sometime between the 6 and 12 August. A telephone wire was hooked up between Cortachy and Glamis and a back-up of a dispatch rider in case the line failed.

'Mr Clynes was a small man, very quiet and shy, dressed in a rather ill-fitting suit and a grey Homburg hat. He talked very little in contrast to Mr Boyd who fidgeted incessantly and still seemed preoccupied with the fear of some plot. "I could not help feeling that his long residence in China was inclining him to view the situation in too oriental a light."'

And so the waiting continued. It seems that by 14 August the hapless Mr Boyd was suffering sympathetic birth spasms. According to Lady Airlie he lost his temper with Clynes the Home Secretary and was in a panic. 'On the morning of the 21st August, 1930, Boyd, wild-eyed and haggard after sitting up all night, phoned Glamis.' Still no news. That night while everyone at Cortachy was dressing for dinner, the phone rang. Glamis calling. Mabell Lady Airlie, in her dressing gown banged on Boyd's door. 'Telephone, Glamis!' She heard wardrobe doors slam. 'I can't go downstairs, I'm not dressed and I can't find my suit!' 'Never mind. Take the call in my room! I'm not dressed either, but it doesn't matter!' Boyd emerged in a dark-blue kimono and rushed into Lady Airlie's room and took the phone. 'What, in an hour . . . we must start at once!' More panic. He was still searching for his suit. Down in the castle hall Mr Clynes was waiting. Boyd skidded up to him. Clynes pointed out to the sunset. 'In such a night did Dido from the walls of Carthage. . .' he murmured. Boyd shooed him into the car. They got to the castle with an hour to spare. And duly confirmed that at 9.20 p.m. Elizabeth had given birth to a daughter. Holding the infant in her arms she looked over the doctor's shoulder and saw the hovering Mr Boyd. She had had enough of him. And so had the Duke of York. (He would later as King abolish the ritual.)

Glamis celebrated the birth with blazing enthusiasm. Bonfires were lit on hilltops to be dowsed by one of the most spectacular storms the castle had seen in years. But pipers saluted the infant, proud that Elizabeth had elected Scotland as the birthplace. Because she and Bertie were convinced it would be a boy they hadn't considered girls' names. They put their heads together and finally Elizabeth wrote to Queen Mary, 'Bertie and I have decided now to call our little daughter Margaret Rose instead of Ann, as Papa does not like Ann – I hope that you like it.' Not exactly an ultimatum but not much leeway there for further discussion. The King, despite his devotion to his daughter-in-law, would rather have been asked than informed. But he settled for Margaret Rose. (According to records, a large number of newly born girls in late August of that year were registered in their surname only, their mothers hanging on for Elizabeth's choice of names.)

The christening took place in the private chapel at Buckingham Palace. The godparents included a bored Prince of Wales, David Bowes-Lyon, Princess Ingrid of Sweden and the spinster sister of George V, Princess Victoria. Swathed in Queen Victoria's lace and satin christening robe, the infant bawled her head off as the Archbishop of Canterbury, Cosmo Gordon Lang, dipped into the 18-carat gold font and sprinkled droplets on a wriggling head. As before, Jordan Water had been sent from the Holy Land. This was to be one of the few ritual privileges the young princess would share with her elder sister. In time she would find herself more and more out on a limb as Lilibet was groomed for greater glory. But sibling rivalry, conscious or otherwise, was a long way off as Elizabeth, the two princesses, and the more settled Duke of York entered some of the most contented years of their lives. They joined the Strathmores at Glamis to celebrate the frail couple's golden wedding. The Duke rode with the Pytchley hunt, glad that an idea that he become Governor-General in Canada, had been dropped. If Elizabeth could have known of the enormous popularity she would enjoy there as Queen Mother she might have persuaded him otherwise.

They had now moved into 145 Piccadilly, the mansion which Elizabeth saw as her first real home. The other places were really for royal transients being shifted around in the dynasty. Now buried under the concrete confusion of Hyde Park Corner, 145 Piccadilly in 1931 reflected all the colours and textures Elizabeth favoured: chintzs, silk-fringed lamps, huge chandeliers hanging from ornate carved ceilings, and all *objets d'art* and gilt frippery amassed on her wedding day. A nursery was installed on the fourth floor where some of the three-tons of toys, dolls, and teddy bears accumulated on the World Tour squeaked or bleated along the silk-hung walls. Alah and an undermaid nicknamed Bobo (Margaret McDonald) took charge of the two princesses. Life for the Yorks was lived in a kind of rose-tinted tranquillity within the laminated insulation of the Court. The fall-out from the Wall Street crash of a year or two earlier was visible in the poverty and unemployment which gripped the country. But royalty and those on the periphery managed to scrape along without cutting down on their nannies, butlers, valets, undermaids, cooks, housekeepers and gardeners.

King George V, delighted to have another grandchild to tickle his beard, decided upon a status readjustment between David and Bertie. David had asked for, and was granted, Fort Belvedere, a huge grace-and-favour house on the southern side of Windsor Great Park. The King decided that his second son deserved equal indulgence. In April 1932, he offered the Yorks Royal Lodge, Windsor. A huge pink-washed pile in magnificent grounds, the King thought it might amuse them for weekends and things. More secluded than Fort Belvedere, it had been previously occupied by Mrs Fetherstonhaugh, a widow whose husband had been King George V's racing manager. (The Lodge had a seductive history, George IV having used it for his private fun with Lady Conyngham.) Elizabeth loved the place and the Duke set about planting azaleas and rhododendrons in the largely neglected gardens. He also stitched a set of chair-covers in petit point, a skill shared apparently by his brother David. One other matter had to be settled – finding a governess for the two princesses.

The Duchess would have preferred to have sent Lilibet to

school. But the King wouldn't hear of it. The third in succession to the Throne must not rub shoulders with other children no matter how lofty their background. (We can imagine what this dyed-in-the-ermine reactionary would have thought seeing today's royal children striding to nursery school as confident as their mothers in front of the cameras.) But if, as the King insisted, the princesses were to have a governess, who?

It was Elizabeth's sister, Rose Leveson-Gower who introduced the answer. She was a close-cropped, no-nonsense Scottish lass named Marion Crawford. The sort of lively, fresh-air fiend the Yorks had in mind, she had been coaching Rose's daughter and came highly recommended. Twenty-two years old, a graduate of the Moray House Training College, Edinburgh, she was interviewed at Rose's Scottish home by the Yorks who had driven over from Glamis. Her initial reaction was interesting. 'For the first time,' she declared, 'I met that long cool stare.' This did not inhibit her from remembering also, 'I was quite enchanted, as people always were, by the little duchess. Petite, there was nothing alarmingly fashionable about her.' Presumably graduates from the Moray House Training College alarmed easily in those days. In any event, 'that appraising stare' or not, she passed the test and was given a month's trial. She survived that and moved into 145 Piccadilly. Nothing about her life with the two little princesses would normally have emerged had not 'Crawfie', as half the world would subsequently and sensationally know her, decided to publish her memoirs.

Learning one day that the King and Queen Mary were coming for tea, 'Crawfie' had an attack of nerves. Worried about her curtsy she went out into the gardens and practised the royal kow-towing in front of a British oak. She, and the tree, duly satisfied, she walked back to teach the three Rs to the future Queen of England.

In those days, 'Crawfie's view of life precisely matched the attitude of her mistress. Everything had to be tranquil, un-ruffled, virtuous, and strictly in line with convention. As the governess recalled, 'It has often seemed to me since, that in those days we lived in an ivory tower, removed from the real world. The duke and duchess were so young and so much in love. . . .' But ivory towers are, at best, illusions. Key figures in the real world outside were closing in to shatter them.

There had been a time before Elizabeth and the Duke had

become engaged when gossip linked Elizabeth's name with David's. They had often danced together. With his Niven-like wit, and what Chips Channon called 'his dentist smile', the dashing Prince of Wales had appealing credentials as a 'date'. But he missed out on her two basics for a husband, decency and fidelity. She had no special affection for Mrs Freda Dudley Ward. Yet she felt sorry for the callous way the Prince of Wales jettisoned her. No flowers or 'thanks for the memory'. Just a curt dismissal of the mistress he'd had for sixteen years, with instructions to the Palace telephone operator not to put through her calls. She was prepared to accept his rejection, knowing the nature of the man. What she found hard, and Elizabeth agreed with her, was that her dismissal should come via a servant. She behaved with greater dignity than her ex-lover deserved. After she was banished from his life, she gave no interviews, wrote no kiss-and-tell autobiography, and burned all his love letters. Her sixteen years with him receive no mention in his memoirs. She died in 1983.

Thelma Furness was a shade more sanguine. It had all been fun, if at times on a somewhat juvenile level. One night at the Fort, David, Bertie and Thelma had 'great fun' hurling plastic records across the Terrace. The sport spilled over into the drawing room until a lamp was smashed. The Prince tired of that as he finally tired of Thelma Furness. Classier than most of the others in his set, Thelma had style. She accepted her fate, grateful at least for her friendship with Elizabeth. As she had said, Elizabeth was 'the woman I would most like to have as a next-door neighbour . . .' That possibility faded when the Prince of Wales dropped her, in favour of an American wife of a naturalized Englishman named Ernest Simpson.

7

There are two women who should never have been thrown together on this planet – Mrs Wallis Simpson and Elizabeth Duchess of York. Wallis was an ostentatious American divorcée and a man-eater of some repute. Elizabeth was her driven-snow opposite, with an inborn reverence for holy matrimony. Even if the Prince of Wales's apocalyptic love-affair hadn't thrust one towards the other, they were never likely to be soul-mates. On the one hand there was the daughter of a Scottish earl with an aristocratic bloodline going back for centuries. On the other, a strong, wilful creature with no particular deference towards the high and the mighty. A smooth poker player and social drinker, Wallis's brittle flirtatiousness and flair for the outrageous wouldn't remotely have meshed with Elizabeth's impregnable serenity. In short, Mrs Wallis Simpson represented almost everything Elizabeth found distasteful in a woman, and the diamond-encrusted divorcée was well aware of it from the beginning. What began as mutual wariness developed into open dislike, and ended finally in cold, unspoken enmity. As Elizabeth would say at the squalliest moment of the Simpson Crisis, 'None of this would have happened if Wallis hadn't blown in from Baltimore!'

The pampered daughter of the wealthy Warfield family, Wallis was born in Baltimore in 1896, four years before Elizabeth. Some of her critics, eager to blame her for the crisis of the century, diminish their case by dismissing her as a raw adventuress with no recognizable pedigree. In fact her grandfather, Henry Mactier Warfield, had been a member of the Virginia state legislature. On her mother's side, the Montagues, there were judges, generals, and others of equal standing. She was christened, Bessiewallis (after an aunt and her father) but dropped the first half in her teens. She married Naval Lieutenant Winfield Spencer in 1916.

A tall, bulky Texan, Spencer's heroic image in aviator uniform hardly squared with his behaviour as a husband. He was a drunk and a sadist. When he left the house he would sometimes hogtie her to the bed or lock her in the bathroom. They separated, became reconciled, but finally were divorced in 1927. Somewhere during their estrangement, Wallis appears to have had an affair with an ardent Argentinian diplomat named Felipe, who danced well and wore a monocle; and then there were two years in China where Wallis made mysterious and exotic excursions to Shanghai and Peking in which other men, including an admiral and a French chargé d'affaires kept her company. (All this was documented in the Simpson Dossier, a full breakdown on Wallis's past, secretly compiled on behalf of King George V.)

Wallis had met Ernest Simpson in Washington a year before her divorce in 1927. He impressed her, she wrote, as an unusually well-balanced man. 'I was attracted to him and he to me.' Son of an American mother and English father, Ernest Aldrich Simpson worked for his father's shipbroking company, Simpson, Spence and Young which had offices in New York and London. Obsessed with all things English – the upper-class English – Ernest served in the Coldstream Guards and returning to New York, continued to strut around with the mandatory bristling moustache, bowler hat and rolled umbrella, and never without his regimental tie. In 1923 he married a divorcée, Dorothea Parsons Dechert by whom he had a daughter, Audrey. After their divorce, Dorothea would say of Wallis, 'She had enough of what it takes to steal a man.' Insult or compliment, Wallis decided to marry Simpson. Despite the Warfield's top-drawer status, they didn't have the funds to underwrite it. Wallis came to London virtually penniless. Simpson promised security if not much else. A year after their marriage in July 1928, they moved to a huge apartment in Bryanston Court, near Marble Arch, London, with quarters for a cook, chauffeur and housemaids. This was base camp for the Simpsons' joint expedition to scale the heights of London society.

It was a campaign that could not be launched on the cheap, Wallis possessing an insatiable addiction to fine jewellery and expensive gowns. She regarded both as crucial to a successful climb to the upper reaches of Mayfair. Fortunately Simpson had the money and was soon manoeuvring the two of them into the places that mattered. With an irony Noel Coward might have appreciated, they were introduced to Thelma Furness. It was she who arranged for the Prince of Wales to meet them. (Introducing a carp to a piranha might have been just as prudent.) Not long after, the Prince of Wales found himself hooked. Worse, he began comparing the two women, much to Thelma's detriment. The mutual sexual excitement which rapidly developed between Wallis and David was plain to see since neither party bothered to conceal it. By all accounts, Ernest Simpson didn't put up much of a fight. Once divorced himself, he probably recognized the signs, accepting that he had become, in the terminology he'd picked up in the Guards, 'surplus to establishment'.

In fact as the relationship developed he seems to have encouraged it, tactfully making himself scarce when they hungrily eyed each other. Another, less attractive notion, is that even as an object of private ridicule he saw some social mileage in having the famous Prince of Wales panting submissively behind his wife. Simpson's tactics soon began paying off. He managed, through influential American friends, to get Wallis presented at Court (first convincing the Lord Chamberlain's office that she had been the innocent party in her divorce). Early in 1933 he and Wallis spent several weekends at Fort Belvedere, the absolute pinnacle for social climbers. The Simpsons occupied Bedroom Number Two. Thelma Furness still held a shrinking hold on Number One. In November 1934, the Prince of Wales got them invited to a State reception at Buckingham Palace on the eve of the Duke of Kent's marriage to Princess Marina. When the list of invited guests was shown to the King and Queen Mary they noticed that the Prince of Wales had included Mr and Mrs Simpson in his party. Whether the monarch discussed this with Bertie and Elizabeth is not known. What is recorded is that the King scored the Simpsons' names out. The Prince of Wales delivered an ultimatum saying if they weren't invited he wouldn't come. That threat failing to impress his father he insisted that including the Simpsons would be good for Anglo-American relations. It was an absurd idea in view of the unfavourable gossip already blowing up on the other side of the Atlantic. But the King finally capitulated, and on the night of the Ball found himself shaking Wallis's hand.

It was the first opportunity for Wallis and Elizabeth to scrutinize each other at close range. The sharp contrast between the two women was beautifully drawn by the gowns they wore. Wallis had armed herself in violet lamé set off by a fluorescent green sash. Elizabeth met fire with ice, favouring delicate orchid pink. It was then, Wallis remembered, that she first encountered the 'almost startling blueness' of the Duchess's eyes, and felt that 'cool appraising glance sweep over her'.

No word was uttered between the two of them. It was not so much a meeting as a prelude to hostilities. Forty years on, the Dowager Lady Hardinge would recall: 'I am afraid Mrs Simpson went down badly with the Duchess from the word go. It may have been the rather ostentatious dress, or the fact that she allowed the Prince of Wales to push her forward in what seemed an inappropriate manner. The Duchess of York was never discourteous in my experience, but those of us who knew her very well could always tell when she did not care for something or someone, and it was very apparent to me that she did not care for Mrs Simpson at all.'

As Ernest Simpson began fading out of the reckoning so Wallis was pushed further into the foreground. This further polarized the growing hostility between her and Elizabeth. Crassly, the talkative divorcée, aware of the Duchess's disapproval of her, began criticizing Elizabeth at private dinners and cocktail parties. Aware perhaps of the way she had been subtly downgraded, she derided the snobbery of the Court and what she regarded as the Duchess's 'goody-goody' image. Reckless, too, she had begun imitating Elizabeth's voice and mannerisms. On a visit to Fort Belvedere early in 1935, Elizabeth is said to have walked into the drawing room just as Wallis was in the middle of one of her imitations. A pretty good mimic herself (today one of the best in the Royal Family), Elizabeth would normally have laughed at the incident. But to be lampooned by this vulgar woman . . . there are certain things Elizabeth, her Scottish blood rising, could neither forgive nor forget.

That episode was significant for another reason. It confirmed what Wallis's critics had asserted all along, that she didn't know how to behave in royal company. Yet even at this stage neither Bertie, nor Elizabeth, read into the relationship anything more than another of David's peccadilloes. It was only when he brazenly projected Wallis into the exclusive inner circles of royalty that Elizabeth began to have serious misgivings. Even when she had married Bertie and became the Duchess of York and a princess she only diffidently put a toe in royal waters. But this creature, with the Prince of Wales as her besotted 'sponsor', was sailing in and making waves. As Chips Channon purred in his diary: 'We had a luncheon party here [Southend] and the plot was to do a "politesse" to Mrs Simpson . . . she has already the air of a personage who walks into a room as though she almost expected to be curtsied to. At least she wouldn't be too surprised. She has complete power over the Prince of Wales who is trying to launch her socially. . . .'

And with considerable success. All invitations to the Prince of Wales for cocktails, dinner, weekends or fun and games anywhere, were more likely to be accepted if the Simpsons were invited. If you wanted *him* you asked *her*. Thus Wallis Simpson peacocked around Mayfair deliciously aware of the turmoil she was causing. Envy, curiosity, hostility, admiration – what more could a famous divorcée ask for? But David was determined that the Court – and essentially that meant the Duchess of York – should grant Wallis more tangible recognition. He had seen the Duchess becoming not merely the King's favourite but a considerable force behind the throne. And must have grudgingly admired her for it. That status had not been achieved by guile. She had become an influential figure just by being herself. She was a steadying influence whereas he was rocking the boat. Moreover, he knew she disliked Wallis intensely. That situation had to be confronted. A State Ball at Buckingham Palace in Silver Jubilee year, 1935, provided an opportunity.

If Wallis had known that the King had earlier had his card marked by a Court official ordered to probe her past, she might have been a shade less jaunty. As it was, the King later expressed his displeasure, dismissing Wallis, according to Kenneth Rose in *George V*, as 'unsuitable as a friend, disreputable as a mistress, unthinkable as Queen of England'. He later growled to Prime Minister Baldwin, 'the boy will ruin himself in twelve months after I've gone'. Wallis didn't fare much better with Queen Mary who was about as welcoming as the iceberg was to the *Titanic* – an analogy which also occurred to Wallis Simpson. As she recalled in her memoirs, *The Heart Has Its Reasons*: 'As David and I danced I thought I felt the King's eyes rest searchingly on me. Something in his look made me feel that all this graciousness and pageantry were but the glittering tip of the iceberg that extended down into unseen depths . . . depths filled with an icy menace for such as me.'

It is not difficult to feel some sympathy for Mrs Simpson. A love-affair with the impulsive Prince of Wales was problem enough for her, for David, and to a lesser degree for Ernest. But she sensed with increasing nervousness that she and the Prince were walking hand in hand into a minefield. And beyond that, the enemies within the Court were deploying further artillery. She didn't fit, it was as simple as that. And she had got off to an abysmal start. A little more deference might have got her over a couple of fences with the stiff-necked grandees at the Palace. A little more finesse with the Duchess of York might have bridged the chasm between them. Intelligent, direct, Wallis Simpson was never going to be the type to genuflect before royalty. She was flattered, but she was certainly not awe-struck. Moreover, David's own behaviour scarcely enhanced the prestige of the Court. The Prince of Wales's almost comical devotion to her was being giggled over in Mayfair and New York. Anyone who has ever tossed a stick for a leaping, obedient dog, would get the flavour of it.

There would come a time when, noticing a momentary frown as one of her fingernails split, David unasked, shot out of sight returning to place a nail file adoringly before her. Later, as King Edward VIII, he would be served drinks by a footman at Fort Belvedere, who came upon him carefully painting Mrs Simpson's toenails beside the pool. The footman, outraged, resigned.

Speculation about Wallis Simpson's extraordinary influence on the Prince of Wales centred on their sexual relationship. No prurient intent here to reprise that speculation, particularly since both these forlorn figures have long since departed. But in probing the sources of the Court's hostility we cannot ignore that secret Simpson dossier prepared for King George V. No one can be certain of these things but one explanation for her extraordinary hold on the Prince was that she was the most successful of all the Prince of Wales's bedmates. That success, according to one observer, is partly attributed to a variety of techniques practised in certain 'houses' in China, a country which Wallis had visited. That 'Chinese Connection' was apparently touched on in the dossier. (We can imagine the effect these revelations would have had on Elizabeth, the Duchess of York. The effect they had on the King, however, needs no imagining.)

A ferociously intolerant monarch, only a woman with Elizabeth's skill at managing difficult people and situations, could have defused him. When his son Bertie had been upstaged by that distinguished gentleman from Afghanistan at the wedding in Rome, he at least kept his irritation to himself. When the same dignitary a year earlier, had been ushered out of George V's presence at Windsor, he called out to the lord-in-waiting, 'Shut that door. I can smell that damn nigger from here!'

The Thanksgiving Service for the King's Silver Jubilee on 6 May 1935, gave Londoners a ceremonial vision of the Yorks and the two young princesses. It was a warm, sunny day. The old King and the upright Mary rode in the State Coach to a burst of cheering from the crowd. He hadn't expected a demonstration like this. He thought his subjects probably respected him. Or if not him, at least the Crown. But it had never occurred to him that they could actually *like* him. As he wrote in his diary afterwards, 'I'd no idea they felt like that about me. I am beginning to think they must really like me for myself.'

Elizabeth and Bertie could have had no doubts about what the crowd thought of them with the Duchess in her favourite powder blue, the two princesses in rose-coloured bonnets, all smiling in the maroon and gold State landau. Later, the Royal Family appeared for the familiar handwaves on the Palace balcony. Queen Mary, usually so controlled, was close to tears. That night, Bertie and Elizabeth, in front of their radio at Royal Lodge, heard his broadcast to the nation. There was a poignancy to his thanks '. . . for all the loyalty and, may I say so, the love, with which this day and always you have surrounded us. . . .'

Elizabeth was moved, but also felt a sense of bitterness. She was devoted to the King and had watched him being worn down not merely by the protracted celebrations, but also by the Simpson Affair. His health failing, Elizabeth felt he should have been spared the scandal and the threat it posed for the Crown. She was beginning to sense too that somehow Wallis posed a threat to her and Bertie. On that score, Elizabeth was resolved fiercely to protect him at all costs. Bertie could hold his own with David. She knew precisely how to handle Wallis Simpson.

The King had made it clear; he hoped David, who privately he called 'a cad' would never marry, in which case the Yorks would eventually have the throne.

He was becoming frailer, but every morning he would look through his binoculars and often see Lilibet waving to him from a window at 145 Piccadilly. There were occasions when he insisted on being driven around London with Lilibet and the Duchess. These were brief but enjoyable excursions. He had never expected much pleasure from a daughter-in-law. Saxe-Coburg marriages over the decades had largely been designed to strengthen old alliances or form new ones. Elizabeth was the one joyous exception. She had put a smile on the face of the Court. He and Mary felt happy when she was around. She may have come into the family without the required blue-blooded pedigree. But she was showing them all! Princess Marina who had married George, the Duke of Kent, possessed all the dynastic credentials but she could never measure up to Elizabeth. (One reason for the King's disenchantment with this forthright aristocrat was her vividly painted fingernails. On arriving at the Palace one day, Queen Mary told her curtly, 'I'm afraid the King does not like painted nails.' 'Your George may not,' Marina responded, 'but mine does.')

King George did not survive to read this tribute to Elizabeth in Stella King's biography *Princess Marina*: 'In a way the Duchess (of Kent) was made more conscious of her own inadequacy by the example of her sister-in-law the Duchess of York. The non-royal former Lady Elizabeth Bowes-Lyon may have been the first commoner to marry into the British Royal Family without it being a morganatic alliance, but she knew better than anybody how to behave. When she became Duchess of York she stunned everybody in royal circles . . . over the way she slipped easily and naturally into her public duties . . . Always smiling, never ever putting a foot wrong, her serene professionalism was so far ahead . . . she set a standard that seemed almost impossible to reach.'

In November, the King's third son, Henry, the Duke of Gloucester, married Lady Alice Montague-Douglas-Scott with Lilibet and Margaret getting another public outing, this time as bridesmaids. In December, Elizabeth went down with pneumonia which ruled her out of the Christmas festivities. But there were compensations. This was the first Christmas they had ever spent alone together. Overshadowing it were the reports from Sandringham that the King's illness was now critical. On 16 January, Queen Mary phoned Bertie at Royal Lodge and asked whether he could come over to Sandringham to help out. He came home three days later to tell Elizabeth that his father was gravely ill and might not last much longer. A telephone call recalled him to Sandringham. On the morning of 20 January 1936, the King received six Privy Counsellors in his bedroom. Seated in an armchair wearing a Chinese dressing gown, he welcomed them with a weary smile. But he was fading rapidly. As she lay in bed later that night, Elizabeth heard the announcement that 'the King's life was moving peacefully towards its close'. But not before he was supposed to have delivered that classic, but un-authenticated one-liner. Either Queen Mary, or an attendant, seeking to reassure the dying monarch, is supposed to have said, 'Your Majesty will soon be in Bognor again.' To which George allegedly rasped back, 'Bugger Bognor!' An alternative version has him whispering a question to his Private Secretary, Lord Wigram, 'How is the Empire?' At 11.15 p.m. the Archbishop of Canterbury, Cosmo Lang, put on his cassock and went into the King. David and Bertie sat comforting the Queen. The Archbishop read the 23rd Psalm and quoted some lines from the Bible. He looked at the King. Only minutes remained. He went out and called the family.

King George V died at five minutes to midnight. When Bertie told Elizabeth she wept. As she said afterwards: 'I miss him dreadfully. In all the twelve years as his daughter-in-law he never spoke one unkind or abrupt word to me.' Heartbroken, Queen Mary went to her room and wrote with touching eloquence in her diary, 'The sunset of his death has tinged the whole world's sky.' Doctors told Elizabeth that she ought to stay in bed. But she felt her place was at Sandringham with Bertie and the grieving Queen Mary who on the King's passing had kissed the hand of her son, King Edward VIII. It was more a solemn ritual than a spontaneous gesture of shared grief. The new King wept hysterically. This surprised those who had never considered David to be nearly as devoted to the King as his younger brothers. While Bertie moved to console him, Wallis Simpson was at a charity showing in a London cinema. News of the King's death was flashed across the screen. Sitting there in the darkness, conflicting thoughts ran through her mind. There was immense sadness for David, but also a chilling prescience as she remembered thinking afterwards, 'I was sure I had a big hurt coming. My head was spinning. But something kept telling me it's going to end now. You're going to know heartbreak. . . .'

Hysterical or not, the new King Edward VIII recovered sufficiently to slip away to phone and break the news to Wallis. 'It's all over, darling. Papa died a few moments ago. I must see you.' Bertie and David flew to London the following day for the Accession meeting of the Privy Council at St James's Palace. In the evening, Bertie and Elizabeth at 145 Piccadilly, were both still numb, perhaps more apprehensive than sad. They had anticipated the King's death, but not the turmoil caused by this controversial creature from Baltimore. They had left the two princesses at Royal Lodge, instructing Crawfie, 'don't let all this depress them more than is absolutely necessary. They are so young. . . .'

Meanwhile King Edward VIII and Mrs Wallis Simpson were meeting at the Ritz. A short sprint away, the Yorks were also holding earnest discussions at 145 Piccadilly. The two separate conversations must have contrasted dramatically. Elizabeth found herself consoling a grieving Bertie who, later than he would have wished, had finally earned the respect and love of his father. Consolation was a shade less evident at the Ritz perhaps. The new King was in turmoil. Passion had collided head-on with protocol. In a few hours, Londoners would be streaming towards St James's Palace to hear the Proclamation. God, how he envied Bertie! Beautiful wife, lovely children, happy, and free! Here he was, a bachelor King, dining in secret with his woman, but trapped. And being trapped, he would hit out in all directions. Defiantly, he insisted that Wallis Simpson stand alongside him at St James to watch the proclamation ceremony, knowing that this would incense the Court, Elizabeth most of all.

As the Anthem played and the crowds cheered, the two women, Elizabeth, the Duchess of York, and Mrs Ernest Simpson, viewed the occasion from vastly different standpoints. Elizabeth, with Queen Mary in mourning, was now, effectively the First Lady of the British Court. Bertie, at least for the time being, was next in line to the throne. He, and therefore, she, would not just be more involved. Past experience warned her to expect the selfish elder brother to unload as much as he could on to her husband. And what could she expect from Wallis Simpson, now elevated to the rank of paramour to the reigning monarch? On existing form, nothing but trouble. If Wallis could reduce the former Prince of Wales to emasculated servility what havoc might she make for her and Bertie?

We know exactly what Wallis Simpson was thinking as she stood alongside the new King. 'It was all very moving,' her memoirs recall, 'but it has also made me realize how different your life is going to be.' The King's reply was unequivocal. 'There will be a difference of course. But nothing can ever change my feelings towards you.'

The day of the funeral, 23 January, placed Elizabeth in the foreground, correctly excluding Wallis Simpson from the royal mourners. Instead, she watched the procession from a window at St James's Palace. In black and heavily veiled, Elizabeth would not have been aware that Wallis had her under scrutiny. The King and his brothers walked slowly behind the coffin, their faces the only glimpse of white against the blackness of the cortège. Elizabeth shared a closed carriage with Queen Mary and the Princess Royal. Marina, Duchess of Kent, followed with other family mourners. George's riderless pony, Jock, clattered sombrely in the procession. And then, deferentially behind ministers, peers, and court officials, came the tenant farmers, the beaters and other countryfolk in their rough tweeds and polished boots. Lilibet, nearly ten, was considered old enough to attend the funeral, but only the last part of it at Paddington Station. From there, the late King would be taken for burial at Windsor.

Crawfie, anxiously efficient, had arrived at the station with the young princess an hour or so too early. They passed the time playing noughts and crosses on GWR notepaper then watched the coffin roll slowly down the ramp. It was a strange experience for Lilibet. Thoughts collided in her mind. Grandpa gone. No more building sandcastles with him on the beach. No more sitting on his knee at Buckingham Palace, pulling at his beard, a hint of whisky and tobacco on his breath. She watched the train move out of the station, turned and clung to the governess. That first experience of death and the final departure stayed vividly in her mind for years.

Not long after the King's death and David's Accession, Elizabeth could see that her brother-in-law intended to pull rank, and not too tactfully either. Within weeks, while Mary was still absorbed in her grief, he summoned Bertie to Sandringham to discuss ways of cutting down expenses there. He cut budgets, sacked workers who had been there for years. And then only informed his brother afterwards. Bertie raised objections but was overruled by his brother, now unmistakeably the King. Elizabeth was angered and shocked by this crude, mercenary behaviour so soon after George V's death. (The full picture of the new King's obsession with money was yet to emerge.) Even more tasteless was the party Edward VIII had at Fort Belvedere not four weeks after his father died. The high-spot of this shindig featured the new King with a bonnet on his head, marching round the table playing the bagpipes with half a dozen other pipers in tow. If Elizabeth shuddered to think what George V would have made of it, Queen Mary could have told her. To the old monarch, David was behaving exactly as he predicted.

Elizabeth had other disturbing thoughts. She knew that sooner or later the King would ask her to receive Wallis Simpson. They had met briefly at Palace functions. Observed formalities but nothing more. That was more than enough for the Duchess of York. Court gossip had become polarized into two opposing factions: the pro-Wallis and the pro-Elizabeth. Chips Channon described it as a 'war to the knife between the past and the present'; another said that Wallis saw the Duchess of York as her arch-antagonist. Thus battle was joined between them revealing an intriguing deployment of opposing forces. In Elizabeth's camp were Helen Hardinge, wife of the late King's Private Secretary, Alex Hardinge; Queen Mary's lady-in-waiting, the Countess of Airlie, the forthright Lady Astor and a formidable line-up of supporting protagonists.

The Hardinges had always been among the Duchess of York's closest friends. Elizabeth had been a bridesmaid at their wedding. Their friends automatically joined the anti-Simpson alliance. '"One of these," Lady Hardinge impishly recalls in her memoirs, "absolutely refused to shake hands with her (Wallis)." "What did you do?" I asked her after they had been introduced at a party. "Oh," she replied, "it was quite easy. I dropped my handbag just as she got to me, so I had to stoop down to find it."'

Leading the Simpson contingent – known as the Ritz Bar set, (the Paris not the London Ritz) – were two of society's most aggressive and influential hostesses, Lady Emerald Cunard and Lady Sibyl Colefax. These were joined by Winston Churchill (who later recanted) and a couple of conspiring newspaper proprietors with questionable motives.

The heavily bejewelled Emerald was variously described as 'twittering', 'squirrel-toothed' and by the admittedly anti-American Harold Nicolson, as 'a third dynasty mummy painted by an amateur'. None of which would have bothered Emerald too much. Her own malevolent wit enlivened, or wrecked, some of the best parties in Mayfair. 'Christmas is only for servants' was a typical opening gambit. Born in San Francisco and christened Maude, she was persuaded to call herself Emerald by a numerologist who believed the change would foreshadow a glittering future. But just in case this soothsayer had miscalculated the numbers, Emerald married Sir Bache Cunard who was forty-three to her twenty-three but rich enough to bridge the gap. Over the years her lunches and dinners – her last address was 9 Grosvenor Square – attracted foreign princes, ambassadors, cabinet ministers, and writers hand-picked for the occasional poison in their prose. George Bernard Shaw, Somerset Maugham, a Sitwell or two, and Evelyn Waugh were typical. Given her appetite for gossip and dangerous liaisons, Wallis Simpson's entry on to the London scene was irresistible. Old enough to have flirted with Edward VII but still able to go weak-kneed in the presence of his grandson, Emerald was staunchly behind Edward and Mrs Simpson. A credible explanation for this was that with Wallis as the King's Consort there might be a role for her as lady-in-waiting or perhaps Mistress of the Robes. Others in the Simpson camp had similar ambitions unaware that they were hitching their wagons to a falling star. When Emerald died in her late seventies, she left instructions for her ashes to be sprinkled over Grosvenor Square.

Her great rival as a hostess, Lady Sibyl Colefax, was a short, slim woman with glinting hair-dos to match her steel-like elegance. She also entertained politicians and a fair share of reigning or deposed monarchs at her famous dinner table in the Division Bell area of Lord North Street. But mostly she favoured distinguished performers like Noel Coward and Artur Rubinstein who were usually expected to play for their supper. She had the edge on Emerald when it came to presentation. She had more style and her magnificent salon reflected it. Understandably too. Sibyl Colefax and John Fowler Ltd, became world renowned as interior decorators.

With both these spry, influential matrons in her corner, Wallis had access to the leading Establishment figures of the day. Some of these saw political advantage in standing by her and thereby Edward VIII. With known Nazi sympathies the new King could be expected to play an important role in any post-Munich accommodation with the Germans. (Both Edward and Wallis had met Hitler, Goering, and had courted Ribbentrop, associations which would have added contempt to the distaste Elizabeth already felt.)

Those facts and other dubious characters had yet to be smoked out of the woodwork. What was beginning to worry the Court – and both Bertie and Elizabeth were aware of it – was the security problems posed by the King's obsessive love-affair. Oblivious to everything else, the King was taking only a meagre interest in State papers. Some were returned uninitialled, and therefore unread. Some came back to Alec Hardinge drink-stained, or ringed by the bottoms of glasses. Cabinet documents were carelessly left lying around at Fort Belvedere in full view of Mrs Simpson and whoever might have been there from the Ritz Bar set. Informed of all this, Prime Minister Baldwin became more selective about the documents sent to the King. Informed of what was happening, the Yorks distanced themselves further from the King and his companion.

If the uninhibited Sybil and Emerald knew of the dangers involved it didn't prevent them blithely continuing their launching parties. Pathetically, the celebrated cuckold Ernest Simpson returned their invitations expressing his regrets that business etc. would exclude him, but not, of course, Mrs Simpson. It became a society joke, 'Ernest Simpson, the little man who wasn't there'.

It would be a mistake to imagine that Elizabeth only had Wallis Simpson on her mind. She had other more important preoccupations, chiefly helping Queen Mary pack up her belongings and move to Marlborough House. It is a melancholy chore for a widow and the Queen was grateful to have Elizabeth with her. A born comforter, her daughter-in-law helped cushion some of the sorrow, and tried to dispel her one fear that the new King might pull the roof down on them all. That danger seemed imminent when Bertie told her casually in the spring of 1936, that the King was coming over to Royal Lodge to show off his new American station wagon. He said he would be bringing some friends.

8

But for his paralysing obsession for Mrs Simpson, the King
might have thought twice about bringing Wallis over for tea
with the Yorks. But he was seeing everything around him with a
kind of kamikaze self-assurance. And if he was aware that his
poodle-like behaviour in public with Wallis was making him a
laughing stock it appeared not to bother him. (One court jester
had quipped, 'King Edward the Eighth and Mrs Simpson the
Seven-Eighths.) Wallis, long accustomed to ordering her men
about, instructed him one evening at the theatre to remove a
large Havana cigar poking out of his front pocket. Friends in the
box nudged each other as Edward sheepishly did as he was told.
Her hold on him was total. It is conceivable, therefore, that it
was she rather than he who suggested they go over to have tea
with the Yorks. She was no longer the King's secret woman.
She was now the dominant figure of the Court, and behaving
like a queen well in advance of any such possibility. Tempting
to go over to Royal Lodge and try that status on for size?

There are several versions of what happened when the un-
crowned King decided to bring Wallis and three house guests
over to Royal Lodge that weekend. The two prime sources are
Wallis Simpson herself, and Marion Crawford the governess
who was virtually banished as a consequence. What is evident
from all published accounts is that the two leading protagonists
honed a sharper edge to their mutual dislike. According to
Wallis Simpson's published recollections: 'That spring David
bought a new American station wagon. He was extremely
proud of it. One afternoon David said, "Let's drive over to
Royal Lodge. I want to show Bertie the new car." There were
three other guests staying at the Fort that weekend and they

went along with us. The Duke and Duchess of York met David at the door. David insisted they inspect the station wagon . . . I had seen the Duchess of York before on several occasions at the Fort and York House. Her justly famous charm was highly evident. I was also aware of the beauty of her complexion and the almost startling blueness of her eyes. Our conversation, I remember, was largely a discussion of the merits of the garden at the Fort and that at Royal Lodge. We returned to the house for tea which was served in the drawing room. David and his sister-in-law carried on the conversation with his brother throwing in only an occasional word. It was a pleasant hour but I left with the distinct impression that while the Duke of York was sold on the American station wagon, the Duchess was not sold on David's other American interest.'

Sarcasm as pointed and elegant as the matador's *coup de grace*. First the disarming preliminaries . . . 'justly famous charm' . . . 'beauty of her complexion' . . . then the fatal thrust.

Crawfie was more felicitous though; according to Penelope Mortimer, there is a significant divergence between the English and American versions of the episode in her book *The Little Princesses*. As she remembered that day: 'He [David] arrived bringing friends with him, among them Mrs Simpson. I looked at her with some interest. She was a smart, attractive woman with that immediate friendliness that American women have. No one alluded to that visit. But it was impossible not to notice the change in Uncle David. He had been so youthful and gay. Now he looked distraught and seemed not to be listening to what was said to him.' But American readers were treated to some additional intelligence, learning for instance that Mrs Simpson appeared to be entirely at her ease and that she had 'a distinctly proprietary way of speaking to the new King' and that 'she drew him to the window and suggested how certain trees might be moved and part of a hill taken away to improve the view.' If Crawfie's account is correct, then it was a piece of breathtaking gall, Wallis telling the King how to reconstruct the Yorks' landscape from the window of the Yorks' home. No wonder she left with the 'distinct impression . . . that the Duchess was not sold on David's other American interest.'

Any objective reflection on that encounter must make Wallis Simpson's other comments seem disingenuous. If the tea party was as bland as all that why did David appear, in Crawfie's words, so distraught, not listening to what was being said to him? And anyone as intelligent as Wallis must have known that peremptorily advising the moving of a tree or a hill in someone else's backyard is a fairly large-scale impertinence. Only Elizabeth's most intimate confidantes would ever know the extent of her anger. But there was worse to come. In July of that year, the King invited her and the Duke of York to a dinner party at York House. The official purpose was to honour Sir Samuel Hoare, then First Lord of the Admiralty. But the real intention was to make Wallis Simpson the centrepiece of an influential Establishment group dominated by Winston Churchill.

By having Wallis (Ernest Simpson sent his regrets) alongside Lord Willingdon, Viceroy of India, Sir Philip Sassoon and an additional helping of peers and peeresses, the King was emphasizing to Elizabeth and Bertie that allegiance to him included her. Churchill, aware that other guests like Alec and Helen Hardinge resented Wallis's presence, enjoyed himself making a little mischief. He took as his theme an earlier Prince of Wales's (later George IV) secret marriage to Maria Fitzherbert which broke the rules of the Royal Marriage Act. The King didn't rise to the bait. Nor did Wallis who presumably wasn't concerned, then, with Constitutional booby traps. The Duchess on the other hand responded casually, 'Well, that was a *long* time ago.' After which Churchill sailed on a different tack with a reference to the Wars of the Roses, Lancaster versus York. Nobody gnawed at that bone and the evening ended without bloodshed.

Elizabeth's frustrations over the Edward and Mrs Simpson affair were intensified by the effect it was having on Queen Mary. The old matriarch was in deep gloom, often in tears. David was increasingly hostile to his mother, seeing her as the one citadel the Colefax-Cunard forces couldn't conquer. Queen Mary was said to have warned Wallis that she risked destroying the Crown. Wallis while conceding that danger pleaded that the King had threatened suicide if she left him.

That exchange merely increased the King's agitation. The residual respect and sympathy for George V's widow; the public's affection for the Duke and Duchess of York and the little princesses; it was all getting a bit too much for the disgruntled monarch. What must have infuriated him further was his misreading of Elizabeth's low profile as meekness. The famous charm, he was discovering, didn't soften the influence she exerted on Bertie, *for* Bertie, or Queen Mary's increasing reliance on her. Events were closing in. True to form, he backed off from the problem, chartering a yacht to take Mrs Simpson and friends cruising the Dalmatian coast and into the Mediterranean. Even in today's moral climate, a new King bobbing around the Med with his still-married mistress might raise an ecclesiastical eyebrow and a question or two in the House. But in 1936, the affair competed with the Spanish Civil War and Hitler's invasion of the Rhineland for the front pages. But only in America. There, gossip writers gorged themselves on the meaty items wired daily from London. 'CUTIE SIMPSON CUTS OUT BLOODLESS BRITISH BLONDES IN ROYAL CHOICE' headlined an over-heated item implying that Wallis had the edge on some of the more eligible British spinsters.

In England an unedifying alliance between Beaverbrook and Rothermere kept the affair out of their papers. No altruism was involved. Just a case of two calculating newspaper proprietors treading water to see which way the tide would run. In principle they were behind the King, but like Churchill, this was largely because of their disenchantment with Prime Minister Baldwin. Others were having second thoughts, notably Sibyl Colefax and Emerald Cunard. By late September 1936, both were receiving troublesome vibrations from the Simpson Scandal. Their friend Wallis and the King were becoming isolated, Edward increasingly erratic and unpredictable. A friend had confided that she'd seen him goose-stepping around in the Simpson's London apartment wearing a German helmet. He frequently wandered around Mayfair without telling his security men or his chauffeur. Whether the two famous hostesses, Sibyl and Emerald, compared notes is not known. But it's clear they were inclining to the view that Edward and Mrs Simpson weren't such a good bet after all. (In the event, both 'sponsors' leapt off the sinking ship, their volte-face scathingly attacked in a famous poem by the late Osbert Sitwell, aptly titled 'Rat Week'.)

If Wallis's proprietorial behaviour at Royal Lodge irritated Elizabeth this was nothing compared with the turmoil she caused on her visit to Balmoral. The King was already in bad odour in Scotland. Early in September he had been asked by the Lord Provost of Aberdeen to open extensions to the city's Royal Infirmary. He declined, giving as his reason that the Court was in mourning for his father. This ignored the fact that the mourning period ended on 20 July, and in any event what applied to him equally affected Bertie. Moreover, official grieving hadn't inhibited him from attending Ascot in June. But logic no longer featured in the King's thinking or state of mind, diagnosed by Bruce-Lockhart as *dementia erotica*. Having backed out of that opening ceremony on the grounds of royal mourning he was spotted on the same day in a muffler and driving goggles waiting for Wallis and her American friends Mr and Mrs Herman Rogers at Aberdeen railway station. Whether the King thought the motoring goggles would prevent recognition isn't clear, though a policeman did reprimand him for leaving his car in the wrong part of the station yard. Later that day the local paper headlined the story: 'His Majesty in Aberdeen – Surprise Visit in Car to Meet Guests'. There were also pictures of the Duke and Duchess of York opening the new Infirmary buildings. That juxtaposition was not lost on Aberdeen, and Scotland, feeling insulted, never forgave him. On the other hand, the popularity rating of the understudies Bertie and Elizabeth soared.

Both had been invited to dinner at Balmoral on 26 September. Bertie, still devoted to his elder brother, accepted though Elizabeth would gladly have pleaded a diplomatic illness. Queen Mary saw the guest list and her heart sank. In addition to Balmoral's usual complement of Court associates and Establishment figures, her son, the King, had brought in his own crowd, Wallis's name appearing in the Court Circular ahead of those of the Duke and Duchess of York. Another gauntlet thrown down in the arena. Shortly afterwards Queen Mary learned that Wallis Simpson had been installed in the suite that had always been reserved for her and George V. An absence of tact as well as logic was apparent in her elder son's *dementia erotica*. And much of this was rubbing off on to Wallis.

Maybe there was nothing wrong in introducing American three-decker toasted sandwiches on to the Balmoral menu. And if each morning she emerged from the George and Mary suite in shorts, well the older retainers at Balmoral could always look the other way.

But Wallis did more than that. She joined the King in a purge of some of the older employees. 'David only told me what he had done after it was over,' Bertie complained in a letter to Queen Mary. Wallis changed household routines that had applied for decades at the castle. She ran a manicured finger along mantel-shelves and other surfaces, visibly displeased at finding dust. The demonstration was unmistakable. She was the mistress of the house. She gave the orders. And though she now knew what to expect, the Duchess of York bridled at the thought of being formally received by Wallis. Descriptions of her reactions to that famous Balmoral confrontation vary. According to biographers Keith Middlemas and John Barnes, 'she openly showed her resentment at being received by Mrs Simpson'. This theme is developed by Michael Thornton in *Royal Feud*: 'With a freezing expression Elizabeth, devoid of her usual smile, walked straight past Mrs Simpson, ignoring her attempted welcome and said, as if to no one in particular, "I came to dine with the King."' The source of this is not identified. It seems the least plausible account. Though nobody disputes Elizabeth can bite as well as smile, that scene was totally out of character. Elizabeth, whether as a Bowes-Lyon, a Queen or the Queen Mother has her own inimitable way of communicating her disapproval.

Her intimates tell of a subtle, unspoken signal which leaves the victim in no doubt whatsoever that he, or she, has boobed. It is not so much a sudden coldness. It's more canny than that; just a fleeting withdrawal of the customary warmth. The late Lord Mountbatten was amused discussing that aspect of the Queen Mother during our talks.

'She has this marvellous way of indicating her displeasure,' he chortled. 'She hasn't got a temper but she is prepared to sulk. If something is done absolutely against what she wants she lets people know it just by being aloof. That is much worse than temper. It is more frightening you see, they know they have displeased her. But the mood just blows itself out quickly.' In this context Sir Martin Gilliatt adds a grace note: 'Basically in life she objects to anything which is cheapened.'

There cannot be any doubt that Elizabeth saw the bizarre antics of Edward and Mrs Simpson as a cheapening of the monarchy. Morals apart, flaunting their love affair around the royal estates, consummating it in the dynastic four-poster; the Bermuda shorts, the three decker-sandwiches, the upheaval she'd caused at Balmoral; no wonder Queen Mary wept. The ultimate indignity was having the woman receive her in Scotland. The Yorks saw the evening out as best they could though it was evident from the King's forced humour that rigor mortis was setting in fast. Even the showing of a Fred Astaire-Ginger

Rogers film, *Swing Time* failed to lift spirits. Jerome Kern's classic 'A Fine Romance . . . This Is' meaning different things to different guests.

The following morning the Royal party went to Sunday service in the rain. The Duchess of York did not join them. The stained-glass windows of Crathie Church must have seemed the wrong backdrop for another confrontation with the woman from Baltimore. The Duke and Duchess were glad to get away, Elizabeth particularly. Her first thoughts on returning to London were about Queen Mary now installed in Marlborough House. Elizabeth comforted her as she coped with Bertie's ambivalence towards his beleagured brother; he felt a deep-rooted affection and pity, but a kind of mute terror at the thought of the royal roof caving in.

If ever Bertie needed strength it was in the weeks running up to December 1936. That strength, which Mountbatten witnessed, was significantly underpinned by Elizabeth. 'She proved her worth. Made him proud of himself. The effect she had on him was very, very profound.' Nevertheless Bertie and Elizabeth felt imprisoned by the situation. Edward and Mrs Simpson were controlling events. Everybody else was expected to fall into line. But to the King the situation was getting nowhere. He decided to ignite the fuse.

A phone call by the Press Association to Alec Hardinge, the King's Principal Private Secretary, on 15 October 1936 initiated the first explosion. Wallis Simpson's divorce petition against her husband would be heard at Ipswich Assizes on 27 October. To give herself the necessary residential qualification she had taken a cottage, Beech House, in nearby Felixstowe. Hardinge checked the story with the King who confirmed it. Alarmed now, Baldwin saw the King at Fort Belvedere on 20 October. His object was to try to persuade the King to stop the divorce proceeding. He knew that once Wallis was free then the throne stood only on quicksand. An hour of talking between them showed the King to be as determined as ever. Whether Baldwin warned him at this, or a subsequent meeting of the catastrophe pending, is irrelevant. More important, at some time during that week, Edward VIII was curtly informed that no Constitutional manoeuvre could enable him to marry Wallis and keep the throne. A morganatic marriage, allowing her the consort's role but no privileges as a queen was equally out of the question. Predictably the King rounded on Baldwin making it clear that throne or not he intended to marry Mrs Simpson the moment she was free. It was then that the Duke and Duchess of York were privately put on notice that the King might cut and run and that Bertie would have to take his place. The Duke was in shock, Elizabeth in a rage. As Duke and Duchess of York they were on the Palace rota, but some privacy was still left to them and the two princesses. As King and Queen it would be goodbye to all that.

The enormity of the threat induced a fierce resentment in both Elizabeth and Bertie, though each had a different target. Elizabeth's fury was directed entirely at Wallis Simpson. The wrong woman, for the wrong man, in the wrong place, at the wrong time. The Duke of York's anger was angled more against circumstances than his brother. But Bertie had this in common with Elizabeth; he didn't want to play King to her Queen. In fact he was totally unprepared for it. At least a stand-in is expected to know the script and in an emergency perform the starring role. George V, with no reason to suspect that his stammering second son would ever be King, had taught him nothing, shown him no State papers, discussed nothing of importance with him. He had virtually excluded him from the inner workings of the Court. And his brother chucking his weight around at Sandringham and Balmoral merely reinforced his sense of being, in royal terms, a second-class citizen. He was frightened now as well as bitter. So as husbands will in these situations, Bertie turned for comfort to Elizabeth. She provided instant balm as with each day the pendulum swung between Fort Belvedere and 145 Piccadilly.

If the King sensed the Duke and Duchess's apprehension it caused him no loss of sleep. His nightmare was the ultimatum his love-affair had posed: the throne or Wallis. The more obsessed he became the more of a pain the whole business of kingship appeared to him. Within a few days he would be wailing to Sir Walter Monckton as they walked towards the Palace, 'I'm not going to let them lock me up in that place!'

On 27 October, Wallis secured her divorce from Ernest Simpson on the grounds of his adultery with a woman (whom he subsequently married) at a hotel near Maidenhead. The British Press under the combined weight of Beaverbrook and Rothermere meekly reduced the story to a few low-key paragraphs. American papers on the other hand, soared into an orgy of wishful thinking. 'KING TO MARRY "WALLY" – WEDDING

NEXT JUNE'. 'KING'S MOLL RENO'D IN WOLSEY'S HOME TOWN' were typical. In France, readers were reassured, 'L'AMOUR DU ROI VA BIEN'. Though this material was kept out of the British papers it filtered into Mayfair gossip which automatically ensured that Elizabeth and Bertie would hear all about it. Whether they heard rumours that Wallis was already seeking to have a department store sew the royal crest on her lingerie isn't known. But Wallis did seem to be behaving as though she were only an eyelash away from becoming the Queen.

If it all looked like indecent haste to the Duke and Duchess of York, the ominous logic was soon explained to them. With a decree nisi on 27 April 1937, that would still be two weeks short of the King's Coronation. They could marry, he could be crowned, and as the King believed, with Wallis on a consort's throne beside him. Those five weeks from 27 October to 3 December were unmitigated misery for the Duke and Duchess of York. Nevertheless Bertie's touch of steel was beginning to show. He declared on 25 November to Sir Godfrey Thomas, the King's Assistant Private Secretary, 'If the worst comes to the worst and I have to take over you can be sure I shall do my best to clear up the inevitable mess – if the whole fabric does not crumble under the shock and strain of it all.'

The fabric the Duke referred to was positively showing cracks, more so at the Fort than at 145 Piccadilly. Even the King's friends thought he was becoming unhinged. Baldwin was certain he was mad. The King's Private Secretary, Alec Hardinge, was always loyal, but his devotion did not extend to humouring an unbalanced monarch. He wrote to the King stressing that not only the Crown but the Government was in peril. To that warning he added a proposal which froze him out of the King's circle permanently. Everything could be saved, Hardinge wrote, if Mrs Simpson went abroad without delay. David reacted with predictable outrage. His response to the letter was to ignore it and its author. Instead he ap-pointed Sir Walter Monckton to act as his spokesman with Baldwin. He also began selling the idea of his brother taking over if the problems became irreconcilable. That notion in-furiated Bertie who complained that he felt like a sheep being led to the slaughter. To Elizabeth, floating Bertie's name merely added impertinence to David's arrogance, and increased the Duchess of York's hostility towards her wayward brother-in-law.

On 29 November they had engagements in Scotland. The Duke became Grand Master Mason of Scotland, the Duchess received the Freedom of the City of Edinburgh. Back in her homeland and breathing the crisp Scottish air, Elizabeth felt the strain of the Simpson crisis slacken. Memories of her years at Glamis brought a soothing sensation which contrasted sharply with the unpleasantness surrounding Fort Belvedere. It was good to hear English as the Scots speak it, particularly when the Lord Provost addressed her as, 'Beloved Duchess, daughter of our northern land, gracious servant of the State, ambassadress of Empire. . . .' Two factors however, gave the Provost's words a true ring to them: first Scotland was genuinely pleased with its Duchess; and second there was an intuitive sympathy for this popular couple trapped by unwholesome events south of the border.

Elizabeth and Bertie took the night sleeper to Euston, pleased with their separate successes in Scotland. The euphoria vanished the moment they stepped off the train at 7.25 a.m. Thursday, 3 December 1936. All the newspaper placards foreshadowed in giant type 'The King's Marriage'. The catalyst for this sudden dam-burst in Fleet Street was a speech by the Bishop of Bradford, Dr Walter Blunt, to a diocesan conference. A chubby-faced cleric few had heard of before, he decided to take as his theme the forthcoming Coronation Service. He didn't leave it at that, however. With a cold ecclesiastical eye directed two hundred miles south to Fort Belvedere, he asked the conference to 'commend the King to God's grace which he will so abundantly need . . . if he is to do his duty faithfully. We hope that he is aware of his need. Some of us wish that he gave more positive signs of his awareness. . . .'

In the furore that followed, the red-faced Bishop protested that when he wrote the draft of his speech he had never even heard of Mrs Simpson, but stuck to his guns once the gossip had reached him. Malcolm Muggeridge likened Blunt to 'an elderly visitor to a Swiss mountain resort, who, wandering aimlessly along in knickerbockers, carelessly kicks aside a stone and releases an avalanche.' Once the local *Bradford Telegraph and Argus* had published a full account of Blunt's words, Fleet Street – essentially Beaverbrook and Rothermere – were forced into removing the gags on their editors. The 'Gentleman's Agreement' which had nothing gentlemanly about it, was dead. Their newspapers, which had cravenly kept on ice news that the rest of the world headlined, were suddenly galvanized into action. The whole Simpson Scandal, the previous marriages and messy divorces, were feverishly written up. Pictures of Edward and Mrs Simpson were hunted out of files and a sudden surge of interest focused on the Duke and Duchess of York. Previously overshadowed by the charismatic Edward, they were suddenly the centre of interest. And not merely with the newspapers. An epidemic of second-guessing began afflicting some of Edward's closest friends and supporters. Some of these were merely society mavericks leaping on to a safer band-wagon. Others ratted on the King, seeing no sense in going down with a sinking ship. But a few, like the late Lord Mountbatten, had a genuine dilemma, loving the man while totally condemning his behaviour. As his biographer Philip Ziegler observed: 'Edward VIII was his best friend but over the years he had begun to recognize the futility and wilfulness which made the King unfit to rule. Mrs Simpson he liked and was amused by, but he had concluded that she would never sit happily on a throne. She had got off to a bad start when she had first gone to stay at Adsdean (their country house) and brought with her a cold chicken from Fortnum and Masons. Edwina who flattered herself that her Austrian chef was among the best in Europe was not enchanted by the gift.'

As he became further disillusioned with Edward VIII so Mountbatten found 'new respect for the future King George VI. In the past he had seen the Duke through the eyes of the Prince of Wales, the honest, loyal, "dear old Bertie". Only as the crisis deepened and the Abdication became more likely, did he begin to appreciate the integrity and radiant decency which were to make the unfashionable brother so much a better monarch than the Prince of Wales would ever have been.' It was that criterion ultimately, which turned Mountbatten away from the friend he hero-worshipped as he said 'like all the others'. How crucial that criterion was to Mountbatten is clear from advice he once gave to Prince Charles. The affection between those two was only marginally exceeded by the love Charles has for his grandmother Queen Elizabeth. Duty was high on the list of many fine qualities Mountbatten attributed to the young Prince in our conversation. He emphasized that he was not in the business of giving advice to any members of the royal family, though I doubt if this inhibited any of them from seeking it. However he did say this to Charles: 'Study the life and times of the Duke of

Windsor. Don't imagine that because like him, you have become a sort of royal pop idol that the British people will always support you. They will back you only as long as you serve the country and do the job.'

On that basis Edward VIII, in that fateful first week of December 1936, failed to measure up to Mountbatten's test. As for Wallis Simpson, you can hardly forgive a woman who brings her own Fortnum's chicken to your lunch table.

The crowds forming outside Downing Street and Buckingham Palace in that December week would have had no idea then of any fatal flaws in their King. They sensed a crisis and that the King was being forced into a corner. Coming out on to the streets was a display of allegiance. Wallis on the other hand received no public benediction but rather the reverse. Bricks were thrown through a neighbour's window in mistake for her own. There were threatening letters and obscene graffiti, 'Down With the American Whore' being one of the nastier examples. Now the King wished he had listened to Alec Hardinge and sent Mrs Simpson abroad three weeks earlier. Not to save his throne, but to clear the field in order to relinquish it. Mrs Simpson went to the South of France to avoid the press and sit out the crisis. Edward, in response to an urgent request from Queen Mary, called on her at Marlborough House. He found the Duke and Duchess of York and the Princess Royal there with her: Bertie was grim; Queen Mary close to tears; Elizabeth, silent but significantly disapproving. She had seen what George V's death had done to the Queen; the grief and nights without sleep. Now all this added strain was draining the strength of an already frail old lady. And if his mother hadn't demanded it the King would probably not have bothered to see her. If there was now to be a family conference Elizabeth wanted no part of it. What concerned her personally was no concern of the King's. She left the room. The meeting was short. Edward announced that he could not live alone as King. He was going to marry Mrs Simpson. If this meant Abdication so be it. He left, making a brief arrangement with his brother to come and see him at the Fort on the 4th.

From that day Bertie commuted frantically between the Palace, Royal Lodge and 145 Piccadilly, looking for those who might manipulate a last minute reprieve. He behaved more like a prisoner striving to avoid the gallows than a prince sidestepping the throne. The following day the King postponed the proposed meeting at the Fort until Sunday the 7th. 'I will tell you my decision then.' A Cabinet session confirmed to the King that they would not legislate for a solution which put Wallis Simpson beside him as his consort. His kingship was over bar the signing. On 8 December, Elizabeth went down with an attack of flu. She was confined to her bed at Royal Lodge with a temperature. A crisis meeting between the Duke of York and Walter Monckton spelled out the situation. The King would almost certainly abdicate. Bertie would become George VI. His head spinning, Bertie went to Marlborough House to brief his mother on the situation. From there he went to Fort Belvedere for a dinner party which had all the dramatic overtones of the Last Supper. Around the table sat the four sons of George V, and the Prime Minister, Stanley Baldwin. The King contrived manic good humour. The Dukes of York, Kent and Gloucester were visibly dejected. By the time the cigars and brandy circulated the three brothers recognized that within a day or two Bertie would be the new King.

The fine print involved in a proposed Abdication calls for a cluster of Constitutional lawyers to work out future status plus smart accountants to consider a King's severance pay and yearly stipend. Within hours Bertie was embroiled with these professionals while Crawfie supplied Elizabeth with hot drinks and tender loving nursing. (Hilariously, during all these solemn comings and goings, the word had got around that none other than Marlene Dietrich was trying to talk the King out of abdicating. Her pleading phone calls and notes unanswered, it was reported that she turned up at the Fort but was gently turned around and sent back to London.)

Bertie arranged one last meeting between his elder brother and their mother. She would not go to the Fort. Instead she joined her two sons at Royal Lodge. It was the final scene of the last act. Driving to London afterwards Bertie, to use his own words, 'sobbed like a child'. The following day, Thursday, 10 December, he kissed his sick wife goodbye and went to Fort Belvedere to witness the signing of the Abdication. At 10 a.m. the brothers York, Gloucester and Kent assembled in the study joined by lawyers and court officials. Beyond the unvarnished wooden desk, tall windows opened out on to a gently sloping lawn. There were several copies of the abdication instrument and of the King's message that would go with it. The brothers smoked and talked in whispers. The King sat down at the desk, dipped his pen in the inkwell, scribbled a signature, then with Chaplinesque irritation announced, 'There's no ink in the damn pot!' He borrowed a fountain pen and signed. 'I Edward Eighth, of Great Britain, Ireland and the British Dominions beyond the Seas, King Emperor of India, do hereby declare my irrevocable determination to renounce the Throne for Myself and My descendants and My desire that effect should be given to this instrument of Abdication immediately.' The King stood up, smiled, and beckoned his brother Bertie to take the chair. He then walked out to take a last look at the flowers he'd planted while each brother laboriously signed a total of fifteen documents with a courtier blotting them one at a time.

There would be other formalities but a reign had effectively been blotted out that morning in Fort Belvedere. Edward had been king for 326 days. (Not the shortest reign in English history. Edward V had reigned for seventy-seven days in 1483.) After his historic abdication broadcast, David had one last meeting with his brothers at Royal Lodge. He recalls it with evident sadness in his book *A King's Story*. 'My brothers walked me to the door exactly as they would have done were I leaving for Balmoral, Sandringham or some other familiar place. On this leave-taking however, it was I who, as the subject of the King, bowed to Bertie.' That night, as J. Wheeler-Bennett records, the man who would be George VI confided to his friend and cousin Louis Mountbatten: 'Dickie, this is absolutely terrible! I never wanted this to happen. I'm quite unprepared for it. I'm only a naval officer. It's the only thing I know about.' It was the wrong tack to take with the man who was to become First Sea Lord. Mountbatten wrote assuring his friend, 'On all hands in the Admiralty one hears the profound satisfaction of the Navy at having once more a sailor King. Heartbroken as I am at David's departure and all the terrible trouble he has brought on us all I feel I must tell you how deeply I feel for Elizabeth and you having to shoulder his responsibilities in such trying circumstances. Luckily both you and your children have precisely those qualities needed to pull this country out of this ghastly crisis. . . .' It was a fairly shrewd assessment as the future would prove.

The reactions of the two women most affected by the Edward and Mrs Simpson affair, Elizabeth and Queen Mary had this in common: both blamed the catastrophe on Wallis Simpson. A few days later when Jim Salisbury, brother-in-law to Lady

Airlie came to commiserate with Queen Mary he found her: 'not weeping as he had feared but furious and outraged. "The person who needs most sympathy is my second son. He is the one who is making the sacrifice!"'

Elizabeth, of course, felt the same. But unlike Queen Mary she made no public utterances of her deep resentment. Close friends are nevertheless convinced that she blames the Simpson Scandal for shortening her husband's life. Tactlessly, someone asked her once whether she had noticed how well the Duke of Windsor looked since he had married Wallis Simpson. The then Queen responded sharply, 'Yes, look who has the pouches under his eyes now!'

For years Elizabeth could not bear even to mention Wallis by name. It was always 'that woman'. (In his letters, Bertie stopped short of writing her name in full, restricting it to Mrs S—.) But the Duchess's continued reticence merely intensified the speculation. What effect did the Abdication and the ill-fated lovers at the centre of it *really* have on her? When I put that question directly to her friend Lord Home, the veteran diplomat said simply, 'she found it all distasteful'. No doubt he would have said more if she herself had been more forthcoming. But as the late Lord Mountbatten indicated, she rarely needs words to draw blood. But speculating on what she might have said in anger to Edward or 'that woman' or both, is irresistible. It was certainly so to playwright Royce Ryton who makes a fine effort of it in *Crown Matrimonial*, putting these words in Elizabeth's mouth in a confrontation with King Edward: 'Everything has to be sacrificed to your vanity, the country, Bertie, the children, your mother, me, the Throne; everything and everyone, so that you can be happy in your private life. You are mesmerised by your own legend.' There is no record of any complaint from Clarence House.

What mattered to Elizabeth on the night of the Abdication was that, brave face or not, she had a reluctant monarch on her hands. Having proved she could become the most popular Duchess on the royal circuit, she had no qualms about becoming a Queen. In Mountbatten's eyes she had all the regal qualities of a monarch bar the dubious criterion of bloodline. But she knew how traumatic events had been to her husband, the new King. He had come to her after that last meeting with David as stricken as if he'd suffered a bereavement. There were other factors which must have humiliated him and therefore hurt her. He was not it seems, the automatic choice to replace his brother. His uncertain speech, nervousness and reluctance to do the job weighed against him. But a close look at the Dukes of Kent and Gloucester hardly made them viable alternatives. The Duke of Kent had been involved in a blackmail scandal involving a young man in France which had been successfully kept out of the newspapers. He had also flirted with drugs. The Duke of Gloucester had no such past, but not much presence either. The brief read-out on him was – 'unreliable'. So it was back to Bertie, of whom Mountbatten would say with evident sincerity, 'He was the most unselfish, friendly, thoughtful, considerate friend you could wish to have. And he had one up on her! She was a wonderful person but he was quite out of the ordinary. I do think she would be the first to say he had an even better character than she. They were marvellous together. She made him what she wanted him to be.'

But the day he came back from saying goodbye to his brother, Bertie was trembling and agitated. Alarm bells must have rung in her mind. Mr Logue, the speech therapist, had better be alerted. Bertie's stammer, though under control, relapsed at moments of extreme stress. Those moments would soon be crowding in.

Hastily too. The monarchy, with an empty chair on its hands, cannot drag its feet. Once Edward VIII had formally relinquished his lien on the tenancy of Buckingham Palace, they couldn't wait to get him off the premises. Within hours he was on a ship bound for France, to join Wallis Simpson at the Villa Lou Viei near Cannes. She had wept constantly throughout the last hours of the Abdication. Whatever dreams she might have had as the love-affair swept towards Niagara, they were unlikely to have had this ending. If there was a touch of venom to her bitterness it is pretty certain it was directed at the woman in bed at Royal Lodge. To Wallis Simpson – if to nobody else – Elizabeth led the powerful opposition which ultimately had them ostracized from the Court. Historians dismiss that but judged her more benevolently than they did Edward VIII. In A. J. P. Taylor's judgement: 'Many people feared, a few hoped, that the abdication of Edward VIII would permanently weaken the monarchy. It did not do so. Edward's former popularity turned out to be as evanescent as the enthusiasm for a film star.' An even more withering indictment came from Alistair Cooke who declared, 'The most damning epitaph you can compose about Edward – as a Prince, as a King, as a man – is one that all comfortable people should cower from deserving; he was at his best only when the going was good.'

All the constitutional apparatus was now being assembled to proclaim Bertie as the new King. The British public, who had previously rallied round the beleagured Edward, behaved like pop fans, switching their allegiance overnight and closed ranks behind his brother. Farewell David, Long Live Bertie. Crowds now clamoured outside 145 Piccadilly for a glimpse of the new monarch. This delighted Bertie who could scarcely wait to tell Elizabeth. Ripples had already reached out to Royal Lodge, where the Duchess was last seen nestling among the pillows, various potions and pills on the antique bed table beside her. The crisis as seen through Crawfie's eyes is worth noting. 'The peace of the house was broken. The cloud had appeared on the horizon. The uneasiness we all sensed in the air grew . . . I do not know what we would have done at that time without the swimming lessons. They were a great diversion and took our minds off other matters.' And then . . . 'One afternoon the Duchess sent for me to go and see her. She was occupied when I reached her room and I stood outside in an alcove by the landing window waiting and watching the crowds gathering below. Then something happened that told me that the abdication had taken place. The bedroom door opened. Queen Mary came out of the Duchess's room. She who was always so upright, so alert, looked suddenly old and tired. Tears streamed down her face. The Duchess was lying in bed, propped up among the pillows. She held her hand out to me. "I'm afraid there are going to be great changes in our lives, Crawfie," she said. "We must take what is coming to us and make the best of it."'

9

Elizabeth had taken to her bed at Royal Lodge as the Duchess of York but by the time she climbed out she was the Queen. The quantum leap from being merely one monarch's sister-in-law to another's Queen Consort had amusing repercussions. Crawfie, always dutifully reverential, was now suitably awe-struck. As events brought her employer ever closer to the throne, she put the two princesses, Elizabeth, aged ten, and Margaret Rose, aged six, through a crash course in curtsying. On 12 December, the day after the Abdication, their father, smartly turned out in the uniform of Admiral of the Fleet, returned home as King to solemn, sweeping curtsies from his two daughters. He bent down and kissed them both. The Queen, touched by the display of affection, noticed how worn and haggard Bertie seemed. He had managed to get through the ordeal of addressing the Accession Council at St James's Palace, but the strain showed. He had spoken to the Privy Councillors in a clear voice, but there were still painful pauses and hesitation. 'Now that the duties of Sovereignty have fallen on me I declare to you my adherence to the strict principles of constitutional government and my resolve to work before all else for the welfare of the British Commonwealth of Nations. With my wife and helpmeet by my side, I take up the heavy task which lies before me. . . .'

A pencilled footnote to the typewritten address, clearly added later by Bertie himself, conferred a Dukedom on his ill-fated brother who would 'henceforth be known as His Royal Highness the Duke of Windsor'. With that title went percentages from Sandringham and Balmoral which brought him about a million pounds in cash, plus a yearly income of around £60,000. Further substantial amounts from undisclosed sources followed the Duke to France. Few Kings outside of Midas coveted wealth more than did the Duke of Windsor. He was no big giver either, except when it came to jewels for his duchess. These were often 'sweeteners' for some disappointment or slight. The most bitter of these was the refusal of the Cabinet to grant Wallis the status of a 'Royal Highness'. This made her a kind of morganatic Duchess, wife of the Duke but little more. The abrasive repercussions from this constitutional freeze-out would grind on up to the start of the Second World War. As the Duchess of Windsor reflected afterwards, 'it was a move to debar me in defiance of all custom from taking my place alongside my royal husband'. One can argue about precedents but it is clear that having both in England, with Wallis hovering around as a Royal Highness, would have been a considerable embarrassment to the new King and Queen. George VI faced hard enough problems as an unrehearsed stand-in without having a struck-off monarch and his consort breathing down his neck.

A more urgent matter as King George VI took his Queen to Buckingham Palace, was the question of the succession. On the face of it, Princess Elizabeth was now heir apparent. But the Act of 1702, while giving elder sons unqualified rights of succession, makes no distinction where the sole heirs are daughters. In other words, legally, both Elizabeth and Margaret could have been co-heirs to the throne. If both had married, the confusion over their status and that of their husbands and children, would exacerbate the nightmare. On 28 January 1937, Mr G. L. le Mander, MP for Wolverhampton, asked the Home Secretary Sir John Simon in the House of Commons: 'Is it proposed to introduce legislation to amend the Act of Settlement with a view to making it clear that the Princess Elizabeth is the sole heir to the throne and does not share it jointly with her sister?' The Home Secretary replied: 'No sir, there is no reason to do so. His Majesty's Government are advised that there is no doubt that in present circumstances Her Royal Highness the Princess Elizabeth would succeed to the throne as sole heir.'

Assuming it was a planted question, the Government considered it would offset any constitutional quibble in the future (though the Home Secretary's reference to 'present circumstances' suggests he wasn't that secure in his argument). But the effect of the Parliamentary answer is significant for a more subtle reason. It sealed Margaret's fate as a second fiddle princess. She would be in the same position as her father had been *vis-à-vis* the glamorous Prince of Wales though by contrast, the strong-charactered Elizabeth never attempted to upstage her younger sister. Virtually out of the running as an heir, excluded from the inner sanctums of the Court, any competent analyst could have forecast future rebelliousness in the life of Princess Margaret.

But in 1937 the relationship between the two princesses was as lively as with any other sisters. 'Let it not be thought,' stressed Crawfie in her memoirs, 'that all was sweetness and light in our schoolroom all the time. These were two entirely normal and healthy little girls. Neither was above taking a whack at her adversary if roused, and Lilibet was quick with her left hook. Margaret was more of a close-in fighter known to bite on occasions. More than once I have been shown a hand bearing Royal teethmarks.' An average day in the life of the royal princesses, *circa* 1937 – normal, mischievous, and totally remote from life beyond the palace gates.

For while the future Queen of England was being playfully bitten by her younger sister, Mussolini had crushed Abyssinia. Hitler had re-armed Germany and was scheming to march into the Rhineland, with Austria pencilled in to follow. Foreign Secretary Anthony Eden had warned Prime Minister Neville Chamberlain of the dangerous disparity between Britain's forces and Hitler's massive arms build-up and was told, according to Churchill, to 'go home and take an aspirin'. A cabal of leading political and industrial figures in this country energetically lobbied on behalf of the Nazis whose jackbooted methods they much admired. The most feted of these was Joachim von Ribbentrop, a former wine salesman who was German Ambassador in London from 1936 to 1937. He was the first to woo Edward and Mrs Simpson, persuading Hitler that this self-indulgent couple could be easily manipulated on behalf of the Fatherland. Critics of the Queen (and later of her as the Queen Mother) have suggested that Her Majesty's objections to Wallis were based on snobbery or anti-Americanism, or both. Those charges are answered as her life unfolds. But would it be snobbery to resent the Duke and Duchess of Windsor visiting Germany and socializing with Goering, Goebbels, and other top Nazis; and hearing that after meeting Wallis Hitler declared, 'she would have made a very good Queen'? Moreover, Elizabeth was bound to object to the Duke of Windsor's disgruntled behaviour towards his mother, Queen Mary. As his withdrawal symptoms became more acute, the exiled Duke began writing letters of such viciousness to his mother that George VI was forced to warn him that if he couldn't write more courteously he must not write to her at all. When he wasn't writing churlish letters, the Duke badgered his brother the King with interminable phone calls. Most of these were about money. At other times the Duke offered his younger brother some unsolicited advice on how to do his job. It may have been well intentioned. It could also have indicated a brooding reluctance to accept the fact that he was no longer King; that his power base was gone and that no one, least of all his brother, would jump in response to orders.

Elizabeth shared her husband's resentment of the ex-King's behaviour. Bertie had been having some success in conquering his stammer. His anger at David's tedious, complaining phone calls was throwing him back to square one. The Duke wanted Wallis to be welcomed into the Royal Family. Both Queen Mary and Elizabeth were adamantly against it. Finally, the King – who as Mountbatten revealed, scarcely made a move without consulting his wife – told David that the phone calls had to stop. 'Are you serious?' his brother asked in disbelief. 'Yes I'm sorry to say I am. The reason must be clear to you.' Which of course it was. The Duke of Windsor knew that there was a strong anti-Windsor faction standing squarely behind his brother. Leading it, were Alec Hardinge, and Sir Alan Lascelles, the former Assistant Private Secretary to George V. Both wanted to obliterate any residual influence Windsor might have mustered in England. The first act was to sever the heads. The next was to ostracize all those who, for different reasons, had slithered around the celebrated pair. Here, as often happens, the Court and the established Church sang the same tune. In an unusually nasty address, Archbishop Lang broadcast an attack on the abdicating King and [his] 'social circle whose standards and ways of life are alien to all the best instincts and traditions of his people. Let those who belong to this circle know that today they stand rebuked by the judgement of the nation which had loved King Edward.' Sibyl Colefax was said to have wept after she heard him. Emerald Cunard shrugged it off with her usual lively disdain. But suddenly they discovered they 'really didn't know Wallis all that well', indicating that they were not likely to be in touch with her now. But the purge was complete. The 'Black List' unequivocal. Both were subsequently *personae non grata* with the new Queen. Other senior figures of the Court known to have lined up with Wallis and David found themselves out on a limb, if not immediately out of a job. Hardinge and Lascelles discovered that Elizabeth was not just the 'plucky little wife' behind the King. She was a formidable ally, ruthlessly protective of her husband. She believed passionately that Bertie would make a great king. She was helping him fight his speech impediment. She would be just as resourceful in helping him overcome the larger impediment in the shape of the Duke and Duchess of Windsor.

This implacable attitude begs the larger question: was Elizabeth as Queen, and later as the Queen Mother, fair in the way she treated the exiled Duke and Duchess of Windsor? Wasn't a certain degree of magnanimity called for? True the ex-King had walked away with a fortune in hard cash and land investments; while 'that woman from Baltimore' was now an English Duchess with a social standing, not to say attractive notoriety, far beyond anything she might have dreamed of. But it was still small change compared with David as King and she as his Consort. A persuasive case is made for the couple by J. Bryan and Charles J. V. Murphy in *The Windsor Story*. In their view at least, the Abdication brought highly desirable spin-offs to the Duchess of York. 'She became famous. She won respect, even popularity; she became the matriarchal eminence of the Court – Clarence House is hers; so is a splendid Grace and Favour house at Windsor. All this she has Wallis to thank for, although the Queenship,' the authors acknowledge, 'was the last thing she wanted at the time, knowing as she did the price it would exact from her husband.' That is, of course, the whole point. In Elizabeth's mind, his distressing illnesses and his cruelly shortened life, were all brought on by the Abdication and the two self-obsessed figures at the centre of it. To suggest that Clarence House, Royal Lodge, fame and popularity in some way compensated for her loss, must have struck her as insulting. The anger inside Elizabeth the Queen simmered for years.

Lord Mountbatten has said that Elizabeth had 'a difficult row to hoe' on marrying the Duke of York. It was harder still on becoming the Queen. As he explained: 'The British Constitution is fascinating. It doesn't legislate against the Consort but it doesn't admit him or her within the Constitution either. The British Constitution which is largely unwritten revolves around the sovereign as a man. If he marries, the Consort is crowned. If, however, it is a woman who becomes sovereign her Consort is not crowned. Nor is he usually given a worthwhile title. But the Duke of Edinburgh brought to the role of Consort his own royal pedigree. Prince Philip himself was born His Royal Highness Prince Philip of Greece, Royal Highness Prince of Denmark, also born a Royal Highness of Great Britain and Ireland. But because of the Act of 1701 he doesn't wear a crown. He has a royal ducal coronet which is a bit more splendid than an ordinary duke's coronet. After he and Elizabeth were married, the Queen (unlike Victoria and her Consort) wasn't bossy and made no attempt to throw her weight about. But the fact was that as Consort, he automatically had to step aside. When he went to the first Privy Council meeting, as is well known, he did not go in alongside the Queen. The Duke of Gloucester went in as the senior member of the Royal Family. Prince Philip came in through another door which created quite a stir at the time. It was not a deliberate snub. It was a complete oversight in the Constitution. They did not expect a Queen to undertake this with a husband in existence. You probably would not have noticed that they once removed the Consort's throne from under the canopy in Parliament. They always have two thrones there. The Consort's is always about three-quarters of an inch lower than the Sovereign's. At that time when the Consort's throne was taken away, the Queen sat alone in the middle under the canopy. Philip sat on a chair outside. Then a constitutional lawyer, a chap called Eady [Sir Wilfrid Eady] pointed out that when the Prince of Wales became of age he would demand to sit in the seat then occupied by Prince Philip who would then either have to be pushed up or down. It was hastily decided to push him up and the Consort's throne was brought back under the canopy.'

Lord Mountbatten then returned to the other Elizabeth – by then, the Queen Mother. 'It is not unnoteworthy,' he smiled, 'that although legally by Order in Council, Prince Philip ranks above the Queen Mother, and must do – nevertheless either through his own modesty, generosity or whatever, nobody has tried to change the order of the Prayers for the Royal Family in the prayer book or the Loyal Toast.' Presumably 'nobody' would dare.

So Bertie's Queen moved into the six-hundred-roomed Buckingham Palace and into a position for which there was no constitutional recognition. Elizabeth could carve out the Consort's role exactly as she saw it. And here she had eager support from George VI. Bertie acted quickly to ensure she enjoy the power and the glory of a Queen. Three days after her accession – his forty-first birthday – he conferred on her the Order of the Garter. Perhaps more significantly, he insisted that except on the most important formal occasions, she precede him. Which she did in style, with the proud, smiling monarch falling in behind. Traditionalists may have gnashed their teeth, but the public totally approved. Bertie was being a gentleman and husband first, King second. A good start to what would become one of the most popular reigns in the history of the British monarchy – and to its splendid aftermath, the long-running love affair between the British people and the mother of the Queen.

Buckingham Palace in 1937 was more mausoleum than mansion; a seedy place, apart from the glitteringly impersonal formal rooms dominated by the great ballroom, 111 ft by 60 ft. Antiquated, run-down, vast – after 145 Piccadilly it had all the cosy intimacy of an underground car park. It required an army of footmen, porters, grooms and sundry characters with titles like Page of the Back Stairs and Chief Yeoman of the Glass and China Pantry. There was an official clock winder and a flower arranger who doubled as a table decker. And a vermin man who Pied Pipered his way round six-hundred rooms. The princesses' governess, 'Crawfie', wrote: 'People think that a royal palace is the last word in up-to-date luxury. Nothing could be farther from the truth.' Her bedroom light could only be operated from a switch out in the passage. The girls' schoolroom on the top floor was dark and gloomy. Glamis Castle was the Ritz compared with this. The Queen marched around all floors dictating instructions for immediate changes. She stacked the place with flowers. 'The scent of roses always brings her back very clearly to me still,' Crawfie wrote. Different species of roses, bright colours, flowered chintzes – the new Queen was determined to let the sun in on the palace's Victorian gloom. The princesses switched to more cheerful rooms, Lilibet sharing hers with 'Bobo', Margaret with 'Alah'. But their schooling had to give way to more urgent preoccupations.

The Coronation of Edward VIII had been scheduled for 12 May 1937. The plans had been so far advanced it was decided to stick to that date. Normally the Coronation follows a year after the Accession. The abdication gave Elizabeth and the King only five months to prepare. In between rehearsals and conferences about the invitations and the planning, Elizabeth had sessions with the Court dressmaker Madame Handley Seymour. The Coronation robe followed the traditional lines created first by Queen Alexandra in 1902 and by Queen Mary in 1911. Lined with white satin instead of fur, the dark velvet was embroidered in gold with the emblematic rose, shamrock, thistle, leek, maple, fern, mimosa and lotus of the British Empire. The dress was white satin cut in the style of the thirties. The ivory satin high-heeled shoes, all-time favourites for her, were also gold embossed with oak leaves and thistle. The jewel in the crown literally was the Koh-i-Noor ('Mountain of Light') Diamond presented to Queen Victoria by the East India Company in 1850. When she tried the whole ensemble on for size and stood before the King, Elizabeth looked stunning. Diamonds sparkled from the ears and the sweeping neckline. Outshining them were the Strathmore eyes smiling out from those soft peach features. Not for the first time – nor the last – Bertie marvelled at his good fortune. Cecil Beaton would one day confess, 'I have such a profound admiration and love for her,' sentiments heightened when he saw her in her Coronation robes, and 'the effect of the jewellery, the fur and the velvet on her startling skin. . . .' But Bertie had beaten the field. She had accepted him without the slightest notion that he would ever be anything more than, initially at least, the least favourite of all George V's sons. Now he was King and he was determined Elizabeth would enjoy all the perks as well as the prestige of a full-blooded queen.

But there were eleventh-hour problems. Elizabeth's crown gave her a headache, not helped by the 106 carat bauble embedded in it. George VI had that problem too, compounded by a barely controllable apprehension of the ordeal ahead. He would have to say a few words during the formal service. He dreaded the thought knowing that having a seven-pound crown on his head would scarcely make it any easier. Again Lionel Logue, the speech therapist, was called in to help, the King's stammer always more marked at impending stress. When Logue left, the King practised with a crown on his head, Elizabeth prompting him. 'Make sure you're always where I can see you,' he insisted. Thereafter, palace officials followed that instruction on all public occasions sitting the Queen within the King's uninterrupted eyeline. Having that reassuring smile in his view at all times was not merely a royal command. It was the bedrock of the Logue treatment. In the fifteen years that followed, the King's eyes would search out hers on every royal ceremony. Contact established, the king would go through his paces like an athlete spurred on by a coach. A subtle exchange of glances followed by an immediate release of tension. The few who were aware of it, found it moving. Recalling Elizabeth's 'profound influence' on his friend the King, Mountbatten, made this simple judgement: 'Yes . . . she proved her worth.'

But come Coronation Day, not even this capable Consort could cover every contingency. Both she and the King had disturbed nights, woken before dawn by engineers testing the loudspeakers. The King's stomach, delicate at the best of times, decided it couldn't handle breakfast. By the time he and his Queen had stepped into the gilt-cherubed State coach, His Majesty's internal butterflies went into formation flying. One of the chaplains fainted and was carried off. The Dean, sweating inside his robes, offered George VI the white surplice inside out. Urgent stage whispers encouraged the puce-faced priest to make a swift adjustment. The King looked at his Queen with a non-expression which expressed plenty. The Archbishop of Canterbury then produced the solemn Form of Service from which the King would read the few essential words; the one sentence he had agonized over for hours in his study at the Palace. His Majesty looked down – and saw that the Archbishop's thumb had obscured the start of the text. He prodded the offending digit which slid abjectly into the margin. At this point nobody expected the Lord Great Chamberlain to attach the vestments and sword belt on to the King without a hitch, least of all His Majesty. The poor chap fumbled and fiddled until the exasperated monarch grabbed the sword belt and buckled it on himself. By now, some observers could only stifle giggles by staring fixedly at the Abbey's reverential stained glass. The St Edward's Crown was put on the wrong way round, then given a 180 degree turn like a diver's helmet, a muscle in the King's jaw signalling dangerous irritation.

The scene that followed would have had a scriptwriter accused of going over the top. As the King made to step forward a bishop behind him stepped on his robe momentarily stopping His Majesty King George VI dead in his tracks. The King glared round and hissed the heavy-footed ecclesiastic off his robe. 'I had to tell him to get off it pretty smartly as I nearly fell down,' he recorded later. Souvenir shops outside the Abbey and near the Palace were offering plaster busts of Edward VIII for one shilling and sixpence (about 7p) but sales were slight. The

Princesses Elizabeth and Margaret wore lightweight coronets and purple robes, miniature copies of the robe worn by their grandmother Queen Mary when she was Princess of Wales at the Coronation of Edward VII in 1902. Lilibet was automatically invited, the Queen deciding it was important that she put a toe into ceremonial waters. Margaret, according to Elizabeth Longford, urgently insisted on going too. It is normal for the younger child to clamour to go with her sister to the party. But it is also possible that even then she was aware that she would have to fight her corner all the way. Her sister was next in line to the throne. The demarcation line between Margaret and her sister was undefined but unmistakable.

On 3 June that year, Edward and Mrs Simpson were married in France, further exacerbating relationships between them and the Royal Family, particularly Queen Mary. That date, the anniversary of George V's birthday, had always been special to her. George had given her the Garter on that day (as Bertie would to Elizabeth on his own birthday). Choosing 3 June for his wedding day was probably pure coincidence, but it wasn't seen that way either at Buckingham Palace or Marlborough House. It reinforced the royal determination to keep this couple off limits in Britain. Elizabeth's cool, arms-length attitude to the Windsors went beyond the pressure the Abdication put on Bertie. The Duke of Windsor's shadow still cast itself over his younger brother. Edward had been the pin-up boy of British Royalty; feted, admired, and totally eclipsing his brothers. Now Bertie, as George VI, had to follow that act. Elizabeth, who had worked hard to convince the new king that he had all the resources of his elder brother, was not prepared to see all that effort put at risk. By insisting that Bertie refuse Wallis the title of 'Royal Highness', Elizabeth virtually ensured that the couple would not come to Britain – since the Duke had made it clear his return was conditional on Wallis being addressed as 'HRH'. The impasse had more important implications for the King and Queen and for the Court in general. It prevented the 'Windsor Faction' getting a foothold in Britain and so undermining the King's confidence, suspended as it was more on a thread than a hawser.

Mountbatten was best man at the Windsors' wedding though he first had to seek permission from the King. It was typical of Lord Louis to want to support his old friend. He was not uncritical, however, regarding the Abdication as gross self-indulgence and David's flirtation with the Nazis disgraceful. But loyalty to friends, regardless, was almost a religion with Mountbatten. Receiving an approving nod from the King he went to the Chateau Candé, near Tours, to stand by the Duke. One biographer claimed that an order went out insisting that nobody with any standing close to the Palace should attend. And certainly when the couple got down to sounding out guests and preparing invitations an embarrassingly high proportion found pressing or last-minute reasons for being absent. Sibyl Colefax and Emerald Cunard would not be coming. Nor would the Windsors' original supporters the Duff Coopers. Several of the Duke's old friends sent their regrets, presumably because, if the 'ban' was true, they might lose the friendship of the Court if not their jobs. In fact there is no evidence at all that the King prevented anyone from going to the wedding. And those acquaintances who did go suffered no reprisals as a result.

By then, the King was confident he had nothing to fear from his brother. Moreover, any influence the Duke of Windsor might have exerted evaporated when in October the couple were entertained by Hitler. It was hardly the time to be seen consorting with the Nazi dictator as Europe rattled on a downhill course towards the Second World War. The picture of them alongside the grinning Führer erased finally the Duke's already fading charisma. As far as Elizabeth was concerned, she began tackling her role as Queen the way she approached every challenge, determined to make a success of it. One thing was certain; whatever previous Consorts had done, Elizabeth would give the job her own imprint. Fortunately the Constitution provides the Queen Consort with most of the perks enjoyed by the monarch. Not inconsiderable items either, like tax exemption and freedom from any of the disabilities of a married woman over property contracts and the like. Her will is kept private. Her wealth and how she disposes of it, is also her own affair. She has her own retinue which includes her Lord Chamberlain, Treasurer, Four Ladies of the Bedchamber, Mistress of Robes, and other ceremonial and business officials all on call at the tug of a silken cord. If this suggests that a Consort's life is hugely over-staffed, a tally of her engagements as Queen and then as Queen Mother over more than fifty years, would come as a sharp corrective. During the run up to the Coronation and for a brief period afterwards, 18,832 dinners were served at Buckingham Palace. At the first State Banquet of their reign the King and

Queen entertained 400 guests in the white and gold ballroom
and supper room of the Palace. Myrtle grown from plants taken
from sprigs of Queen Victoria's wedding bouquet were in some
of the centrepieces on the table. Thousands of roses were
specially forced at Canterbury to be in perfect bloom for the
occasion. The red roses blended with the solid gold plate in the
ballroom where the King played host, upstaging the paler pinks
consigned to the supper room silver over which the Queen
presided. It was an irresistible opportunity for the new Consort
to show what she could look like as the Queen of the Ball.
'Exquisite' was the favourite adjective of that night. She wore a
gold brocade gown embroidered in a leaf design. Diamonds and
rubies gleamed from her tiara and necklace. The now famous
Smile completed the fairy-tale ensemble. She was stunning and
the society writers drooled on for days. In the context of what
Churchill would call 'The Gathering Storm' it was all blissfully
unreal. In less than two years many of the royal folk present
would be under siege or in flight; Princess Juliana and Prince
Bernhard of the Netherlands, Crown Prince Frederick and
Crown Princess Ingrid of Denmark, Crown Prince Olav and
Crown Princess Martha of Norway, and Crown Prince Gustav
Adolf and Crown Princess Louise of Sweden. It would take a
little longer for brutal events to crowd in on Crown Prince
Michael of Rumania and Prince Regent and Princess Paul of
Yugoslavia.

The nation hugely enjoyed its new 'royals'. In the months that
followed, the King and Queen played to full houses everywhere, the monarch noticeably three paces behind, beaming
with pride of ownership. Also noticeable, at least to the sharp-
witted diarist Chips Channon at the State Opening of Parliament in October, was that, 'the King seemed quite at ease and so
did the Queen. She has become more matronly, and as she toyed
with her jewels, I looked at her and thought of old days when I
called her "Elizabeth" and was even a little in love with her.'
Elizabeth's concern at that time was the impending Christmas
broadcast by the King from Sandringham. Bertie would not just
be speaking to the people of Britain, his words would be
broadcast throughout the Empire, the United States and South
America. Elizabeth was perturbed by fairly widespread comment about the King's health. Bertie had gone some way to
rubbish it. As *Time* magazine quoted him in March 1937,
'According to the papers, I am supposed to be unable to speak

without stammering, to have fits, and to die in two years. All in all I seem to be a crock!' It was an engaging disclaimer and revealed a new and relaxed confidence. Elizabeth was determined that he would sound that way in his Christmas broadcast. She called in Logue and the three of them conferred as in a stage rehearsal; she the producer, Logue directing, the King the star. Again it was a case of the King taking strategic pauses, controlling his breathing, but above all keeping in his eyeline those reassuring Strathmore eyes.

He spoke through two microphones placed on pedestals of Australian walnut on his study desk, wired via the Court post office to the entire English-speaking world. Fortified by roast Norfolk turkey – fattened, killed and plucked on the estate – the King waited for the intimidating 'on' signal to glow red then spoke for only four minutes. Short by normal standards but long enough decided the 'producer' and 'director'. He was slightly nervous at first, but then his voice strengthened, his diction loud and firm. The speech, inevitably, was strong on platitudes. But he said what millions wanted to hear. There was evident emotion in his voice as he concluded: 'And so to all of you, whether at home among your families – as we are – or in hospital, or at your posts carrying out duties that cannot be left undone, we send our Christmas greetings and wish you, under God's blessing, health and prosperity in the years that lie ahead.' Some said he sounded like his father. Bertie must have preened at the comparison. The feed-back to Elizabeth was that the four-minute effort had been a triumph. At dinner one evening, Lady Airlie, who was sitting next to the King, told him how she had enjoyed his broadcast. She said how well written she thought the script had been. 'He looked across at the Queen,' Lady Airlie remembered. 'She helps me,' he said proudly. She added this: 'The King was a devoted father to both his daughters. He spoiled Princess Margaret and still continued to treat her as an *enfant terrible*. But Princess Elizabeth was his constant companion in shooting, walking, riding – in fact in everything.'

With Elizabeth pushing buttons behind the scenes, the new monarch dragged the monarchy – specifically the Palace and its protocols – into a fair approximation of the twentieth century. The Queen bought modern paintings to replace some of the gloomier old masters on the palace walls. She had Handel's own harpsichord which had been gathering dust in a palace cellar brought out, restored, and put where everybody could see it. (It is now on permanent loan to the National Trust.)

She bought a Wilson Steer study of Chepstow Castle knowing that the artist was threatened with blindness. Sir William Llewellyn, the then President of the Royal Academy, whom the Queen consulted about her collection, called on Steer. He told the near-sightless artist how much the Queen liked his painting and how she had taken personal charge of its hanging at Windsor Castle. It was a thoughtful gesture which gladdened the twilight of a fine but ailing artist.

Derby Night, June 1938, was another ritual caught up in the Palace 'revolution' that had to change. For years this exclusive party had been a boisterous stag shindig for the King and his racing cronies at the Jockey Club. But with the Queen becoming increasingly interested in the Turf, wifely lobbying led to the event being transferred to the Palace, wives attending.

The King may have had the highest motives for the bold change of an age-old custom. The truth was he hated going to parties without his wife. He loved to show her off, and as at the State Ball, Elizabeth stole the show. As one paper lyrically reported, 'Most dignified among them was the Queen, a lovely figure in a crinoline of white Duchesse satin, panniered with draperies and flounced with silver lace. She wore the Order of the Garter and her tiara and necklace were of rubies and diamonds with bracelets to match.' Elizabeth obliged supremely well, everything about her proclaiming she'd been born to it.

Later that year a State Visit to France planned for 28 June, had to be postponed. On the 22nd Elizabeth received an urgent phone call from her brother David. The ageing Lady Strathmore had suffered a heart attack. The Queen, who made twice-weekly visits to her mother at the Strathmore's flat in Portman Square, rushed over. She could do little more than hold her mother's hand. At 2 a.m. the following day, with Elizabeth, David and her royal son-in-law present, Lady Strathmore died. She was buried during a rainstorm at Glamis in a grave surrounded by rhododendrons. Standing back from the mourners at the memorial service at St Martin-in-the-Field was the Honourable James Stuart. Lady Strathmore's death was a great personal loss to Elizabeth. More a clan than a family, the Strathmores had always been close. But Elizabeth's relationship with her mother had a particular intensity. Pride, dignity, discipline and guts were the constituents of the Strathmore credo. The inspiration came from Lady Strathmore. Elizabeth would become its chief exponent. The first discipline: dry your tears. The next: get on with the job. But there was now the delicate problem of protocol. It was decided that the State Visit to France should still proceed but three weeks later than planned. After the funeral the Queen huddled with her new designer Norman Hartnell over the lively and colourful wardrobe he'd created for her visit to France. The King demonstrated a surprising interest in the clothes Elizabeth wore. Apparently he gave Hartnell a Cooks' Tour of the Palace's art collection focusing eventually on paintings featuring the Empresses Eugenie of France and Elizabeth of Austria. Both wore crinolines, the style in which the King loved Elizabeth most. A King does not tell the Royal Dressmaker how much he admires his Queen in crinolines unless he expects the character to exit, trance-like, with hooped skirts spinning in his mind. Hartnell did just that, though by a pleasing coincidence he also liked to see the Queen in crinolines and had driven away from the Palace with various designs swirling romantically through his thoughts.

Thus all the gowns had been completed when Lady Strathmore died. But when Hartnell met with Elizabeth both agreed that the gorgeously hued creations hardly squared with a Queen in mourning for her beloved mother.

The shrewd couturier had known that the gloomy Queen Victoria had surprised everyone by insisting on a white funeral. He clutched at that straw. 'Is not white a royal prerogative for mourning Your Majesty?' Hartnell asked, treading eggshells. Elizabeth graciously conceded that one did not argue with precedent. The decision was taken. The entire collection was re-made in white.

The cross-channel trip to France on 19 July in the royal yacht the *Enchantress* proved uneventful except for a vignette which only an incisive gossip like Diana Cooper could – and would – reveal. *En route* to Portsmouth there was a minor crisis. The King had forgotten his hot-water bottle. This item – as Eleanor Roosevelt would later discover – was one of the King's essential travelling prerequisites. Diana Cooper recalled how 'A frenzied message preceded the royal party's arrival telling the ship to provide one. A child was dispatched to Boot's Cash Chemist on a bicycle before it was realized that he would never edge his way back through the crowds and the guards but the clever Puck got back in forty seconds. He should get a medal. . . .'

The account of how the Queen, more specifically her magnificent Hartnell creations, had Paris gasping in admiration has been exotically documented both here and in France. We can get a fair idea through the spellbound eyes of Elizabeth Longford and the aforementioned Diana Cooper. According to Lady Longford, 'Paris went mad over the Queen's trousseau, a perfect expression of her temperament and beauty. At the Bagatelle garden party her white dress of cobweb lace and tulle trailed like thistledown on the green grass, while the feathers on her sweeping hat dipped in unison. There was a sensation when she opened her gossamer parasol. . . .' But wait. . . . 'Each night's flourish,' Diana Cooper recorded, 'outdid the last. At the Opera we leant over the balustrade to see the Royal couple shining with stars and diadem and the *Legion d'Honneur* proudly worn, walk up the marble stairs preceded by *les chandeliers* – two valets bearing twenty-branched candelabra of tall white candles. At Versailles,' the awe-struck Diana continued, 'we lunched at the Galerie des Glaces with thirteen glasses apiece for thirteen precious wines all bottled on the birthdays of presidents and kings. . . .' Considering the time and place, July 1938, France, the gigantic extravagance and euphoria had all the jaunty overtones of the orchestra on the *Titanic*.

As thousands swarmed along the streets of Paris their cheers were drowned by the insistent roar of engines. A formation of British and French fighter planes soared overhead in a salute to the royal couple. In less than two years both squadrons would be together again on other business.

10

One of the Queen's first unpublicized engagements on returning to London from Paris was to visit Mrs Ronnie Greville at whose country home she and Bertie had spent their honeymoon. It was an instance of Elizabeth's strong loyalty to old friends especially when they were ill or fading from the social scene. Maggie Greville was both. Moreover she had been the target for considerable derision because of her simpering genuflexions to royalty; which was a shade unfair since she had a genuine affection for Queen Elizabeth or as Beverly Nichols described it in *The Sweet and Twenties* an 'unaffected love of the lady'. Whether she was aware of this or not it mattered little to the Queen whose only concern was that her old friend was ill and needed cheering up. Within hours of returning across the Channel she went over to Maggie's flat in Charles Street, Mayfair, brought some goodies, sat by her bedside and told her all about the Paris trip. To have the Queen of England fussing around, straightening the pillows, dishing the gossip was ecstasy to Maggie Greville. She wept buckets after Elizabeth left. 'Oh what it would be to have a daughter like that!' she sighed. If the doting hostess saw the Queen as a kind of Fairy Godmother we ought to concede she was just one of many. It is probable that the long-running love affair between the British people and this Queen, had its origins on the eve of the Second World War. From the moment she and Bertie decided to hang around and endure the bombing like anybody else, the British people slipped an affectionate arm through hers. It has been there ever since.

In late 1938 Prime Minister Chamberlain had begun his ill-fated shuttle diplomacy between himself and Hitler, designed to buy time if not achieve peace, Czechoslovakia being surren-dered as an inducement. Elizabeth, who was fourteen at the outbreak of the First World War, had a flashback of images and emotions. Was it all going to happen again? 'Unthinkable' was the word used by those who were nevertheless thinking it. She would have a different role now as Queen, if the worst were to happen. Her anxieties were shared by Bertie who faced the responsibilities of a King and of a father of two young daugh-ters. In Sunday chapel at Windsor, Elizabeth's prayers had a more personal intensity.

As before, despite warnings from Churchill and others, the British war machine responded with the casual, unhurried pace of a veteran London copper. Makeshift trenches were dug in London's parks by grinning navvies who were convinced they'd have to fill them all in again. The capital's forty-four anti-aircraft guns were rolled out into the autumn sunshine, a couple visible from the Palace windows. Air-raid sirens were given a try-out over the radio so that listeners could distinguish between the warning and the 'all clear'. The Fleet was alerted and 38 million gas masks were distributed throughout Britain. But even while the King and Queen, the two princesses, and the ageing Queen Mary were trying them on there was still this pervasive feeling that Britain was merely going through the motions; that some-how a deal would be struck and the soil shovelled back in the holes in the Royal Parks. So it was still business as usual. At the end of September the King and Queen were scheduled to go to Clydebank to launch the world's largest liner, the *Queen Elizabeth* named in honour of the Consort. At the last minute, with the political situation tense, the King stayed in London, the Queen going to Clydebank alone. On her return from the launching, Bertie showed her a letter from President Roosevelt inviting them both to Washington in May 1939. (At approxi-mately the same time, Neville Chamberlain stood on a windy British airfield brandishing the note signed by Hitler which promised 'peace in our time' – for less than a year in fact. The King and Queen had previously been invited to Canada by Prime Minister Mackenzie King. The USA would now be tagged on to the six-week tour, but scarcely as an afterthought. This contact with the then neutral USA was politically crucial as Hitler turned his eyes, and guns, towards Poland. The King's role would be to overcome resistance from America's powerful isolationists, convince Roosevelt that Britain, as America's first line of defence, had the guts and the will to fight a war. Roosevelt, aware of the internal criticism and suspicion of Britain, hoped that this display of friendship would silence it. A strong hint of residual anti-royal if not anti-British feelings in the US appeared in the powerful and widely circulated magazine *Scribners*. It demonstrated the anger still rumbling on over the Edward and Mrs Simpson affair. The attack was venomously personal: 'An important fact about public opinion in the United States is that a large part of the country still believes that Edward, Duke of Windsor is the rightful owner of the British throne and that King George VI is a colourless and weak personality largely on probation in the public mind of Great Britain as well as of the United States.' A singularly unpleasant insult which then gave itself away. 'We do not of course know what plans have already been made, but we suggest that before the departure of the King and Queen there should be some public evidence of their reconciliation with Edward and the Duchess of Windsor,' adding this final impertinence, 'this should preferably take the form of their being entertained at Buckingham Palace particularly with the former Wallis Simpson being named, "Her Royal Highness".'

No doubt, the usually reticent Elizabeth might have commented, 'over my dead body!' had she not made up her mind long before not to respond in public to attacks like these. George VI, apprehensive over the demands the tour would make, relied as always on Elizabeth's canny behind-the-throne strength, backed up by Logue, the speech therapist. More than ever before, the King's voice would have to be strong, clear, and convincing.

And behind Logue, there was Norman Hartnell, commanded to produce the half-dozen changes of clothes each day – sixty dresses in all – a Queen seems to need for a six-week State Visit abroad. Light stuff for the hot weather, sturdier numbers for the chilly train rides across the Rockies at night. As ever, at Bertie's insistence, crinolines dominated the ensembles. While Hartnell's dressmakers pored over patterns, Eleanor Roosevelt in Washington wondered what was required to feed, house, and entertain a King and Queen of England. The USA would be no pushover for their Majesties. Canada, one of the family, was expected to pay homage to its Queen on the grand scale, and did so. In America, Washington in particular, the word had got around about the bizarre requirements – actual or notional – of the royal couple during their stay at the White House. To the backwoodsmen who still regarded Britain as the 'old enemy', any fawning, bowing and scraping would be an outrage. Apparently Eleanor Roosevelt had received a secret memorandum from the American Ambassador in Paris, William Bullitt, listing some of the royal couple's alleged likes and dislikes gleaned during their trip to Paris. The diplomat advised the First Lady what furniture the Queen was supposed to have favoured; the way the bedcovers were expected to be folded; warned her to have a hot-water bottle in the royal beds (the temperature in the capital hovered close to ninety at the time). The firm supplying their Majesty's tea had a bottle of London's water analysed to see if it could be reproduced exactly in Washington. It failed the test and for better or for worse, Elizabeth and Bertie drank the local brew.

Still nervous, Eleanor Roosevelt had the British Ambassador's wife, Lady Lindsay, over to the White House to discover if there were any other important requirements. 'Yes,' replied her ladyship, 'the King must be served at meals thirty seconds ahead of the Queen.' As she records in her memoirs, 'I told Franklin that British protocol required that the head butler, Fields, stand with a stop-watch in his hand and, thirty seconds after he and the King had been served, dispatch a butler to serve the Queen and myself. He looked at me with firmness. "We will not require Fields to have a stop-watch. The King and I will be served simultaneously and you and the Queen will be served next."'

These absurdities reached the ears of the acerbic American politician and diarist, H. L. Ickes, who commented frostily in *The Secret Diaries of Harold L. Ickes*: 'Some of the things the King and Queen apparently expect seemed to be ludicrous. The sheets had to be of such a sort and the coverings of the King's bed had to have a reef in them at the foot of the bed. I came to one conclusion . . . that if the King and Queen of England think they are slumming when they come to visit the President and Mrs Roosevelt at the White House and Hyde Park then they ought to stay at home. Moreover, unless they are willing to accept the hospitality of the country in the manner in which that hospitality is customarily extended, they ought to stay at home.' (Strong stuff, but Mr Ickes' disdain could not survive a direct eye-to-blue-eyes confrontation with the Queen. When that happened this same critic dipped his pen in honey to declare: 'The King and

Queen were gracious and made a very good impression. She seemed quite lovely and exceptionally good-looking.')

We can be certain that the King and Queen did not remotely consider they were slumming, assuming either or both of them had ever seen one; nor would they have been aware of the maladroit behaviour of their courtiers who, incidentally, also informed the President's wife that the King did not like capers or suet pudding. Mrs Roosevelt's deadpan response to this was 'we did not often have suet pudding in the United States and that I really did not expect the King to like capers.' The farce did not end there. In preparation for their weekend at Hyde Park, the Presidential home on the Hudson River, Franklin's mother, Mrs Sarah Delano Roosevelt, called a plumber in to buff up the bathroom and install a new lavatory seat. When he sent the bill after the King and Queen departed, Mrs Roosevelt (the elder) thought the price exorbitant and refused to pay. The angry plumber stormed into the house, unscrewed the seat, and later exhibited it in his shop window with the logo, 'The King and Queen Sat Here'.

Inevitably, Elizabeth and the King ate hot dogs at a Presidential picnic on the banks of the Hudson (referred to in the Franklin D. Roosevelt Library as 'perhaps the most famous picnic in American history'.) Elizabeth, with Bowes-Lyon delicacy, wanted to use a knife and fork on her hot dog which looked somewhat out of its depth on a silver plate. Roosevelt grabbed her wrist before that crime could be permitted. 'Just push it straight into your mouth, Ma'am,' advised the President of the United States. It was said at the time that Mother Roosevelt's English butler elected to take a vacation during the royal visit, reportedly because he couldn't bear the thought of their Imperial Majesties descending to chomping on an American sausage. But the reason advanced by Eleanor Roosevelt for the butler's absence was because he was told that the black butlers from the White House were being brought in to assist him. The idea of coloured people serving his King and Queen so shocked him he went on holiday rather than witness it.

Understandably, then, nerves were as taut as fiddle strings on the night of the famous dinner. The President's mother had augmented her china by borrowing extra plates, expensive stuff, from her stepdaughter-in-law, Mrs James Roosevelt. Unfortunately, half-way through the dinner the serving table collapsed, the china crashing to the floor. There was a shocked silence broken only by Mrs James Roosevelt's involuntary shriek, 'I hope none of *my* dishes were in there!'

Meanwhile, the British colony in America, anxious to fly the flag, decided to broadcast a special radio show from Hollywood to coincide with the picnic. As David Niven recorded, 'We rehearsed for days and bashed our brains out being loyal and talented. Olivier gave the "Into the breach . . ." speech from *Henry V*. Brian Aherne recited Rupert Brooke's "The Soldier", C. Aubrey Smith, Nigel Bruce and Roland Young sang "Three Little Fishes"; Reggie Gardiner imitated a train, and the rest of us, Vivien Leigh, Flynn, Cary Grant and myself all did something. I had an unexpected moment alone with Her Majesty a few years later and asked how they had all enjoyed our efforts. "Oh, wasn't it awful," she said, "the battery on the President's hearing-aid ran down just before the show came on."'

Behind all these diversions, history of a kind was taking shape. The President and the King strolled away to talk about Hitler's threat to Europe and therefore the New World. The President outlined to the King what America was prepared to contribute in the event of war; mostly naval patrols in the Atlantic to protect Britain's vital supply ships. Throughout their discussions, the King scribbled some notes on a scrap of paper. These jottings, now locked away in archives, are handwritten evidence of how the Grand Alliance against Hitler was born. It was evidence too of George VI's negotiating skill over hot dogs on the edge of the Hudson River.

Throughout the whole of their trip, the King and Queen spoke daily by phone to the two princesses in England. They had read the British newspapers which unanimously described the tour as a triumph. One American newsman wrote, 'Give the Queen a crowd and she mows 'em down!' One US Senator at a Congressional Reception stood back from the Queen, then pumped the King's hand exclaiming, 'My, you're a great Queen-picker!' Elizabeth had an abundance of anecdotes to share with her daughters – and her diary. She could tell of the night the Royal Train, winding through the Canadian mountains from Chilliwack to Jasper, stopped at a small station for servicing. A crowd gathered. Then as the King and Queen stepped out to stretch their legs, a young man led the crowd into singing, 'When the moon comes over the mountains' (the said satellite having shimmered in on cue). He had a pleasing voice in the style of Nelson Eddy, a favourite of the Queen's.

Irresistibly, she took up the refrain with the King joining in. A brief, moonlit interlude north of the Okanogan mountains of Canada. A short chorus for tenor, random choir, and the King and Queen of England. There must have been the odd gulp among the affectionate cheers which sent the Royal Train chugging away into the darkness.

Elizabeth learned an important lesson on that trip; to be careful about throwaway comments, even one as harmless as announcing that one of her favourite dishes was chicken. It resulted in:

Luncheon at Quebec's famous Chateau Frontenac, Breast of Chicken. Windsor Hotel, Montreal, Squab Chicken. Ottawa, Mousse of Chicken. Toronto, Fried Chicken. Winnipeg, Halves of Chicken. Regina, Breast of Saskatchewan Chicken. Edmonton, Breast of Chicken. Fredericton, Combination of Chicken, Truffles and Mushrooms. And Charlottetown, Broiled Breast of Spring Chicken. It was reported that a Manitoba farmer hearing that the royal train would stop for one night alongside his hen-coop, transported his entire flock to another part of his farm so that their Majesties should not be disturbed by the early morning crowing of the roosters.

The North American tour was by any standards a roaring success. Four million people had turned out to cheer them in New York. Washington's high society noted appreciatively Elizabeth's regal yet uncondescending manner and the fact that despite the gruelling schedules there was never a crease in her dress nor a hair out of place. The Queen spoke impeccable French in Quebec, and overran the time allotted to a foundation-stone laying because she overheard a couple of the masons talking in a Scottish brogue and couldn't resist chatting with them about the old country.

Media headlines and supporting prose glowed with genuine admiration, even affection. This did not happen by accident. The Queen worked at it with round-the-clock energy and determination. There was no automatic assumption of good-will; certainly not in America where Elizabeth was well aware of the pro-Simpson faction glowering in the shadows. She conquered North America by being an appreciative guest, a polite and inquiring visitor, and every inch a Queen. 'They have a way of making friends, these young people,' wrote Eleanor Roosevelt, a quality not to be underrated as the last summer of peace darkened into autumn. Meeting Mackenzie King two years later, the Queen made an unusually candid comment on the State Visit. 'That tour made us as King and Queen,' she declared. 'It came just at the right time.' What did she mean? One person's speculation is as good as another's. But consider the stakes: Canada was about to be drawn into a war it felt, initially, was largely Europe's business. America had to be wooed and won against powerful lobbying by isolationist and anti-British factions. A bad speech, a sign of hesitancy and/or weakness by the King, a negative performance from the Queen, and Roosevelt might have found it tougher to unlock American money, ships and materials. In the event, the King's speeches were clear and well delivered; not surprising, considering the time he spent alone with the Queen going over them. He got on well with the Washington politicians. And as his notes indicate, he knew what he had come to say to the President. It diminishes nothing to assert that he could never have pulled it off without Elizabeth acting as his resourceful ADC. That the tour 'made them' is probably true; but only in the sense that a challenge was offered and skilfully met. Canada could now preen it over the US, realizing, as it did, that the King and Queen belonged to them. Moreover America had seen Britain's King and Queen face to face and liked what it saw. The few remaining combatants in the Edward and Mrs Simpson camp were finally routed.

Mrs Rose Fitgerald Kennedy, the formidable mother of the late President, provided the most eloquent footnote to the Queen's visit. It was written years after in her published memoirs when Elizabeth had become the Queen Mother. Rose Kennedy was a woman with an awesome independence of spirit. She had met probably every world leader. She had suffered a painful bereavement. She was no Anglophile either, so anything approaching sycophancy would not be her style. This accolade, therefore, must be the genuine article: 'In my lifetime I have met quite a number of great ladies. I suppose that Queen Elizabeth the Queen Mother of England would be at the top of my list, almost anyone's list of women in public life who have managed the rather delicate balance of being themselves, being natural and unaffected and open and womanly, while also using their minds, their education and their intuitive as well as intellectual comprehensions in a responsible way. . . .'

The King and Queen had sailed out across the Atlantic on the *Empress of Australia*, the King declining to sail in the battleship

Repulse so as not to rob the Navy of valuable fire power in the event of war. The Navy's gain was by no means the royal couple's loss. Mr Abe Toole, the catering superintendent on the *Empress of Australia* had laid on haggis, Black Sea caviar, thirty-three cases of wine from the King's private cellar, His Majesty's hand-rolled Havana cigars and the silver cigar cutter, and ninety varieties of cheese. The Queen's private suite 145 on the port side had a sitting room, veranda and gold-fitted bathroom, which the *Daily Express* at the time earnestly assured its readers were 'no bigger than the rooms in an LCC working-class house'.

One of the reasons given for the monarch to travel aboard a warship instead of a luxury liner was because of serious Foreign Office concern that the Germans might stage a midAtlantic hijacking. In fact the trip was uneventful apart from freezing fog which hid the many icebergs floating in the area. As Queen Elizabeth wrote to her mother-in-law, Queen Mary: 'We very nearly hit a berg the day before yesterday and the poor Captain was nearly demented because some kind cheerful people kept on reminding him that it was about here that the *Titanic* was struck, and *just* about the same date! . . .'

Their return home on the *Empress of Britain* faced no such hazards or delays. Which was just as well. They ached to be with their children again. After all the ceremonials, the public hand-shaking, the speeches and the imperial rituals, they badly needed to bear-hug the two princesses. No nonsense now of dockside formalities intervening. On 22 June, the two eager princesses were ferried out into the Solent on the destroyer *Kempenfelt* to greet them. 'Crawfie', of course, was there and tells us, 'Every-one else was kept out of the way for their very joyful reunion,' coded language for the wild hugging, kissing, excited chattering and 'stand back, let me look at you' ecstasies expected of parents and kids separated for longer than was bearable. Crawfie did reveal however, that, 'the Queen, very slim, said how much the children had grown; the King could hardly take his eyes off Lilibet.' At Southampton, it was the turn of the crowds on the dockside to shriek their welcome. And so on to London and that mandatory balcony appearance which drew from Harold Nicolson, 'We lost all our dignity and yelled and yelled. The King wore a happy schoolboy grin. The Queen was superb . . . in truth one of the most amazing Queens since Cleopatra.'

August 1939 . . . and both the King and Queen knew in-

Left: King George VI at the microphone at Buckingham Palace on Coronation Day, 12 May 1937. (BBC)

Below: Queen Elizabeth broadcasting from Buckingham Palace, November 1939. *(Daily Mail)*

Left: Queen Elizabeth in 1937, the year of the coronation. Photograph by Dorothy Wilding. (Camera Press)

Below: The Royal Family appear on the balcony at Buckingham Palace after the coronation, 12 May 1937. (Press Association)

Above & below: The King and Queen visit the bombed areas of East London, April 1941. (Central Press Photos)

The widowed Queen Mother being driven into Buckingham Palace in her car after the burial of King George VI at Sandringham. (Fox Photos)

The Queen Mother goes fishing in the Waikato River during her tour of New Zealand, 29 April 1966. (Central Press Photos)

Above: Cockney Gerry Branch kisses the hand of the Queen Mother on her tour of Smithfield Market, April 1966. *(Evening Standard)*

Below: The Queen Mother, patron and president of the Royal College of Music, at its Annual President's Concert and Prize-giving together with her eldest grandson Prince Charles. *(The Times)*

Above: The Queen Mother with her granddaughter Princess Anne at Royal Ascot, June 1969. (Central Press Photos)

Below: The Queen Mother had a warm smile as well as a sugar lump for regimental drumhorse Dettingen. (North News and Pictures)

The Queen Mother at the inauguration of the new Lloyds Building, November 1981. (Photo Source)

tuitively that the forthcoming annual trip to Balmoral might be blown apart by events. The King had planned a weekend on the Royal Yacht *Victoria and Albert* taking the Queen and the two princesses on a trip to the Naval College at Dartmouth. He invited Mountbatten whose young nephew Prince Philip was a cadet there to join him. Lilibet was then thirteen with a slim figure and thick silken hair over the famed Strathmore complexion. Prince Philip at eighteen, was carved in the same heroic mould as his uncle Louis Mountbatten and in his naval uniform must have looked, at the very least, irresistible. Reams have been written about the famous encounter between this attractive pair at Dartmouth. Lord Mountbatten was not only present, he had more than a passing interest in the outcome. The man who commanded navies was no mean matchmaker. A view shared by his biographer Philip Ziegler who reflected, 'It is hard to believe no thought crossed his mind that an admirable husband for the future Queen Elizabeth might be readily available.' Mountbatten's version of the Dartmouth encounter therefore must be the one to take on board. 'What happened was this. In early 1939 the King was going down to Dartmouth in the Royal Yacht and because Prince Philip was there at the time he asked me to accompany him. Now because of flu or something like it, the two Princesses were not allowed into the college chapel. So when the King and Queen went into the chapel they stayed behind in the Captain's House at the College. Then this young Viking came in. Pure Dane. He was just eighteen, she was thirteen and she was knocked every way. The colour drained from her cheeks then she blushed furiously and she never took her eyes off him. They corresponded during the war. She knitted socks for him. Since then she has never looked at anybody else. She fell head over hells in love with him. And still is to this day.'

In 1939 then, though Princess Elizabeth was only thirteen, Mountbatten, with a shrewd eye on the Royal Family of the future, gently steered the handsome Philip and the young Elizabeth towards a shared horizon. But all plans, dreams, hopes and first loves were deferred indefinitely as German troops massed on Poland's borders. On Tuesday, 29 August, the Queen returned from Balmoral leaving the two princesses behind. With plans in hand to evacuate millions of the capital's children there seemed no point in bringing Elizabeth and Margaret to London. Commuters at Euston station surprised by this unexpected arrival of the Queen, smiled and waved. Nurses at the University College Hospital crowded out on to the street to cheer her limousine. At Buckingham Palace, the Queen found the King in a tense and gloomy mood. He had twice been briefed by the Prime Minister, Neville Chamberlain, about Hitler's responses to British warnings over Poland and shared the grim information with her.

Both he and Elizabeth remembered personal experiences in the First World War. It had been a war largely fought on battlefields. They sensed that Hitler would draw no fine distinction between combatants and civilians. On 30 August, the King made booster visits to the War Office to see the underground bomb-proof Operations Room; then on to the Air Ministry to look at miniature planes being pushed croupier-style on large horizontal landscapes. Back at the Palace the Queen listened to broadcasts urgently appealing for volunteer stretcher bearers and first-aid workers. Suddenly khaki became the dominant colour in London's streets. Kerbs were painted white, windows sheeted over as the capital prepared for the blackout. The Queen rarely left her husband's side as Chamberlain commuted between the House of Commons and the Palace, signalling the final countdown to war. There was a brief, bizarre, eleventh-hour intervention by the Duke of Windsor, appealing to King Victor Emmanuel of Italy for peace. To the King and Queen who had seen the Duke and Duchess publicly consorting with the German Führer, the appeal was as short on sense as it was on taste. By 1 September, the Fleet was at war stations; the Army at full strength; the RAF at immediate war readiness. On the morning of 3 September, at 11 a.m. the Second World War had begun. Kings know what is expected of them in war. Their Consorts tend dutifully to fall in line. Elizabeth was never going to be merely that sort of Queen.

11

There had been one small, spontaneous gesture by the Queen on her visit to France which few thought particularly significant except, curiously, Adolf Hitler. Elizabeth and the King had gone to Villers-Bretonneux for the unveiling of a memorial to the 11,000 Australians who were killed in France in the First World War. That July morning a French schoolboy had picked a large bunch of red poppies from the fields and presented them to her. The Queen paused before the memorial then scattered the poppies on the grass around it. Hitler watching that scene on a newsreel in Berlin, made this scowling assessment: 'the most dangerous woman in Europe!' Since Her Serene Majesty was doing nothing more threatening than tossing flowers around, what could the Führer discern behind that disarming smile? What had the Queen done to disturb if not unnerve the German dictator? The eight-months so-called 'phoney war' which followed Chamberlain's declaration on 3 September, offers a clue. Post-war German papers, retrieved after the fall of Berlin, indicate that Hitler, encouraged by Ribbentrop, believed that Britain's will to fight in that first year, could be weakened by manipulating the Windsors against the British Government. The reward for such service to the Third Reich – assuming Germany won the war – would be the Duke's reinstatement on the throne, with the Duchess installed as his Queen.

The stratagem had several strikes against it, the most decisive of which was the attitude of this 'most dangerous woman in Europe'. Even before the outbreak of war, urgent discussions took place at Balmoral to decide what future role, if any, the Duke of Windsor would have. Neville Chamberlain was one of the guests. He raised that question with the King who immediately insisted that the Queen should be brought into the discussion (confirming Mountbatten's earlier comments that his friend the King rarely took a major decision without consulting Elizabeth). We do not know precisely what the Queen said to the Prime Minister concerning the Duke and Duchess of Windsor. What is known is that the Queen later went for a walk in the grounds of Balmoral with Sir Walter Monckton who was then mediating between George VI and the Duke of Windsor. Elizabeth left him in no doubt about her feelings towards the ex-King. Monckton took the hint and immediately after, the visit by the Duke of Windsor to England planned for that November was postponed. Another clue to the intensity of the Queen's attitude was provided by her one-time Lady-in-Waiting, Mrs John Little Gilmour. Innocently, she asked the Queen whether the Duchess would accompany the Duke of Windsor if he came to England. Elizabeth's 'quick anger' startled her. 'No certainly not; wouldn't receive her if she did,' was the surprisingly harsh reply. 'May I make this known, Ma'am?' the Lady-in-Waiting asked: 'You certainly may,' the Queen replied.

Unequivocal and uncompromising. Understandable too, perhaps, as the Queen observed what nearly three years of unsought kingship had done to her husband. His features were gaunt and strained, the shadows heavy under the eyes. Yet his first wartime broadcast – Elizabeth on hand by royal command – was a considerable success. Speaking in clear measured tones he gave his words an intimacy that struck chords with the listening millions. 'I send to every household . . . this message, spoken with the same depth of feeling for each one of you as if I were able to cross your threshold and speak to you myself. For the sake of all that we ourselves hold dear, and of the world's order and peace, it is unthinkable that we should refuse to meet the challenge. . . .'

That same theme was echoed in his Christmas broadcast, which was another triumph though as usual, Bertie hated doing it. (Nervousness so besieged his stomach, the Christmas turkey was usually sent away untouched.) But the nation hung on his words. His stammer had virtually disappeared. He was the right King, at the right time, married to exactly the right kind of Queen. The euphoria of victory, particularly a victory gained at enormous cost in lives and human suffering, tends to encourage myths, distort basic truths. The written accounts of the King and the Queen in the Second World War suffer from an excess of fawning hyperbole. Though to be fair, they themselves must have winced at some of the more laudatory froth whipped up around them. King George and Elizabeth did not demonstrate the kind of heroism for which medals are struck, ticker-tape thrown down from skyscraper windows. They themselves would be the first to concede they were no braver than the thousands who crawled out of the bomb rubble of London or, say Coventry, and then turned back to rescue the many still trapped. But they were no less courageous either. The King did all he could to get on to the battlefields of France, the bulky figure of Churchill standing immovably in his way. The Queen was not compelled to stay in London when the raids were at their most savage. She could have stayed at Windsor or pleaded a headache when the blitz became uncomfortably noisy. Instead, she went out into the smoking streets even before the last wail of the 'All Clear' had faded.

Inquiring about an old lady weeping by a pile of rubble, the Queen was told that the woman's pet terrier was too frightened to come out. 'Leave it to me,' the Queen said, 'I'm rather good with dogs.' (She had a half a dozen at the time.) She knelt down and coaxed the shivering animal out into the daylight. Wars may not be won by royalty. But a much-admired Queen acting this way on the bomb-blasted streets, was as good a booster-shot as any to the war effort.

Like every other mother, fear for the safety of the two princesses was the Queen's dominant emotion. The massive evacuation of London's children to safer havens in the country was, like Dunkirk, one of the great rescue operations of the Second World War. The majority of the evacuees arrived on strange but welcoming doorsteps, tear-streaked, apprehensive, gas-mask boxes swinging awkwardly around their necks. Some from the highly vulnerable East End of London were sent overseas, A. J. P. Taylor noting there was shipping space only for 2,664. 'Meanwhile 11,000 women and children from the richer classes went privately at their own expense. Members of the government (and university professors, he is quick to point out) sent their families on this unseemly scramble. The Royal Family,' he declared, 'set a spotless example,' repeating the Queen's most famous comment, 'the children can't go without me. I can't leave the King and, of course, the King won't go.'

Go where? The late Lord Mountbatten remembered the situation clearly. 'Although, I was always told, Winston Churchill had determined to send them [the Royal Family] to Canada in a battleship if Hitler landed, they had never, in my knowledge, agreed to it. The King was not prepared to run away, though it never came to the test. One other thing, the Queen was extraordinarily kind to my mother. She was only fifteen when her mother, Princess Alice, died. The Queen conceived the idea of having her down at Windsor to stay there. It was very kind and thoughtful of her.'

It was during the most devastating incidents of the blitz in 1940 that the Queen played her best role, finding just the right words to go with it. When Buckingham Palace was first bombed (it was hit nine times) she surveyed the wreckage and said, 'I feel we can now look the East End in the face.' In fact the East Enders, blitzed to hell though they were, did not require to see the Palace hit in order to convince them that the Queen cared what happened to them. And when a bomb destroyed the Palace chapel, the blast dangerously close to the King and Queen, Londoners reacted as angrily as if their neighbours' homes had been hit.

So Elizabeth went out on to the streets, substituting a helmet for that oyster-shell hat to mingle with first-aid workers and stretcher bearers bringing the injured and the dead from shattered cellars and piles of masonry. Pictures taken of the Queen on the blitzed streets of London indicate more than a token royal presence. A *Daily Mirror* picture, dated April 1941, and showing the Queen exchanging smiles with East Enders, had this caption: 'Look at this photograph – the King and Queen, the cop, the kids, the crowd – and not a gloomy face among them!' Elizabeth toured munition factories, steel works, and air stations ending the war knowing more about pressure valves, gauges and flight angles than is strictly required of the average 'royal'. She autographed Lancaster bombers aware that many of those signatures would go down with the crews. She visited hospitals and casualty centres and opened allotments defiantly fashioned out of bomb sites. Only she and her aides knew how many cabbages she ceremoniously planted or scrubbed carrots she nibbled in a gesture of royal admiration. Everywhere, that flowered hat, the three-quarter sleeve and the three-strand pearls identified her as uniquely as the V sign and the big cigar hallmarked Winston Churchill.

In the late 1980s, this regal appearance by leading politicians at disasters; a cursory glance at the wreckage then the mandatory two-shot for the cameras at the injured's bedside, has attracted a fair amount of cynicism; a feeling that hype was more evident than humanity. But in the blitz from 1940 onwards, there was an obvious integrity to the gestures of royal sympathy. When the Queen picked her way over the smoking beams to squeeze an outstretched hand, no Londoner doubted her motives.

Since she and the King had made it clear that flying off to Canada was not an option, arrangements had to be made for their protection. The two princesses were considered reasonably safe at Windsor. But with the King and Queen insisting on staying in London every day, they were given a bodyguard drawn from the Household Cavalry and the Brigade of Guards known as the Coats' Mission (after their commander Colonel J. S. Coats). It was equipped with automatic weapons and armoured cars on permanent standby ready to rush Their Majesties to one of four secret houses located outside the capital, in Dorset, Worcester, Scotland and North Wales. Hand-picked personnel were placed at strategic points around Buckingham Palace to deal with a paratroop attack. All this military nurse-maiding was frustrating to the King who was eager, if required, to fire a couple of shots in anger himself. He created a shooting range in the garden of Buckingham Palace. He, the Queen, officials and servants shot at targets with revolvers and tommy-guns, footmen solemnly passing the ammunition. Elizabeth announced that she was quite prepared to fight to the end, and 'not go down like the others', an apparent reference to Europe's capitulating royalty. Churchill, who was delighted by this kind of talk, presented the King with an American short-range carbine. It was His Majesty's lasting regret that he would never raise its sights on a descending German paratrooper.

The King's frustration at not being allowed to go where the action was would lead to some spirited correspondence between himself and Winston Churchill. It was tragically underscored on 25 August 1942 when George, Duke of Kent, the King's younger brother, was killed in an air crash. A pilot with the RAF, his Sunderland Flying Boat had crashed into a mountain on a flight from Invergordon to Iceland. Recording in his memoirs the shock he felt at the time, the King emphasized with capital letters the fact that his brother had been 'killed on Active Service'. He felt somehow upstaged. Kings ought not to be immune when younger brothers get killed in action. Shooting at dummy targets in the Palace grounds was a poor substitute.

With Britain soldiering on alone, London became the haven for several royal refugees. Queen Wilhelmina of Holland arrived one day with just the clothes she stood up in plus a tin hat. With her were her daughter Princess Juliana and a couple of grand-daughters, Beatrix and Irene. They were housed, clothed and fed at the Palace under the supervision of an attentive royal landlady. King Haakon of Norway arrived, then General de Gaulle who merely behaved as though he was a king – a posture which Churchill shrugged off as his 'cross of Lorraine'. On 7 December 1941, Japan had attacked Pearl Harbor ending America's valuable but covert assistance to Britain and bringing her officially into the war. Less than a year later, Eleanor Roosevelt arrived to check on welfare arrangements for US troops sta-tioned in Britain and also to see how women coped in wartime. The visit was an eye-opener to this shrewd American observer then recording her impressions in a lively newspaper column. Reading between the lines, this Roosevelt was publicly impressed, privately amused. 'I had been worried by the thought of having to visit Buckingham Palace, but I finally told myself that one can live through any strange experience for two days. . . .'

It must have been strange to her to find that given the Queen's own apartment for her stay there was only a single-bar electric heater against the bitter cold which blew through the Palace like an Alaskan blizzard. Unaccountably spartan even in peace-time, the Palace in 1942 must have seemed like a distressed area to the shivering First Lady. The shattered windowpanes in her room had been replaced with bits of wood and strips of isinglass. A messenger was installed outside her door to pilot her through the maze of corridors for meals in the dining room. A large woman, her heart sank when she saw a plainly marked black line midway around the interior of the bathtub warning her that hot water being scarce, she exceeded the limit at her peril. Even more quaint was the fact that she ate wartime's standard issue bread and her modest portion of the Palace's weekly meat ration off solid gold plates. The fact that royalty had ration books and clothing coupons like everybody else, obviously impressed her. But there must have been a lingering thought – having been frozen to near death visiting Queen Mary at Badminton – that the English Royals enjoyed their ritual shivers, and wore their goose-bumps as a badge of courage. It was just as well nobody informed her that rats driven out of bomb-shattered sewers had taken London's softest option, moving into all floors at Buckingham Palace. Mrs Roosevelt was, by all accounts, highly relieved to get back to Washington.

Did she and the Queen talk about the Duchess of Windsor? Hardly likely, the President's wife having been briefed by the American Ambassador John G. Winant on the Queen's implacable resentment of Wallis Simpson. The resentment was mutual, more intense now on the Windsors' side. The Duke, shunted away in the undemanding if not demeaning role of Governor of the Bahamas, envied his brother's increased stature and glowing popularity. The Duchess gazed coldly at the Queen who, in her view, had soured the abdication, and deprived her and the Duke of a respected place in society on British soil. Not that she is that explicit in her memoirs. But her words can scarcely have any other meaning: 'All that he [David] ever specifically asked for was a fairly simple thing; that I be received, just once, by the King his brother, and the Queen, in order to erase by that single gesture of hospitality the stigma attaching to my never having been received since our marriage by the Royal Family, his family. . . .'

Hard not to feel a pang of sympathy for the woman who wrote those words. Vain, jewellery-mad and imperious she may have been, but there could be no doubt about her devotion to the unpredictable Duke. Yet to expect the Queen to receive her publicly was not the 'fairly simple thing' the Duchess imagined it to be. A family life overturned; a major Constitutional crisis; the effect of both painfully etched into the face of the King; a 'gesture of hospitality' would be hard to extract from the Queen. But the compassion was there, and would eventually be offered. Meanwhile with the war on there was a much greater need for charity nearer home. One of the Queen's cousins, Lilian Bowes-Lyon, had become one of the East End's unsung heroines. Few knew of her relationship with the Queen as she worked among the ruins helping to put lives as well as homes together again. One of the more immediate problems was replacing the furniture in houses that had been burned away in the blitz. Lilian approached her cousin the Queen who gave instructions for suites of furniture to be sent from Windsor Castle; wardrobes, chairs, beds, tables that had been around early in Victoria's reign. The apples never fell far from the Bowes-Lyon tree.

In November 1944, the Queen's father, the Earl of Strathmore died. He was eighty-nine. A gentle and kindly old man, he faded as unobtrusively as he had lived. The Queen had been much closer to her mother Countess Strathmore. Yet she wept at the graveside at Glamis where his ashes were buried. There are always tears, and a void, when finally both parents have gone.

The daily routine, leaving the Princesses at Windsor Castle at 8 o'clock each morning, and returning there for dinner at night, had its dangers. Along the route to the Palace there were landmines, several unexploded bombs, the risk of gas explosions from pipes fractured in the raids. 'It was an occupational risk,' the King wrote afterwards, 'nobody is immune.' It was this constant threat which prompted the Queen to write those two letters to the Princesses to be opened only if the worst happened. They were written with Elizabeth's customary composure, a quality which the King regarded almost as his lifeline. There was a lively example of it one night at Windsor Castle. The Queen had gone up to her bedroom when suddenly a man appeared from behind a curtain and threw himself at her feet. In a frenzy, he grabbed her ankles and, as the Queen recalled afterwards, 'for a moment my heart stood absolutely still'. Then that composure took over. Knowing that if she screamed he might attack her, she calmed him down, sat on the bed and listened to what he had to say. A soldier, he had lost his entire family in the blitz. Near demented, he had deserted. On the run, he had panicked all the way to the Castle believing he might get a sympathetic hearing from the Queen. Her comment, 'poor man, he meant no harm, I was sorry for him,' suggests good thinking on the poor chap's part. Anybody who knows the lady would lay odds that she asked the Army to take a lenient view of the affair.

At last, the war against Rommel turning in Britain's favour, the King was allowed by Churchill in June 1943, to visit the troops in North Africa. The flight was not without risks. The route, via Gibraltar, was identical to the one taken eight days earlier by the plane in which the actor Leslie Howard was shot down. Hearing this, the King continued with his packing but quietly called lawyers, checked on his will, made sure his affairs were in order. Elizabeth paced around waiting for news of the flight. There were reports of fog in the area around Gibraltar; sudden changes in the flight plan; a landing in Africa then an unscheduled take-off again. 'I imagined every kind of horror,' she wrote to Queen Mary. 'I walked up and down my room staring at the telephone.' Bertie returned two weeks later, sunburned and safe. But there were further anxieties for the Queen. As D Day approached the King became restless. He knew that at the back of Churchill's mind lay an idea to accompany the invasion forces on to the beaches. The King, whose wartime service at the Battle of Jutland was all too brief, promptly decided that he would go too and told Elizabeth so. The Queen had mixed feelings. She backed Bertie in his eagerness to make a D Day appearance alongside Churchill on French soil. She was also a wife and a mother with private fears of what could happen. Churchill displayed similar ambivalence. The old warrior, though secretly intrigued by the chivalrous vision of a King leading his troops into battle, knew that the Cabinet would oppose any such plan. The ultimatum, 'If you go, I go' had too much muscle behind it. 'This was perhaps the only occasion,' A. J. P. Taylor wrote, 'when Churchill was overruled by the monarch he served.'

But he was genuinely touched by his relationship with the King and Queen. Often lunch with them was interrupted by a raid. They had to scramble with their plates and glasses down into the Palace shelter, Winston lagging behind to collect his cigars. Churchill was impressed by the King's grasp of state matters, and by the Queen's strong support in the wings. No mistaking the sincerity behind the Churchillian prose: 'I have been greatly cheered by our weekly lunches in poor old bomb-battered Buckingham Palace and to feel that in Your Majesty and the Queen there flames the spirit that will never be daunted by peril, nor wearied by unrelenting toil. This war has drawn the throne and the people more closely together than ever before, and Your Majesties are more beloved by all classes and conditions than any of the princes of the past. . . .'

Hyperbole to some, the plain truth to others. The fact is, when the buzz bombs came, their guttural roar cutting out into a terrifying silence, the King and Queen were as vulnerable outside the shelter as anyone else. When the V1 rockets followed, they could never be sure, commuting between the Palace of Windsor, where this random atrocity would strike. If there was no time to get to the Palace shelter, the Queen would take cover in a narrow corridor behind the Belgian Suite. Palace servants were frequently in there ahead of her. There was a bad Sunday morning when the Guards Chapel near the Palace took a direct hit. More people pray in war time. The Chapel was crowded. One hundred and twenty-one members of the congregation were killed, many of them friends or acquaintances of the Queen. She and the King heard the news at Windsor Castle. 'It was the only time during the whole war,' Marion Crawford remembered, 'when I saw the Queen really shaken.' She was certainly shocked by the death of a nephew John, son of her eldest brother and Strathmore heir, killed in action. And by the news that another nephew was taken as a prisoner of war.

If 'Crawfie' hardly ever saw the Queen shaken it was because in the Bowes-Lyon style, Elizabeth had been raised on the principle of not wearing one's heart on one's sleeve. As Lord Mountbatten indicated, she rarely gave a clue to her true feelings, keeping dominant emotions like grief, displeasure, or fear to herself. Becoming Queen, which in essence demanded a performance of sorts, necessarily increased this reserve. As playwright Arthur Miller argued, loneliness is the penalty of celebrity. He clearly had in mind his doomed wife Marilyn Monroe, who suffered this sense of isolation all her professional life. Elizabeth, as Queen and later Queen Mother, managed her surface radiance often despite fatigue, painful feet, and sometimes an aching heart. Certainly it is a performance. But no one could say this Elizabeth has not done her best.

Cynics argue that this 'radiant, warm and compassionate' public image is a mask behind which a harder, less pliant personality exists. A close examination of their indictment reveals a ton of innuendo to an ounce of fact. 'Blind and uncritical acclaim is, when it comes to the crunch, worthless,' wrote Penelope Mortimer. True. Conversely, blinkered and highly selective disparagement is just as bad.

The Queen's war, as for every other surviving participant, was not all fear and gloom. There were the Christmas concerts at Windsor, Margaret at the piano, the Queen leading the chorus in 'Roll Out the Barrel' and 'Run, Rabbit, Run'. There were birthdays to celebrate too. Princess Elizabeth was eighteen on 21 April 1944. One gift, from the King, was her appointment as a Counsellor of State. A small but significant step on the road to the throne; and another indication to Margaret of her diminished place in the royal pecking order. But she was never short of love. Her father, who himself had been upstaged by an elder brother in line for the throne, understood Margaret's problems which went beyond sibling rivalry. There were rituals and status symbols which involved Elizabeth as heir but denied her younger sister. She had her own lady-in-waiting, her own coat of arms, her own secretary, her own flag. As a Counsellor of State, when Churchill dropped by the Palace, he and Lilibet would often saunter off to discuss serious matters while Margaret hovered aimlessly at a distance. Occasionally the King would show his elder daughter secret State papers which increased Margaret's feeling of being left, constitutionally at least, out in the cold. The elder Princess, now a Junior Transport Officer in the Auxilliary Territorial Service, was put on the 'royal circuit', visiting factories, opening charity bazaars, a life in the spotlight for a future Queen. It was the Constitution which made the sharp, arbitrary distinction between the two princesses. If it left the younger one with a chip on her shoulder, too bad. (Margaret was also crisply downgraded Below Stairs being nicknamed 'P2' by the palace servants.) George VI who had suffered miserably as a second-fiddle prince, unquestionably over-compensated in his handling of Margaret. Usually undemonstrative, he went overboard responding to her fierce show of affection. She would frequently throw her arms around his neck in an uninhibited display of love which neither the King – nor the Queen – could resist. Both recognized that there might be problems in the future. Neither could foresee how shattering these would be. On this subject, Lord Mountbatten's comments are interesting for what is implied rather than said. 'Princess Elizabeth and Princess Margaret developed along *completely* different lines. Elizabeth is very different from her sister who was brought up in a very spoilt way. The elder daughter's life has been one of serious dedication. She was totally dedicated to becoming Queen one day. Not necessarily looking forward to it with any sense of joy, but realizing that this is what she would be required to do.' If the implication of this is that Margaret was not as seriously motivated as her sister, she could scarcely be blamed for it. Elizabeth was groomed for everything, she for nothing.

And now this handsome lieutenant Prince Philip had taken to dropping in at Windsor on leave. Jealousy would never be one of Princess Margaret's faults. But she must have suffered a jolt of envy at the glances exchanged between the (then) bearded Viking and her starry-eyed sister, now an attractive, well-groomed, infatuated nineteen year old. Margaret, observing all the signs, giggled at her sister's sudden concern over her appearance. Long interludes playing romantic records. Philip's portrait on her dressing table. Flushes of colour in her cheeks whenever his name was mentioned. Parents are usually slow to pick up signals, and the King and Queen, caught up in the thought of approaching victory, would hardly have noticed them at all.

The Axis death throes came first. On 28 April 1945, Mussolini and his mistress were shot by partisans, their bodies displayed hanging upside down in Milan. On 29 April in a singularly gruesome betrothal, Hitler married his mistress Eva Braun in his Berlin bunker, then killed her and himself the following day. Their bodies were later incinerated in a yard outside. On 7 May 1945, Germany surrendered unconditionally. The day after, Churchill announced to Parliament Victory in Europe. It was now the King's job to make his VE Day broadcast to the nation. It had to be a speech to match the occasion. Apart from Britain, the world would be listening. The Queen called Lionel Logue to the Palace. There were several rehearsals before and after dinner. Then, as Logue himself recorded, the Queen came into the room where he and the King sat. 'She turns at the door, and says: "*in your growly voice*". The Queen in her white dress stands at one window, and I at another, and we both stand rigid for the first two sentences, but the King's voice is gathering strength and power and we glance at one another and smile. And so we stand until the end. I know the Queen was praying. I was too.'

'We want the King! We want the Queen!' the surging thousands chanted outside the Palace railings. Beyond them, millions danced and sang on the streets. London's landscape had been brutally reshaped. The City had been partially erased. The remains of bombed-out buildings made craggy silhouettes on the skyline. Pot-holes, craters and mountains of rubble completed the moon-surface desolation. But Londoners were ecstatically and uninhibitedly happy. Thirty-thousand or so civilians had been killed by German air raids, more than half that number in London. Homes had been destroyed, lives shattered, countless nights spent in freezing shelters or in Underground stations. It was now over. Relief was the dominant emotion.

'We want the King! We want the Queen!' There was no refusing that insistent Wembley roar. And so they appeared on that famous balcony, flanking a beaming Winston Churchill. Beside the Queen, Princess Elizabeth in uniform. Alongside the King, Princess Margaret. The Queen's familiar ensemble proclaimed, 'Business as usual' – the feathered, upswept hat, three-quarter-sleeved coat, and three-strand pearls all lit by that 1,000 kilowatt smile. The family took a half-a-dozen curtain calls. Finally, with a last hand-wave they disappeared off the balcony. The Queen would have been glad to kick off her shoes, drink her first peacetime gin and tonic. A chance now for the family to relax together; to forget the war and talk about the future, the young Elizabeth's in particular. It was a matter of some irritation to the King. First Mountbatten, and now King George of Greece, were dropping hints about this young sailor prince. 'Dammit, a gal just doesn't go off and marry the first chap she falls in love with!' appears to have been His Majesty's initial reaction to the proposed match. But that 'first chap' being a Mountbatten, different 'rules of engagement' applied.

12

It was – if we ignore the home address at the end of the Mall – a fairly typical family dilemma. Elder daughter falls in love with handsome sailor. She is twenty, he twenty-five. Both could claim a string of other ardent admirers. In her case, young Guards officers and born-in-the-purple gallants who could ride, shoot, and hunt and who were not irksomely short of ready cash. He, a tall, war-ribboned naval lieutenant, was similarly a dream catch. Girls, it seems, had relentlessly thrown themselves at him, 'daughters of publishers, sultry-eyed steel heiresses, girls with strings of department-stores and farming fortunes . . .' to quote one biographer, Basil Boothroyd. Mother just 'wants her daughter to be happy'. Papa likewise, but he can't adjust to the reality that his lovely elder child has grown up. A woman. He fights a rearguard action, advancing those familiar arguments . . . 'needs to experience more of life . . . meet more people . . . travel perhaps, to get a more objective view of things.' There are family conferences at which the younger daughter loyally closes ranks with her sister. All things being equal, the problem could be amicably settled over a sherry in the drawing room or a pint at the pub. But all things are not equal. With the family home being Buckingham Palace, and Papa the reigning monarch, the daughter and the sailor would have no easy voyage into matrimony. The man who married the young Elizabeth would one day be Consort to a Queen. A union of man, woman, and a dynasty. How good she would be as a Queen could not be unaffected by the quality of the person she chose to marry.

Accounts of when and where Philip actually proposed, and was accepted, vary. The favourite is summertime, Balmoral,

1946. It is the favourite because many years later, the Queen, so
it is said, revealed that 'this took place beside some well-loved
loch, the white clouds overhead and the curlew crying'. Who
hooked whom by the well-loved loch, may never be known.
The point is academic since Boothroyd, Philip's authorized
biographer, asserts that the proposal was made at a large public
luncheon in Edinburgh. And that the bit about the loch, the
white clouds and the curlew were part of a passage on the
beauties of Scotland. Historians would not argue the point.
What mattered was that two highly agreeable and well-matched
adults had decided on a life together. But they would have to
wait a while. By royal command.

The King's decision was supported by his mother, Queen
Mary who told her lady-in-waiting, 'I suppose my son is wise.
After all he had to wait long enough for *his* wife, and you can see
what a success their marriage is.' She also confided, 'They have
been in love for the past eighteen months, in fact longer I think. I
believe she fell in love with him the first time she went down to
Windsor, but the King and Queen feel that she is too young to be
engaged yet. They want her to see more of the world and meet
more men. After all she is only nineteen and one is very
impressionable at that age.' But rumours of an engagement
persisted, resulting in a terse statement from Buckingham
Palace in September, categorically denying it. That took care of
the Press. But what equally concerned the King and Queen was
that Philip realize that delay implied nothing personal. In fact the
King and particularly the Queen, liked him from the start.
Philip, born on the island of Corfu in 1921, was the son of Prince
Andrew of Greece. He was educated at Cheam, Gordonstoun
and the Royal Naval College, Dartmouth. A strong character,
intelligent, independent, with his famous uncle's indifference to
danger on a horse or in a battleship, Philip had well earned his
wartime decorations. He was a 'royal' too, and – as Lord
Mountbatten underscores – he would always be the master in his
own house.

One element in the delay was George VI's known possessive-
ness. This was a throw-back to his own affection-starved childhood. Marrying Elizabeth gave him more than an enriched sense
of identity. In the simplest terms, she made him happy, and
boosted his confidence at the most crucial moments of his life.
He now enjoyed a cosy and satisfying equilibrium in his life. It
was not merely that he thought Princess Elizabeth wasn't ready

for marriage. Everything was going so well he was reluctant to let her go.

In the event, a long-standing overseas obligation fortuitously delayed the engagement. A year earlier, their Majesties had been invited to visit South Africa by the Governor-General, Gideon Brand Van Zyl. That invitation was now taken up, the King officially on hand for the State Opening of Parliament on 27 February 1947. Princess Elizabeth and Princess Margaret would, of course, come too. Lilibet and Philip would be apart for four months in a tour covering a total of 10,000 miles. The strength of the romance was obviously going to be tested on the anvil. The royal party sailed away from a freezing Britain run by Labour, the Churchill Government having been massively rejected in the post-war electoral landslide. The fact that they were sailing away to sunshine when bomb-blasted London was atrophied under fourteen-feet snowdrifts and sixteen degrees of frost, inevitably induced some hard feelings among the population. Unemployment was high, there were power cuts, and many old people had died in the cold. It was hardly the most tactful time for the Royal Family to sail out on the Navy's latest battleship, the *Vanguard*. Accompanying the royal party was the usual complement of high-born courtiers plus two personable equerries, Lt Commander Peter Ashmore, a young bachelor sailor who had served in destroyers, and Wing Commander Peter Townsend, older and married. Both were good riders and dancers which must have helped the two Princesses cope with the grinding formalities of the tour – though perhaps for different reasons. It is unlikely that the Queen was ecstatic over the tour. Travelling for four months by car, train and plane in a turbulent country gearing itself to cut and run from the Empire, hardly made for sweetness and light – two imperatives in Elizabeth's scheme of things.

There were some uncomfortable moments. The Queen described one incident as 'the worst mistake of my life'. She and the King were touring by car through the Reef towns – George VI not in one of his best moods at the time – when a tall and bulky Zulu burst out of the crowd and rushed towards their open car, shouting and gesticulating. He grabbed at the car, a shining object in his other hand. The King paled, the Queen repeatedly beat the fellow off with her parasol which broke in two. The police leapt forward and knocked the man unconscious. 'Within seconds,' eye-witnesses recorded, 'the Queen waved and smiled, as captivating as ever.' Not so the Zulu. All he had intended apparently, was to give her a ten-shilling note as a birthday present for Princess Elizabeth.

Like it or not, the Queen put her best smile forward on the Tour even winning reluctant approval from Boer War veterans. When one of these red-necks told her he could never quite forgive the British for having conquered his country, she smiled back, 'I understand that perfectly. We feel very much the same in Scotland.' The King, however, found it impossible to appear cheerful when clearly he was not. The late James Cameron, a reporter of distinction, covering the trip for the *Guardian*: 'No two personalities could have been more different than those of the King and Queen. She was then, as now, composed, eager, on top of every situation; he was tense, unbearably nervous, alternating diffidence with sharp bursts of temper.' (What my late colleague Cameron would not have known, and possibly not the King himself, was that his short-fused demeanour was probably due to approaching illness. By the end of the tour he had lost 17 lbs.)

At Outshoorn, the centre of the ostrich-feather trade, the King was required to snip the tail feather of a selected bird. More nervous than usual he was all fingers and thumbs with the clippers and nicked a quarter of an inch off the ostrich's backside. 'At which,' Cameron reported, 'the creature let forth an indignant squawk. Enter the Queen, stage right, as usual in total smiling command. She took the clippers from her husband and there and then did an absolutely expert featherectomy.'

All in all the trip was a success. The mighty diamond companies of South Africa had given the two princesses farewell gifts of the finest diamonds as though these were no more than a bag of sugared almonds. But the King, Queen, and all members of the party were glad to get home. Not least Princess Elizabeth who had dutifully put her romance on 'hold' in deference to the King. Four days before they were due to sail home from Cape Town, on the eve of her twenty-first birthday, she broadcast a birthday message to the Commonwealth. The speech was well received, most of all by Earl Mountbatten. When he spoke about it, it was almost thirty years later. Yet with almost uncanny recall, he was able to quote it verbatim.

'I remember that coming-of-age broadcast. She said, "I declare before you all that my whole life whether it be long or short shall be devoted to your service and the service of our

great Imperial Commonwealth to which we all belong . . ."' It
was Mountbatten's kind of language. It confirmed what he had
felt all along. She was in every sense, her mother's daughter.
'What do I think about her? Pure gold right through.'

In the first week of July, the Queen decided, as mothers do, to
inflict a little arm-twisting on the King. Philip would make a fine
son-in-law. He had become a naturalized British subject, re-
nouncing his rights of succession to the Greek and Danish
thrones. He would now call himself Mountbatten. Everything
was now set fair. His Majesty could no longer ignore his
daughter's Cloud Nine radiance. He invited Philip to dinner at
Balmoral on Tuesday, 8 July. The Princess smiling hugely, told
Crawfie, '"He's coming tonight!" She kissed me and danced
away.' The next morning, Lilibet was brandishing an engagement ring, a large square diamond with smaller diamonds on
two sides. On 10 July the engagement was officially announced.
The wedding would be on 20 November. The Palace announced
that the bride would be allotted a hundred extra clothing
coupons for her trousseau and her bridesmaids twenty-three
each. The allocation somehow stretched to a wedding gown of
white satin sparkling with pearls and crystals, embroidered with
stars and garlands of roses intertwined with ears of wheat.
(Norman Hartnell, who was detailed to make the frock, roamed
the London art galleries in search of classic inspiration. 'Fortunately,' he wrote, 'I found a Botticelli figure in clinging ivory
silk, trailed with jasmine, smilax syringa and small white rose-
like blossoms.' And no clothing coupons involved.) Needing
'something borrowed' the Princess seized on her mother's
sunray tiara. The wire frame broke as the bride-to-be was trying
it on for size. She became agitated. The Queen calmed her. 'We
can get it fixed, and anyway,' she reassured her, 'there are other
tiaras.'

And so to the altar at Westminster Abbey on 20 November
1947. On that morning, I was able to claim what may be
laughingly described as a world exclusive, namely that a half a
dozen hot-water bottles, three-feet long would be strategically
deployed in the coach for the comfort of the father and the bride.
The source of this un-startling intelligence (given to me in my
capacity, briefly, as court correspondent for the London *Daily
Mirror*) was a boilerman then working at Buckingham Palace.
This takes us some way from the altar but I make the digression
to illustrate the then Queen's strong influence on the Palace's

dealings with the Press. She would not have forgotten her innocent 'revelations' to a reporter on her engagement; and her subsequent embarrassment reading the breathless outflow the following day. This led to a strong directive from George V to be more circumspect in future and resulted in a clam-like reticence that persists into her ninetieth year. The conduit by which the media received the anodyne royal communiqués of the day, was then, as now, the Palace Press Office. The exceedingly courteous breed therein would always have a problem. Royals at that time, never gave interviews. (The Princess of Wales's comment on the Duchess of York's pregnancy, 'You know this family. We breed like rabbits' would have sent the Press Office of forty years ago into shock.) The Royal Family insisted nothing remotely personal ever be disclosed. Certainly not their opinion, politics, or even their favourite colour, food, or tipple. This was frustrating to newspapers, particularly in the immediate post-war period when stories about royalty were devoured by the millions. Years later, an outspoken Prince Philip would turn a refreshing candour (not to mention a water hose) on the media. His son, Prince Charles would be even more forthcoming, and controversial. But at the time of his parents' wedding, even the most innocuous information was as hard to extract as wisdom teeth. So we, whose job it was to make bricks without straw, did the best we could with 'sources close to the palace' – a euphemism for anybody who knows somebody within cantering distance of the Palace.

These sources were not so difficult to come by. When you live, work, or play alongside royalty, history underfoot (or as in the case of my boilerman, overhead) there is often an irresistible urge to spill the beans. This, despite the fact that confidentiality is a condition of employment. Mostly, the Palace smiled behind its hand at this clandestine activity. In fact royals themselves have often 'leaked' stories the way government ministers do to 'safe' and favoured journalists, the two terms being synonymous. So if a Mistress of the Bedchamber or Yeoman of the Lower Staircase, was known to have passed on a harmless little piece of unattributable information to a paper, no blood was split or questions asked. These insiders rarely divulged anything for gain. It was mainly for the excitement, gossip being a fairly universal addiction. On 19 November, the eve of the royal wedding, every bulletin, every paper was dominated by the excitement of the hour. Suddenly, the boilerman had become personally, if somewhat circuitously, involved, and bubbling to tell someone. His phone call on the eve of the wedding was therefore cathartic. The tone conspiratorial.

'I have some information.'

'Yes?'

'They said it's going to be cold tomorrow, right?'

'Who is this?'

'I can't tell you that right now. But . . .' he lowered his voice, 'I have been ordered to put six hot-water bottles in the coach.'

'What coach?'

'The Irish State Coach of course! The Royal wedding! That's what they asked me to do.' I sensed irritation and soothed him.

'Why would anybody ask you Mr. ? . . .

'Moon.'

'Moon . . . to put hot-water bottles in the Irish State Coach tomorrow morning? I mean, why you?'

'Boilerman, (pause for effect) Buckingham Palace!'

'Ah.'

'The hot-water bottles,' he continued importantly, 'are of aluminium, 3ft long and . . . are you getting all this?'

'Of course.'

'. . . and will be filled with boiling water and placed under the seat and floorboards. On their return . . . (Mr Moon was now dictating) . . . in the Glass Goach the same number of hot water bottles will be installed in the same way.'

Scarcely the sort of information which would have forced say, *The Times* – then – to change its front page. Nevertheless that paper and the rest of Fleet Street would – and did – pay generously for anything that contrasted with the torpid prose of the Palace hand-outs. The first edition of the *Daily Mirror* Thursday, 20 November 1947 (price one penny) led its front page: HOT BOTTLES FOR BRIDE'S COACHES. Harry Moon (not his real name, anonymity being the name of the informants' game), was ecstatic. He gazed long and proudly at the first paragraph. 'The Irish State Coach, in which Princess Elizabeth and the King to-day drive to the Royal Wedding at Westminster Abbey will be heated with special hot water-bottles 3ft long.' His words. Just like he said. True, more significant items soon elbowed the hot-water bottles off the front page of later editions. But he had made it.

The Palace, caught up in the wedding excitement, was amused and asked no questions. Which was unfortunate since from then on nothing could stop him. His last communiqué was in November 1948, the night before Prince Charles was born. He had kept up an hour-by-hour commentary on the preparations for the birth. ('Princess Elizabeth was taken to the Buhl Room where Sir William Gilliatt and a team of doctors and nurses were waiting . . .' He later added a few grace notes; the baby weighed seven pounds six ounces, it was a forceps delivery, and Philip had passed the time playing squash. There was an additional snippet five days later: Doctor Jacob Snowman, a leading exponent of the art, had been called in to circumcise the baby.

How a boilerman could acquire such intimate details intrigued the Palace sufficiently to dismiss him a few weeks later. His was a short and happy career. Since then, the odd butler, valet, or Palace char has sought to exploit his or her brief moment of modestly-paid glory, their so-called 'revelations' upsetting nobody, least of all the Queen. The same could not be said of Marion Crawford – 'Crawfie' – whose book, *The Little Princesses* proved that those who seriously offend Her Majesty, do so at their peril. A case could be made for Miss Crawford arguing that her book was no more than the sugary reminiscences of a reverential Royal governess. Artless, naïve, it nevertheless hit the best-seller list. But missing from the English edition were a few odd lines including some not un-flattering references to Edward VIII and Wallis Simpson as they were then, on a visit to Royal Lodge. Those deletions reveal the other side of the coin. They show the subtle but formidable power of a disapproving Queen supported by influential friends . . . in this case, the late Nancy Astor.

Viscountess Astor was the Queen's kind of woman. Born in Virginia, USA she came to England, married the 2nd Viscount Astor of Cliveden. A fearless champion of women's rights and social reform, she swept into politics to become in 1919, the first woman to sit as a member of the House of Commons. Conservative MP for Plymouth until 1945, she and the Queen became close and dependable friends. Nancy knew everybody who mattered, particularly publishers, Lord Astor having at one time a controlling interest in the *Observer* newspaper. Just how Nancy Astor was able to receive a copy of Crawfie's manuscript is not clear. But on glancing through it, she instantly sent it to the Queen. Her Majesty's reaction was forcefully expressed in a letter she sent in reply. Its purpose was to seek Lady Astor's help in getting 'the most inaccurate and dangerous bits' removed from the text. The letter was written from Buckingham Palace in a strong, purposeful hand on lavender notepaper.

> My dear Lady Astor,
> Thankyou so much for sending on the manuscript of Miss Crawford's story. Perhaps you have heard the whole thing has been a great shock to us. We have worried greatly over this matter and can only think that our late and completely trusted governess has gone off her head, because she promised in writing that she would not publish any story about the daughters and this development has made us very sad. We have to trust people completely and such a thing has never happened before. I shall be grateful if you can help and I am so terribly sorry that I cannot give the story my blessing.
> I am, yours affec,
> Elizabeth R.

The tone of the letter suggests it was written more in sorrow than in anger. But soon after, Crawfie vacated her 'grace-and-favour' house close to Kensington Palace and retired to a white-washed cottage on the edge of the River Dee in Scotland. She had broken the royal 'House Rules' on confidentiality. Her 'excommunication' apparently was complete.

Clouds never hovered long over Elizabeth's internal land-scape. She and the King had celebrated their Silver Wedding in April 1948. Twenty-five not uneventful years. Both she and the King were entitled to be elated at the quality of their marriage. Certainly the Queen could claim that as far as her marriage vows were concerned she had more than honoured her side of the bargain. Her pledge of love – well Bertie would gladly testify to that. In sickness . . . ? Nobody had been more attentive and concerned than she. Fidelity, forswearing all others . . . ? Not a question to be asked of this Strathmore. Faithfulness, like all the other cardinal virtues, was intrinsic to the breed. Not that this attractive and flirty-eyed Queen did not have her male admirers. It would have been no compliment to her to have suggested otherwise. Confronted by that direct gaze and teasing persona even in her mid-years, few men would not have found the encounter mildly disconcerting. Certainly the late Kenneth Clark, the distinguished art connoisseur 'might have been a little in love with her' if his biographer Meryle Secrest is correct. But it takes two to tango and in this respect the late Lord Clark, Surveyor of the King's pictures, was dancing on his own. He was a frequent guest at Windsor Castle. Cultivated, witty, he and Lady Clark were good company for the King and Queen. Clark persuaded the Queen to commission paintings by lesser-known artists. He talked her into having her portrait painted by Augustus John. That venture failed. There was little rapport between the artist and the subject. John attempted 'reality' but the 'fairy princess' image kept surfacing on the canvas. The picture was never completed. Eventually the Queen received it, and was said to have liked it. Augustus John shrugged it off as one of his failures. The episode did not diminish the Queen's regard for Clark's judgement nor his appreciation of her rare qualities, 'not the least of which,' his biographer notes, 'were her sense and innate good taste'. Lord Clark advised the Queen on the decor of Buckingham Palace which outside of the state apartments was a drab arrangement of nondescript rooms and corridors. He changed the pictures around at Hampton Court. It is clear he made a distinct impact on the improved interior of the Palace and the Castle. The Queen, it seems, made quite an impact on the handsome connoisseur. 'When he [Clark] talked about their romantic friendship in retrospect, he said that they saw as much of each other as they dared, adding that the King became unreasonably jealous and twice made scenes, once at Windsor Castle and again at Buckingham Palace.' But this 'revelation' appears to have more ego than evidence to support it. 'Perhaps Kenneth Clark was assuming more than was warranted from the Queen's lively interest in art and what another called her mild flirtatiousness "in a very proper romantic old-fashioned Valentine sort of way".' And like Valentines, to be smiled over occasionally, and then briskly be put back in the drawer.

The Silver Wedding was celebrated with a drive in an open State landau to St Paul's. As the Queen smiled and waved her way along the two-mile route, the consensus held that she had never been happier. With Princess Elizabeth and Philip sailing serenely into marital bliss, plus the bonus of a grandson, there was much to be happy about. The King had conferred the Order of the Garter on his elder daughter, (slightly ahead of Philip so that Elizabeth would have seniority). He had written to her after their honeymoon, 'I have watched you grow up all these years with pride under the skilful direction of Mummy, who as you know is the most marvellous person in the world in my eyes. . . .'

But these were the words of an increasingly ailing monarch. He had been troubled for some months with cramp in the legs. The pain of it often kept him awake at night. Doctors diagnosed arteriosclerosis with the risk of gangrene threatening the possible amputation of his right leg. They explained the narrow options to the Queen. The anxiety she had felt for months about the King's health now turned to alarm. But after minor exploratory surgery, the pain subsided. The threat of complications, leading to an amputation, disappeared. She no longer had to wear that reassuring smile in the King's presence. The prognosis seemed encouraging. She could now enjoy being a grandmother. December at Sandringham brought a bonus. Princess Elizabeth fell sick with measles. The Queen, who would now have Charles to herself, hid her glee behind expressions of maternal sympathy. At Christmas the family were together, playing charades, or 'The Game' as it became known to participants which over the years included Prime Ministers, Judges, Peers of the Realm and other Establishment luminaries, press-ganged into wearing funny props and acting out assorted characters. Churchill was an unwilling performer, growling to himself like a bulldog overdue for its feed. 'The Game' has persisted through the decades, mostly at Christmas at Windsor Castle. Some participants have worn assorted costumes, the Queen once sporting a fake beard. A Prime Minister (unnamed) marched around with fire-tongs doubling as a shouldered rifle. Their Lordships Carrington and Hailsham are reported to have been among the 'cast'. Neither was eager to be drawn on the subject.

The King was now well enough to conduct an Investiture of the New Year's Honours. Behind the scenes the Queen arranged for the ritual to be bent slightly so that Bertie could conduct it sitting down. The ceremony went well and in the first two months of 1949 the Queen felt a surge of optimism. There was no longer any talk of operations or worse, of an amputation. But in the first week of March the King's doctors confided that they were still concerned about the King's condition and that they would have to operate. Her problem, familiar to many women similarly placed, was how to hide her anxieties both from the King and her daughters. She managed this well. The Queen parades a variety of emotions in public. Grief has never been one of them.

In March 1949, in the Buhl Room where Charles was born, the King underwent surgery to free the flow of blood to his right leg. The Queen sat out the hour's procedure in her private apartment with Princess Elizabeth, Margaret and Prince Philip. As Marion Crawford noted in her ill-fated memoirs, 'The Queen was quite distraught with anxiety. She could speak and think of nothing else until the operation was safely over.' The surgery went well. Convalescing, the grateful King called the surgeon, an amiable Scots Professor James Learmouth to his bedside. He produced a sword from under his pillow. 'You used a knife on me, now I'm going to use this on you.' The surgeon rose off one knee, a Knight.

But his life, as King, would have to change. The Queen knew that even before Learmouth spelled it out to her. Between them, she and Princess Elizabeth would have to share some of the burdens. The Princess deputized for him taking the salute at the Trooping of the Colour. The Queen took over some of his speeches. He was determined to be as mobile as possible. For the 'shoot' at Balmoral, the King had a special harness attached to a pony which pulled him uphill. He could now take a gun like the others. Two hundred and sixty-three deceased grouse confirmed that his faltering legs hadn't affected his aim. Slowly walking with him arm in arm in the heather, the Queen must have felt a sense of role reversal. Originally, it had been her strength that he had called on in the years before and immediately after the Abdication. Illnesses apart, he had emerged a strong monarch, a wise father, and as supportive of her as she was of him. There was plenty she could lean on now. But as she studied his gaunt profile, the occasional flicker of pain in his eyes, she must have wondered how long that strength would last. She would have to be strong enough for both of them. Some months earlier, her eldest brother Patrick, the 15th Earl of Strathmore, died. He was only sixty-five. The funeral at Glamis, where her mother lay buried, would have evoked predictable emotions. The Countess's gifted mind and sympathetic shoulder would have been poignantly missed that day. Soon, 4 August 1950, the Queen would be fifty years old. That landmark was preceded by exciting news fluttering out of Clarence House where Princess Elizabeth and Philip now lived. The Princess was pregnant. Nature and other calculations permitting, maybe the infant might arrive on her mother's birthday. In the event, Princess Anne was a late runner, arriving at 11.45 on the morning of 15 August. Margaret was thrilled. She hoped for a niece. Now perhaps the papers would stop calling her 'Charley's Aunt'.

13

Rarely separated from the King for a moment longer than he would tolerate, the Queen could see the painful deterioration in his health. While doctors came, scrutinized X-rays and then murmured back to Harley Street, Elizabeth remained the King's chief nurse, and his hope. It was not an easy role to play. The protracted trauma of seeing her husband physically under siege, his defences crumbling, was affecting her profoundly. But Queen Consorts are obliged to keep their heartache to themselves. Anxiety, dismay, and apprehension – there was no doubt how she felt. But in the back seat of the Royal limousine, or in the busy corridors of the Palace, a 'brave smile' was requested and delivered. She and the King had seen 1950 out with a fling. The Servants' Ball at Buckingham Palace had this dainty-footed grannie in her element, being swept around the ballroom in a succession of her favourite dances. In the azalea-banked ballroom on the first floor she danced the rumba, the samba, and, her Scottish blood up, the Gay Gordons and the Eightsome Reel. This vision of her in gold tulle crinoline, a diamond tiara gleaming under the chandeliers, would have stayed with the King long after the lights were dimmed. The King partnered Margaret's housemaid Isabel Ross for the first number, a foxtrot. The Queen danced a valeta and the St Bernard's Waltz with two of her pages, Jack Crisp and Jack Kemp. This pair of Jacks confirmed what Lord Home, her friend and Scottish neighbour, had discovered before them: 'She was as light as a feather. A beautiful dancer.'

The royal excitement faded with the dancing. The Queen piloted an immensely weary monarch back to his room. The servants stood silent, watching them go. They must have sensed overtones to that Last Waltz.

In the autumn of 1951, the royal couple's stay at Balmoral was cut short. The King was seriously ill. He was taken alone, down to London for urgent medical examinations. The Queen followed soon after. She now knew the King had lung cancer. It had come as a shock. The thrombosis in his leg had been bad enough. Now this. His pallor, the visible loss of weight – any intelligent wife would have been able to read the signs. Even she, now, could not contrive a public smile. For the first time as Queen she avoided the crowds anxiously milling around the Palace gates and took the side entrance instead. On 23 September the King was operated on for a lung resection. The Queen asked for, and was told the truth. There were risks. There was always a danger of a thrombosis on the operating table. But there were no options. The Duke of Windsor who had slipped quietly into London, joined his mother, the ageing Queen Mary, at Marlborough House. He would not exchange many words with his brother's wife. She would not openly accuse him. But he knew where she would lay some of the blame. Yet it is doubtful whether she gave a thought for him or Wallis Simpson as surgeons prepared for the operation in the converted Buhl Room. It took two hours. The King's entire left lung was removed. The Queen was at his bedside the following day. He was still sedated, but managed a wink. No words were exchanged. She kissed his forehead then returned to her rooms. Philip and Elizabeth came to the Palace. She was grave but controlled. Margaret, with no appearances to keep up, was close to sobbing. But six days later she was able to smile to reporters at London Airport before boarding a flight to Scotland: 'It is all very good news!' And so it seemed. The Queen who had scarcely left the King's bedside took a walk in the Palace gardens. Friends have explained to me that this was the way she invariably confronted emotional crises. Walking, sometimes miles, alone. In the same week, Princess Elizabeth and the Duke of Edinburgh were at Ascot.

The world took this as the ultimate confirmation of the monarch's recovery. The *New York Daily News* rushed out the splash headline, 'KING OK'. Six weeks later he and the Queen were at London's Victoria Palace for the Royal Variety Show where 'God Save the King' was sung with all eyes on the Royal Box. That October, their daughter Elizabeth and the Duke of

Edinburgh, left England for a tour of Canada and the USA, sailing out on the *Empress of France*. One item in the Princess's baggage was reluctantly carried abroad. It was a sealed envelope containing the Draft Accession in the event of the King's death. But that prospect receded further every day. The Queen gave a small lunch in December to celebrate the King's fifty-sixth birthday. That night at Windsor, the Queen had called in their favourite entertainers, Peter Sellers, Tony Hancock and the ventriloquist Peter Brough. The grandchildren, Charles and Anne dropped by with presents. Hugs and hearty laughter all round. 'Sunrise, sunset' goes the reflective lament from *Fiddler on the Roof*. And certainly the sun appeared to have risen now. False dawn or not, the Queen seized on the King's merriment as a good sign. And though his Christmas broadcast took two days to record, the huskiness and shortness of breath painfully evident, it was a triumph.

But a casual remark of his which she overheard, struck home. Some tactless character had suggested to him, 'Why not let the Princess read the message for you?' The King replied, 'My daughter may have her opportunity next Christmas.'

But that prospect still seemed remote as doctors, on 29 January 1952, gave the King the 'all clear'. To him, and no less to the Queen, it was another reprieve. Alone together, they made plans which included a recuperating holiday in South Africa. The following evening the family celebrated at a gala showing of *South Pacific* at the Theatre Royal, Drury Lane. It was an evening many would remember. When the National Anthem was sung, the whole cast lined up on the stage to join in. The audience stood and cheered. The King turned his head and smiled at the Queen. She squeezed his hand. It was a celebration, but also a farewell. Princess Elizabeth and the Duke of Edinburgh would fly off the following day for a tour of East Africa, Australia and New Zealand. The King saw them off at London Airport. Thousands witnessed the parting on television as the King, bareheaded though seriously ill, waved until the Princess's plane disappeared in the sky. Two days later, 5 February, he and the Queen were at Sandringham, enjoying the added treat of having the two grandchildren with them. It was a crisp, bright morning. The wind had dropped. It was a perfect day for a shoot and the King was looking forward to it. The sharp February air had brought a touch of pink to his cheeks. He looked strong enough for the Queen to feel she could let him go. She and Margaret had been invited by the local artist Edward Seago – one of her favourites – to lunch and a cruise on the river thirty miles away. The Queen was uncertain but the King pressed her and Margaret to go. When they returned in the evening the Queen found the King in good form. He had shot nine hares and a pigeon partnered by Lord Fermoy whose wife, Ruth was one of the Queen's most intimate friends and lady-in-waiting. After dinner the King and Queen sat by a radio listening to reports of the Princess's African tour. Concerned about Roddy, his golden retriever, who had picked up a thorn in his front paw, the King went out to the kennels twice during the evening to make sure the animal was in no pain. He told one of the grooms, 'Poor Roddy, he and I are both too keen on shooting for our own good. But we had a fine day, didn't we?'

Before dinner he took his three-year-old grandson Charles on his knee and told him of the famous Treetops house in East Africa where his mother and father were spending the night. The future heir is said to have suggested, 'we could have a tree-house here'. The King laughed. 'We'll see,' he said. The grandchildren were taken up to bed. The King sat for half an hour listening to Margaret playing the piano. He felt tired and kissed her goodnight. They talked for a few moments longer on the balcony. He said he thought he'd better go to bed. A valet brought him some hot chocolate. He read a magazine for an hour or so until after midnight. A watchman in the garden looked up and saw the King fastening the latch on the bedroom window. Then darkness. Sometime during the early hours of Wednesday, 6 February 1952, George VI died. Peacefully, Not the lingering, ravaging death he feared and the Queen dreaded. A swift and apparently not too painful coronary had mercifully intervened.

When Gwen Suckling, the Queen's maid brought in morning tea, Her Majesty was already awake. A moment later she was told that the equerry on duty, Commander Sir Harold Campbell needed to talk to her urgently. Instinctively, the Queen guessed that this request, so early, could only mean bad news. Campbell told her that the King was dead. She went in to see her husband, and allowed herself some momentary anguish. Bertie was gone. Her grief, she well knew, would be endless. But there were things to do at once. She went to his study and from there ordered a constant vigil outside the open bedroom door. 'The King must not be left,' she said. Observing that calm and self-control, the equerry would say afterwards, 'I never knew a woman could be so brave.'

Many women, of course, have been that brave. They would admit, however, that such courage is perilously poised. A chance comment, a glimpse at a photo or a mutually treasured object, and the floodgates open. It was that way with the Queen. Perhaps needing desperately to hug someone she went to the children's nursery. Pleased by this early visit, Prince Charles clamoured to know when grandpa was coming to play soldiers with him. The Queen could contrive no answer. Instead she clung to him more fiercely, the tears showing. 'Don't cry, Grannie,' he said.

14

When a Sovereign dies the monarchy must not drag its feet. The Throne does not function on auto-pilot. There can be no delay in the Succession. At 2.45 p.m. East Africa time, on the day of the King's death, the Duke of Edinburgh took the Princess for a stroll along the banks of the Sagana River. He told her that he had received a message from London. Her father had died in the night. Half-expecting it, the Princess nevertheless broke into tears. But her grief, unlike her mother's, would have to wait. Formalities apart, she was now the Queen of England. She and the Duke walked back to their hotel. Prescience or practicality had persuaded her to include a black outfit in her African wardrobe. She asked her maid, Bobo MacDonald, to unpack it in readiness for the flight back home. Silent crowds lined the roads as she and Philip drove to Nanyuki for their flight connection to Entebbe and then London. Meanwhile, in their apartment at the Waldorf Hotel, New York, the Duke and Duchess of Windsor contemplated this distressing second-act curtain in the drama of the Abdication. The Duke, clearly shocked, announced that he would go to the funeral, alone. He left New York on 7 February, sailing to England on the *Queen Mary*. Invited or not, the Duchess would not have wanted to risk a confrontation with Bertie's widow, now the Queen Mother.

It was a damp, blustery day when she and Margaret walked together to the church of St Mary Magdalene in the grounds of Sandringham House. Only a few days earlier the King had knelt there in a pew beside them. On 8 February, the bells tolling at St Paul's and Windsor, the new Queen attended her Accession Council. Later, she and Philip drove to Sandringham. The Queen Mother and Margaret who, respectively, had waved goodbye to a daughter and a sister, now genuflected to a Queen. Royal custom demanded the ritual Lying-in-State at Westminster Hall. The picture of the three leading mourners, Queen Mary, the Queen Mother and the Queen, all in severe, veiled black, dominated the front pages of the newspapers of the world. It is not difficult to imagine their emotions, underscored by the presence of the Duke of Windsor. Queen Mary suffered because mothers do not expect to bury sons. The Queen Mother's grief was aggravated by the bitter conviction that the King's death need not have come so early. The young Queen mourned the death of an affectionate father. But turning to the future, there must have been the subconscious thought that for her, in a sense, 'the party was over'. She had pledged in her coming of age broadcast, 'my life, long or short, will be dedicated entirely to the good of the Commonwealth'. The Constitution was now calling in its markers. It was a sudden change that would dramatically affect not only her life but Philip's and the children's too. Lord Mountbatten in his commanding yet avuncular style, played a crucial behind-the-scenes role in the young Elizabeth's transition from Princess to Queen. He understood her feelings as the massive machinery of state clanked into action around her. 'I can't think how that marriage survived this early death of the King. It was going marvellously, then suddenly he died. Philip was First Lieutenant on the *Chequers*. She came out to join him in Malta and they lived in our house for about three months. She then went home and had Princess Anne. Life was wonderful for them. They had these delightful children. They were a very happy family. And then this supreme disaster befell her when her father died at a ludicrously early age (56). She was shattered by it. She and Philip had a right to expect a minimum of ten more years – twenty more years if the King had lived to my age – instead of which she suddenly had the burden of the Sovereign thrown upon her. Prince Philip had been due to command a bigger ship. But now he couldn't. He suddenly found himself edged out because of the enormous demands being made on the new Queen. It was not done consciously. As Head of State she was involved in so many duties. He had to make his own life and I think, don't you, he has been very skilful in the way he created it.

'When the King had his operation, I thought the Queen was going to pass out. She was in despair, worried, distraught. Then he recovered. That moment she was gay, she was happy. Then the world collapsed. She had this pre-run of anticipatory misery, then the sun shone. Suddenly he died, without any warning at all. Both times caught her absolutely hard. I was in England when he died. She bore up marvellously . . . marvellously.' Part of her strength, he said, came from the support she received from the Strathmores. 'They were a large, devoted and united family. She had all her family and friends to lean on. But make no mistake, her sorrow was very grave and very deep. Yet she has never done this Queen Victoria thing, parading around that frightful public grief. I am absolutely certain she feels it now [we were speaking a quarter of a century later]. Wherever she goes, wherever she is, she misses him. When we meet it's always, "Ah Dickie, how nice to see you. You are the only person left who really knew him." She always said that. Then we start reminiscing, mostly about the amusing incidents that we shared with him. We both loved him.'

And both were there to say goodbye. In dismal weather, on Friday 15 February 1952, they saw the King's coffin on a gun carriage moving slowly along the Mall. On top lay the Imperial State Crown on a purple velvet cushion. And a wreath of white flowers, 'for my dear husband, a great and noble King'. Big Ben tolled fifty-six bells, one for each year of the King's life. Finally at Windsor, where shopkeepers had draped their windows with purple and black, the King was buried. 'The Queen was courageous,' James Cameron wrote, 'that we have been told five hundred times, but she *was*.' Courage is no cure for loneliness, however. But it reinforced the Queen Mother's determination that the painful emptiness would not show. Only her family and her most intimate friends would ever understand the depth of it. Of these friends, the late poetess Edith Sitwell and her lady-in-waiting, Ruth, Lady Fermoy, offer revealing testimony. The Queen Mother had frequently attended Edith Sitwell's poetry readings during the war. In the autumn after the King's death Edith sent her a copy of an anthology which had just been published called *A Book of Flowers*. The Queen Mother wrote to her from Scotland: 'It is giving me the greatest pleasure. I took it out with me and started to read it sitting by the river. It was a day when one felt engulfed by great black clouds of unhappiness and misery. I found a sort of peace stealing round my heart . . . I found a hope in George Herbert's poem, "who could have thought my shrivel'd heart could have recovered greenness . . ." And I thought how small and selfish is sorrow. But it bangs one about until one is senseless, and I can never thank you enough for giving me such a delicious book wherein I found so much beauty and hope, quite suddenly one day by the river.' Eloquent and graceful. Pity the strictures of the Court prevent this gifted lady from sharing more of her feelings and thoughts with a wider public. There's still time. She's only ninety.

The fact that she found hope in the anthology was precisely what the astute Edith Sitwell had intended. But the Queen Mother would need more than poetry to help her 'shrivel'd heart' recover its greenness. Ruth, Lady Fermoy, like Lord Mountbatten, was loyally on hand during the early, painful days of her widowhood: 'Why did she work so hard after the King died? Partly because, like any widow, her life was in pieces. Everything to which she had devoted herself seemed to be at an end. I worked for her at that time and because I had recently gone through the same experience I could appreciate what she was suffering. Loneliness is the hardest thing to bear, not having by you the one person to whom you can say anything and everything. This was probably worse for her because, as Queen, she had many friends but not many intimates – the reserve she had learned as Queen made her lonelier than others would otherwise have been. To resume work was the right and natural decision for her.'

Work, for this energetic fifty-one year old would be no problem. She had been raised to regard it as a virtue. In essence, her duties would be largely ceremonial as before. But now her power base had vanished at a stroke. With it went all the perks, prerogatives and regal authority she enjoyed as England's Queen. As the new Queen prepared to move to Buckingham Palace, her mother did some serious thinking. When she became the King's Consort fifteen years earlier, she had tailored that undefined job to her own liking. She would now have to engage in similar constitutional elbow-jogging as a royal widow. Officially she was the Queen Dowager, the title 'Consort' ceasing to exist on the King's death. But the term 'Dowager' had a faded-lace, over-the-hill ring to it. Not for her. Instead, she asked that she be called 'Queen Elizabeth the Queen Mother' a request which no one who valued a quiet life was about to deny her. She would remain a Queen; she would still be called 'Her Majesty' and permitted to sign herself 'Elizabeth R'. (There was a minor sacrifice. Anybody who plotted her assassination when she was Consort was guilty of treason. This no longer applied.)

In the Royal Households she is styled Queen Elizabeth, her daughter, the Queen.

In the scramble to keep the seat of the throne warm once a monarch has gone, the Court does not concern itself with the emotions of the principals involved. In effect, a daughter was – albeit unwillingly – serving an eviction order on her mother. There was always a room for her at Buckingham Palace of course. If that prospect had been floated it would have been instantly rejected by the Queen Mother. Her determination not to cramp the Queen's style; to exit quickly and let her daughter take centre stage, was entirely in character. Lord Home had been one of the many who had been impressed. 'She moved out – out of London – soon after the King died. I think she felt she did not want to get in the way of the new Queen. She supposed that living in London, so close at hand might be an embarrassment. She also believed that any popularity there might be around ought to be directed towards the Queen.'

Early in March, the Queen Mother instructed officials at the Palace to start collecting all her belongings together. It was a six-week operation, every item having to be detailed as either state or personal property. All this fussy labelling and itemizing by pin-striped officials ignored the emotional wrench all widows suffer when they have to pack up and go. But where to go – and to do what?

It was said of her late husband that he would have been only half a King without her. Without him, she must have felt equally diminished as a woman. Perhaps more so. Her strength and most vibrant influence had been as a wife. That role gone, apprehension overlaid the grief. She might have wondered like all widows on their own, whether friends would leap to accept her invitations as they had done when she was Queen. In fact from Day One of her widowhood – the beginning of a third life – friends were standing in line begging her to come over. One thing all of them knew, she would not bring a lump in the throat to the party. This refusal to give way to her feelings perturbed a royal physician. 'I wish Queen Elizabeth would break down,' he said. 'This incredible self-control will take its toll.' But the sense of loss cut so deep, her instinctive urge was to escape into a frenzy of assorted engagements. She flew to Scotland to inspect the Black Watch before it left for Korea . . . and remembered that it was in this famous regiment that her brother Fergus had been killed in 1915. A month later, offered a chance to go on the inaugural flight of a Comet, she grabbed at it. With her on the flight were Princess Margaret and Group Captain Peter Townsend. Game for anything, she took the test pilot, John Cunningham's seat at the controls. Given the go-ahead to take the aircraft into Mach optimum speed, she watched the needle creep towards the dangerous red sector. Suddenly, according to the pilot, the plane began 'porpoising', in other words hovering close to the plane's stability limits. The pilot respectfully suggested to Her Majesty that she ease the throttle back a bit. On landing the pilot admitted, 'had the porpoising gone on much longer the structural strain might have precipitated a rupture – I still shudder every time I think of that flight.'

That trip to Bordeaux and back momentarily took her mind off her problems. But while Clarence House was being prepared for her she was still obsessed with the urge to stay away from London. Friends with whom she stayed at Caithness in Scotland mentioned a dilapidated pile for sale along the coast called Barrogill Castle. A sixteenth-century stronghold with walls six feet thick, turrets, fifteen bedrooms and five bathrooms, it was steeped in history, saturated with damp and decaying with dry rot. It was built by the 4th Earl of Caithness in 1570, funded, it's believed by a grateful Mary Queen of Scots, the Earl having served on the jury which acquitted her lover Bothwell of murdering Earl Darnley. Mouldering and overgrown, prospective purchasers took one look, and ran. Exposed and wind-battered on the shore not far from John O'Groats, it offered nothing more than solitude. The Queen Mother yearned for nothing less. She bought it, restored it, furnished it, renamed it the Castle of Mey (its original title) and has joyously tramped the shores and hills around it ever since. With its two mock cannon, quiver of gnarled walking sticks in the hall, chintzes, four-posters, and a collection of shells personally scavenged by Her Majesty, it is the only really private home she has had since she was a child. The Caithness locals standing outside their slate cottages, love to catch a glimpse of her in her blue mackintosh and wellies, leaning into the freezing wind, one hand on her crumpled fishing hat. Tramping along the beach with her corgis, or a lone figure in waders fishing for salmon in the freezing waters of the Thurso river, the Queen Mother was as contented as she could ever hope to be. But this far-flung tranquillity, of spring 1953, was short-lived.

On 24 March, that ram-rod of a matriarch Queen Mary, died

at the age of eighty-seven. She had buried a husband and three sons and had remained an uncompromising though mild-natured figure to the end. She and the Queen Mother had got on well. Both were dutiful wives with the patience to cope with volatile husbands. They also shared a passionate belief that the Monarchy had to be protected always – above all from scandal. Fortuitously, Queen Mary died before the Margaret-Townsend Affair had exploded into the headlines.

A month before her sister's Coronation, Margaret had told her and her mother that she wanted to marry Group Captain Townsend. He was sixteen years older than she and was a divorcée with two sons; a love-match almost as ominous in its constitutional implications as the Edward and Mrs Simpson crisis seventeen years earlier. The Queen Mother was appalled by the affair. First, because she was convinced that it would be a marriage hamstrung by too many problems from the outset. Second, because a scandal of this magnitude at the time of the Queen's Coronation would be fatally damaging to the throne. But when she rode with Margaret to the Abbey in the glass coach, the Queen Mother hid her apprehensions behind that all-purpose, public smile. Yet she had no illusions about the strong-willed princess beside her. All the signs pointed to a confrontation which the Queen Mother knew the Crown had to win.

The most bizarre aspect of the controversial romance was the way in which the secret was blown wide open. Townsend was standing alone in the annexe of the Abbey when Princess Margaret came up to him. 'She looked superb, sparkling, ravishing,' he recalls. They chatted awhile and then Margaret innocently flicked a speck of fluff off Townsend's uniform. It was the sort of intimate, reflex action of a wife or a sweetheart, as meaningless, or significant, as onlookers cared to make it. The said onlookers included a sharp-eyed reporter, Donald Edgar. He duly reported what he saw. Never had a speck of fluff weighed so much, or travelled so far. Reports of the incident made headlines in New York after which the British Press felt free to advance. What many had suspected, speculated upon, appeared to be true. The Margaret-Townsend affair was now in the open. The Queen and her mother braced themselves for the onslaught.

In different circumstances, the Queen Mother might have regarded Peter Townsend as an ideal prospective son-in-law despite the age gap and non-royal pedigree. Tall, well-mannered, athletic, he had been a brilliant fighter pilot credited with several daring 'kills'. It was the sort of derring-do which, together with his strong profile and steady blue eyes gave him a high 'eligible bachelor' rating. In 1941 (Margaret was eleven) he met a brigadier's daughter, Rosemary Pawle. They married in July of that year after a two weeks' courtship. It was the familiar wartime scenario; handsome young fighter pilot, life-expectation minimal, seizes whatever happiness fate offers before zooming away into the clouds, plucky wife waving proudly through her tears. Townsend was one of the luckier of the 'Few'. He survived, his known bravery and agreeable manner steering him into influential quarters. He was introduced to George VI who was looking for an equerry. Convention required applicants to be impeccable types from the aristocracy. The King ignored the rules. Moreover Townsend seemed a discreet character behind the 'air ace' charisma. Their first conversation disclosed an added and decisive qualification. Townsend stammered. The rest of the applicants knew when they were beaten. Group Captain Peter Townsend, DSO, DFC, moved into the Palace and proved to be a piece of perfect casting. He was not only a highly efficient courtier. He managed skilfully to keep the sometimes irascible monarch off the boil for which the Consort was eternally grateful. She may well have identified herself with the King who said once, 'I'd have liked to have had a son like Townsend.'

He was good to have around, particularly on the South African Tour of 1947 with Princess Elizabeth pining for Philip and Margaret a capricious adolescent. She and Townsend danced, walked, talked, and went riding together. Margaret was seventeen, smoked cigarettes from a tortoiseshell holder, and splashed herself with Schiaparelli's 'Shocking' perfume. Riding into the sunset over the Zambesi, standing silently together by the Victoria Falls; whether Townsend was aware of it or not, the Princess found the handsome equerry more exciting than she dared admit. But the King and Queen would not have had the slightest notion of a 'situation' in the making. What they might have observed a year or so later, was their daughter's growing disenchantment with characters who would later be identified as 'The Princess Margaret Set'. This included a cluster of Earls and old Etonians representing a sizeable chunk of the nation's private wealth. The Earl of Dalkeith, the Duke of Buccleuch, Lord

Porchester, Billy Wallace, 'Sonny' Blandford, Colin Tennant, the Hon. Peter Ward (plus the late Peter Sellers as 'Court Jester') – the 'Set' giggled its way around those exclusive night haunts, the '400', Les Ambassadeurs and the Embassy Club. But when the King died, Margaret missed her father dreadfully, and tired of that sport. With her sister now Queen, Prince Charles the next in line, she was in limbo, out in the cold. And in love with a man who, subconsciously at least, she must have seen as a strong, reliable father-figure. As for Townsend's feelings towards Margaret: 'She was a girl of unusual, intense beauty . . . centred about large, purple-blue eyes, generous sensitive lips, and a complexion as smooth as a peach. She was coquettish, sophisticated, generous, volatile, attractive and lovable; behind the dazzling façade a rare softness and sincerity.' These are the bedazzled Group Captain's own words from his autobiography, *Time and Chance*. He goes on: 'I was but one of many to be so moved. There were dozens of others.'

In December 1952, two months before the King died, Peter Townsend divorced his wife Rosemary. He cited the banker John de Laszlo, son of the artist whose fairy-tale portrait of the Queen Mother remains the most popular. With Townsend free, Margaret raised the temperature of the romance. Her sister the Queen was ambivalent, wanting Margaret to be happy but not if it meant rocking the royal boat. The Queen Mother was less pragmatic. The idea was unthinkable. The issue became polarized as it had with Edward and Mrs Simpson: the Crown on the one hand, an ill-fated love affair on the other. The impasse hardened Margaret's sense of isolation. The birth of Prince Charles had edged her even further out of the royal reckoning. There was another subtle demotion. She was voted off the Regency Council. This parliamentary manoeuvre was hustled through the Commons once the danger of Margaret marrying a commoner emerged. She would soon be twenty-five, at which age she no longer required the Queen's permission to marry. There were compelling reasons for believing that Margaret and Peter Townsend were prepared to sit it out until then. But for her to marry a commoner and remain on the Regency Council – especially if the Queen died prematurely before her children came of age – would be constitutionally intolerable. Philip, and the Queen Mother, were placed on the Regency Council and Margaret was even further out in the cold.

Caring mothers tend to blame themselves if their daughters'

lives sail into rough waters. Maybe the King, who spoiled her, and the Queen Mother, who indulged her, were partly responsible. But how much of this spoiling was compensation for the brusque way in which Margaret had been squeezed out of the picture? As the Queen Mother saw it, here was her daughter in her early twenties with no role, little status, her self-esteem taking a beating. And in love with a man she could never marry. Queen Elizabeth was a strict observer of the rules but she was still a mother, as Townsend confirms: 'The Queen Mother listened with characteristic understanding . . . without a sign that she felt angered or outraged . . . or that she acquiesced. She was never anything but considerate in her attitude to me. Indeed she never once hurt either of us throughout the whole difficult affair.'

But all the Queen Mother's sympathy could not stop the avalanche which followed this broadside in the *People*: 'It is high time for the British public to be made aware of the fact that newspapers in Europe and America are openly asserting that the Princess is in love with a divorced man. It is quite unthinkable that a royal princess . . . should ever contemplate a marriage with a man who has been through the divorce courts.'

Winston Churchill, who initially had backed the wrong horse in the Edward and Mrs Simpson Affair, was not about to repeat his mistake. Townsend suddenly found himself posted as air attaché in Brussels (an echo of James Stuart's 'banishment' to Oklahoma). Before that abrupt posting, Townsend had been the Queen Mother's Comptroller at Clarence House. He said 'goodbye' to her. Then tactfully, she left the room, so that he could have a few minutes alone with Margaret. In the same month, the Queen Mother and the unhappy Princess left for a tour of Southern Rhodesia and Uganda. The couple's separation was swift, brutal, but effective. There was a request which was granted instantly. Margaret and Peter could phone, and write to each other, but actual contact was forbidden. Meanwhile Margaret made a public show of renewing old acquaintances with Billy Wallace, Peter Ward and the rest. But the atmosphere in Clarence House was heavy with Margaret's moods which swung from indignation to anguish. The Queen Mother, still desperately missing the King, had to put those feelings aside in order to cope with the problem.

If she did not 'throw the book' at her daughter as some say she should have done it was because she recognized that Margaret had a legitimate grievance. When the question of her marrying Townsend was first raised with senior officers of the Court, the Princess was given clear signs that once the Coronation was over, a way might be found for her and Townsend to marry. It was this encouraging nod which made her pursue what manifestly was a doomed relationship. But there was still room for some sensitive, cloak-and-dagger support from the Queen Mother.

When she heard that Townsend was in London on a brief visit, the Queen Mother invited him for tea. And since Margaret also lived at Clarence House, it would not just be tea for two. Peter would not go straight to Clarence House. He would go to Harrods' Book Department. At a pre-arranged section of it – we do not know whether it was 'Romances' or 'Constitutional History' – Townsend would be joined by Sir Norman Gwatkin from the Lord Chamberlain's office. Both men would then drive, in Gwatkin's car, to Clarence House. The plan worked perfectly. The three sat down to tea, the Queen Mother pouring. She decided not to linger over the buttered scones, and left the couple on their own. Despite all the clandestine planning, news of the meeting filtered out. A headline in New York juicily announced, 'Meg Sips Tea with Peter, Mom Makes It A Crowd'.

By October 1955, all Britain's newspapers were screeching into the act, with Church leaders delivering further fusillades from the pulpit. The Queen Mother spelled out the situation to the two beleagured parties. There was a meeting at Clarence House on Tuesday, 25 October. Margaret and Townsend had a long talk then finally conceded the battle. The following day the Princess called on the Archbishop of Canterbury at Lambeth Palace to tell him what he had prayed to hear: she had made up her mind not to marry the Group Captain. Announcing this on Monday, 31 October, the Princess continued with the mandatory humility: 'Mindful of the Church's teaching . . . and conscious of my duty to the Commonwealth, I have resolved to put these considerations before any others. I have reached this decision entirely alone, and in doing so I have been strengthened by the unfailing support and devotion of Group Captain Townsend . . .' On the face of it, a total, and unconditional surrender: two people in love, sacrificed on the triple altars of the Church, the Crown, and the Establishment.

But long afterwards, when asked by one of her closest friends why she and Townsend had not gone through with it, Margaret's reply, according to Nigel Dempster, was a crisp, astonishing, 'He didn't want to.'

15

Coping with Princess Margaret's post-Townsend dejection could not have been easy for the Queen Mother. But one published comment suggesting that 'the broken romance added to the sorrow of her widowhood' is hard to accept. There was no additional sorrow over a love affair of which she herself disapproved. It was all over now, and though the Queen Mother was sympathetic, she held the view that good or bad, one has to get on with life. Her own remedy for bouts of heartache or despair is to work, or walk them off. Her friend Ruth, Lady Fermoy has seen that therapy in operation. 'In the years I have known her – since 1931 – the Queen Mother has suffered many sorrows and tragedies. It seems to me that she prefers to confront them alone. She loves taking her two corgis (currently Ranger and Dash) out with her several times a day when she's in the country. And I feel somehow that those walks are not only good for her health. She uses them to work things out. Also she has this amazing ability to cope with any situation. It may sound impossible to believe but it is what I have seen myself. When there has been some unpleasantness or a very tricky situation which either affected herself or someone near to her, she has this capacity to deal with it. I have never seen it fail.'

This flair for exorcising her sorrows in a long tramp with the corgis, is crucial to this mettlesome widow. Old campaigners remember being danced into near-exhaustion or forced to walk until they dropped, their jaunty tormentor always a yard or two ahead. Lord Home was an early sufferer. A thin, stooping near-ninety year old himself, reminiscing about the Queen Mother brought smiles and a touch of colour to his lordship's tightly-drawn features. 'The old Queen Mary had total dignity but she was not accessible to the crowd. The Queen Mother also has this dignity but when she gets among people she has that irresistible quality that lifts everybody up.'

Lord Home remembers well her tireless penchant for walking and dancing – and the fact that no one could keep up. But he must have preferred that to the Queen Mother's charades, a delight to her and the family, but a self-conscious ritual to a couple of distinguished but less sporting guests. They did not object to Elizabeth dressing up as Charlie Chaplin, moustache included, but felt that goose-stepping in as Hitler went beyond their official brief. That aside, an invitation to join the Queen Mother's house party at the Castle of Mey was a rare and prized opportunity. 'Riotous' was the general descriptive of those royal shindigs. And not surprising since Her Majesty was a zesty, unflagging, irrepressible widow of sixty at the time. She liked having young people around her; a past or present equerry, Bowes-Lyon nieces and nephews, ex-Eton schoolchums of David's, as long as they would 'muck in' and not object to a brisk walk to the top of a mountain and back. The days would be spent mackerel fishing, catching crabs, or taking picnics a mile or two's stroll into the country. The Queen Mother's delight in these al fresco blow-outs suggests an image of a royal home-maker in frilly apron, and rolled-up sleeves, toiling ecstatically over a hot stove or an outdoor barbecue. That image is tempting but wrong. According to Lord Mountbatten who was permanently on her list of chosen guests, 'I have never known her cook. The cooks are Prince Philip (the chef), Princess Anne (the kitchen-maid), and the Queen as a kind of scullery-maid. Princess Anne is at least allowed to cook the sausages. What the Queen does is, she hands up the dishes, serves it around – then the Queen Mother comes in and takes her food.' Well, she has, as they say, paid her dues. I imagine the aforementioned chef, scullery-maid, and kitchen-maid would like to be dishing it out to the lady at least until the end of her century.

But if she disdained to cook the supper, Her Majesty was always eager to sing for it. Her tastes in music go from Gershwin to Bach; 'Daisy Daisy' to the songs of Benjamin Britten. But she can take or leave flamenco. Fidgeting at the sight of a Spaniard clacking the floor with his heels, she murmured to her companion, 'can we turn the hose on him?' Ruth, Lady Fermoy, who sacrificed a promising career as a concert pianist for marriage, has firsthand knowledge of the Queen Mother's passion for music. 'She became patron of the first King's Lynn Festival with which I was associated. It was a great success and she sent me a telegram from Scotland: "Do let's have another festival if you can bear it!" It showed she had a real interest in it. Her musical tastes go from Olde Time Music Hall to Mozart. She has an incredible memory for some of the musical comedy songs she heard when she was young. She knows the verses of "If You Were The Only Girl In the World", "Blue Skies" and all the good tunes by Noel Coward and Cole Porter. She knows, oh so many of the songs Harry Lauder used to sing.' She hesitated, wondering perhaps whether she was betraying a confidence, the ultimate sin in the Queen Mother's canon. But then she smiled. 'I don't think this would be indiscreet . . . it's nothing at all . . . it's merely that often at the end of quite a tiring day or after some event, she would usually start singing something, then she does the verses, and the lady-in-waiting joins in. She loves a sing-song around the piano. The guests whoever they might be gather round, she's the sort of leader, and we'd sing all kinds of things. She has,' said this one-time student of Cortot's, 'perfect pitch. It's still such a young voice and absolutely in tune.'

Admittedly, the Queen Mother will sit hands clasped, teeth clenched, through Stockhausen or a hectic Elizabethan madrigal on behalf of some needy cause. But I suspect that among her eight Desert Island Discs 'Dolly Gray' and 'Let's All Go Down the Strand' will brazen it out with Beethoven, Bach and Brahms. One of the perks of royalty is having musicians over to the house to play (the way Mozart cut his musical milk teeth). 'She loves it when somebody comes and plays in her own home,' Ruth, Lady Fermoy, said. 'I'm thinking more of amateurs rather than professionals. It's informal, and she enjoys encouraging them.

'Benjamin Britten once made a very interesting remark to me. The Queen Mother goes to the Aldeburgh Festival on many occasions. Britten was a composer and musician of the highest order and not given to saying nice things about people unless he really meant it. He said of her, "She is quite extraordinary because you know, and I know, that she has had little formal musical training. But on no occasion have I ever heard her say anything that isn't very perceptive and sensitive in her reactions to what she has heard."' That sensitivity would involve Britten personally years later. Virtually a dying man, he wanted to compose a piece of music as a gift to the Queen Mother on her seventy-fifth birthday. He had chosen one of Burns' poems for his friend Peter Pears to sing as part of the birthday recital. The performance was given in Lady Fermoy's house in Norfolk.

'The Queen, Princess Margaret, and the Queen Mother arrived,' Lady Fermoy said. 'Then Benjamin Britten came with his nurse. He was already a very sick man. The performance was memorable and terribly touching, because of the music itself, and also because it was painfully evident that this extraordinary genius was so very ill and obviously not meant to live much longer . . . I could cry about it now. I have never forgotten the way he looked at the Queen Mother as he said "goodbye".'

Peter Pears would remember that parting too, and seeing tears in the Queen Mother's eyes as he sang a Schumann love song. Afterwards he wrote, 'It was awfully touching on that birthday. Ben was obviously very moved. As we were leaving he asked, "Ma'am, may I kiss you?" and he touched her cheek.' Britten died ten days later.

The Queen Mother loved to have the grandchildren to herself. Exercising the indulgent prerogative of a grandparent, she shovelled chocolate cake into the boy prince, and selected party frocks for the younger princess. There has always been a special intimacy between Prince Charles and his grandmother. It was forged early on when, first during the illness of George V, and later when the new Queen and Philip had overseas commitments, she played a key role in the infant's upbringing. If she had had her way it is unlikely that her sensitive, artistic grandson would have gone to his father's old school, Gordonstoun. The regime at this renowned establishment isolated as it is on the north-east coast of Scotland, perfectly reflects its motto, '*Plus est en vous*' (There Is More In You). Pupils are encouraged to find that last extra effort to prove they are capable of more than they realize. But the Queen Mother believed in Eton which aims at the same goal but by a less aggressive route. Having Charles to herself for long periods the Queen Mother saw and admired the sensitivity which others mistook for weakness. She knew that he did not need to make a frenzied leap from one Scottish crag to another to prove his manhood. As with most grandmothers, distance was no object when it concerned her schoolboy grandson. She happily travelled between London and Scotland. Stuffing him with toffees in the back of her royal limousine – where the Queen couldn't see them – was a perk no royal command would take away from her. She sent her equerry to Hamley's toy store to buy a load of magic tricks. If he is the only heir to the British throne who can apparently pass five coins right through the palm of his hand he has George VI's widow to thank for it. She lunched him and his schoolchums in her special coach on the royal train, recording the scene on her cine-camera. When he had whooping cough she hovered anxiously over him with cough lozenges in her handbag. His appendicitis made her cancel all her engagements. His interest in the cello caused her to flex her fingers again on the piano so that she could accompany him.

But there has always been more than grandmotherly adoration in her relationship with Charles. She likes his style and approves of his vision of a better-looking Britain. If one day he acquits himself well as a King, this wise and concerned grannie ought to appear somewhere in the credits. Given the average grandmother's right to speak, the Queen Mother could offer an intimate and informative profile of the future monarch. Similarly, her verdict on the Duchess of Windsor might clear up some of the overworked myths and misconceptions. But for these thoughts and feelings we will have to wait for the publication of her diaries, probably in the next century.

What, for instance, would she say of her nephew Timothy Bowes-Lyon, the 16th Earl of Strathmore? This unfortunate second son – his brother John Patrick was killed in action in 1941 – had been a problem Bowes-Lyon almost from his schooldays. He left Stowe school with a reputation for chasing after the dormitory maids, and an early interest in hard drinking. This latter diversion became an addiction when he was hit by family tragedies. He succeeded to the Earldom in 1949. In the bachelor years that followed he became an alcoholic and an epileptic. It was at the clinic where he went to 'dry-out' that he fell in love with Mary Brennan, a nurse there. They married in June 1958. She became the Countess of Strathmore. There is no record of the Queen Mother, or any other Bowes-Lyon of note, attending the wedding. Not long after, a newspaper discovered Mary's father, Peter Brennan, working as a steward behind the bar of a Leicester club. The daughter the Countess bore in 1959, died at Glamis three weeks later. The Countess committed suicide eight years later. She was one of the Strathmores few, if any in the family, cared to talk about. Least of all its most prestigious member.

Whatever her private emotions about the Timothy Bowes-Lyon tragedy, the Queen Mother's several preoccupations must have muted their effect. The Queen, thrown in at the deep end herself, was more than grateful to have a mother who actually enjoyed the planting, conferring, stone-laying, launching, signing, and unveiling that comes with the royal package. It is not merely that she has carried out this grindingly repetitive routine for much longer than your average stoic could endure. She does the job well. The press clippings held on her by newspapers are of Himalayan proportions. No ordinary file could handle them. They are listed under: Army (Colonel in Chief twenty-five regiments); Art and Artists (sponsorship, encouragement of); The Blind; British Legion; Chelsea Pensioners; Darts (charity); Dogs; Education; Empire; Youth Sunday; Evacuees (World War Two); Exhibitions; Flags; Flying (Helicopter, Concorde); Girl Guides; Health (hospital visits etc.); Housing; Motherhood Safer Campaign; Opera; Parliament; St John's Ambulance; Toc H; 1939–45; Air Raids; Armaments; American troops (visits); Canteens; Civil Defence; Merchant Navy; Nursery Schools; WVS; Red Cross – and this merely covered the first twenty years.

Considering that she would carry on like this into her eighties – and after a couple of major operations – it raises the question: how does she do it? One clue she gave to Michael Foot, the veteran Labour politician, was this: 'When you get as old as I am you have a great inclination to have little sleeps all the time, short catnaps. Don't do it. You must keep going!'

The Queen Mother's trip to the USA in 1954 to receive the proceeds of the fund honouring George VI had her being voted by one of the New York tabloids, 'Queen of All Hearts'. She stopped the traffic on Fifth Avenue; caused a near riot in Saks Department Store, salesgirls and customers stampeding on all floors. She was introduced to Senator McCarthy and Richard Nixon at the British Embassy in Washington. (Having shaken hands with her, the discredited Senator muttered, 'She's sharp!') The Eisenhowers played host to her and were royally smitten. Columbia University conferred an honorary Doctor of Laws Degree and had her blushing at the citation: 'This noble Queen whose quiet and constant courage . . . sustained a nation and inspired a world.' But she blushed redder at this unsolicited accolade from a New York taxi driver which Cecil Beaton overheard: 'If she wasn't a Queen there's many a man who'd like to marry her. She'd be a pleasing handful at playtime.'

Zimbabwe, Zambia, Malawi (they were not so called at the time); Montreal, Vancouver, Honolulu, and Fiji . . . Cocos, Mauritius, Uganda, Malta, Rome, Paris. In the run-up to her sixtieth birthday the peripatetic grandmother happily became the first member of the royal family to fly round the world. Anti-royalists argue that the entire ritual of sending our royals to smile, wave and shake hands around the world, is irrelevant and a waste of money. At the most sanguine, it was 'nice work if you can get it'. 'Royal Soap Opera' was how Malcolm Muggeridge once described it. That jibe was a pin-prick compared with the broadside which exploded into print on the eve of the Queen Mother's fifty-seventh birthday. The author was a young and controversial peer Lord Altringham, editor and owner of the *National and English Review*. He published a piece which excoriated the Queen's entourage, 'the tweedy sort . . . a tight little enclave of English ladies and gentlemen'. He dismissed the Queen's style of speaking as 'a pain in the neck; like her mother, she appears to be unable to string even a few sentences together without a text. The personality conveyed by the utterances which are put into her mouth is that of a priggish schoolgirl, captain of the hockey team, a prefect and a recent candidate for Confirmation.' Appearing over an August Bank Holiday weekend when hard news is scarce, this juicy coconut was lavishly milked by the national press. The elderly Lord Strathmore was shocked. 'Young Altringham is a bounder,' he declared, the ultimate condemnation by one peer of another. Altringham did not endear himself to the Queen nor to the Queen Mother who was understandably furious. Years later both he and Muggeridge would rethink if not eat their words. The Queen Mother may not have converted them, but she continued to astound them. The ultimate penitent, as we shall see, will be Mr Willie Hamilton MP, Castigator Royal to the Monarchy.

Attacks on royalty in general do not disturb the Queen Mother's sleep. Malicious or mischievous gossip about individual members are another matter. Mud must not be seen to stick. Only once did she lose her temper with the Press. It happened while she was touring Rhodesia and Nyasaland in 1960. A story in the *New York Daily News*, picked up in Africa, suggested that the Queen Mother was thinking of marrying again. It identified the prospective bridegroom as her seventy-four-year-old Treasurer Sir Arthur Penn. A couple of British newspapers ran the item though they must have known it to be totally absurd. She ordered Colin Black, her Press Officer on the tour to tell the reporters that the story was 'complete and absolute nonsense'. 'That's her last word on the subject,' Black said, though he indicated Her Majesty hadn't been so regal in the language she used.

She returned to England to a more benign piece of news. Princess Margaret had fallen in love with a gifted photographer named Anthony Armstrong-Jones. The Queen Mother was probably running out of soothing antidotes for a failed love-affair. She was delighted to see Margaret shining-eyed and smiling at last.

Anthony Charles Robert Armstrong-Jones entered the inner circles of royalty at the right time and with the right credentials. Most of the attacks on the monarchy as it moved into the sixties were aimed at its stuffiness, snobbery, and in-built class distinction. Easy to blame the leading performers, but wrong. A family business which has functioned triumphantly for a thousand years cannot suddenly change the merchandise or its style. But it can get dangerously out of touch. And the Queen Mother was one of the first to acknowledge this. She is said to have named 'Mrs Dale's Diary' as her favourite radio programme, explaining, 'I try never to miss it because it is the only way of knowing what goes on in a middle-class family.' (Years later a couple of her hard-working grandchildren, Charles and Anne, proved there were other ways to get to know the people.) The Townsend affair which washed a fair amount of royal linen in public, gave the monarchy an implacably fossilized image – and Palace advisers much to think about. At the same time that the Beatles swept in the 1960s, Tony Armstrong-Jones did likewise with the Royal Family. They were glad to have him aboard.

As a commoner and therefore an 'outsider', he was bound to get the Queen Mother's endorsement as a prospective son-in-law. She had also entered the 'royal enclosure' without the required blue-blooded pedigree. A photographer, with a studio converted from an ironmonger's shop in Pimlico, next to the Sunlight laundry, Armstrong-Jones was born to inherit more talent than money. His father was a successful QC, his uncle, Oliver Messel, the distinguished stage designer. That talent was not immediately evident. His prep-school headmaster, unable to discern it, hedged his bet with, 'Armstrong-Jones may be good at something but it's nothing we teach here'. Tony left Cambridge without qualifying as an architect, but with an intuitive skill behind a camera. He took a six-month apprenticeship with the famous photographer Baron. It confirmed his skills but more valuably, jostled him around influential company. Nevertheless it was his photographs not social leverage which brought his first royal commission – to take the official eighth-birthday portrait of Prince Charles. This pleased the Queen sufficiently to have him take the whole family group. He went to the Palace and, refreshingly underawed, he had the Queen and the rest smiling easily into his lens. The Queen Mother warmed towards this agreeable chap with his questioning eyebrows over a broad, toothy smile. Margaret, who'd met him socially at a friend's dinner party in Cheyne Walk, was attracted to him for other reasons. He treated her as a woman who just happened at the time, to be fourth in line to the throne. He changed her lifestyle dramatically. No other heir to the throne would be seen in heavy goggles and motorcycle gear on the back of a 500cc Ensign.

No need to reprise in detail the sequence of events which brought these two frisky, independent lovers to the altar at Westminster Abbey. The Queen Mother's role in the affair, however, was intriguing. With the Townsend debacle still haunting Clarence House, she and the Queen were concerned that Margaret shouldn't have to suffer another traumatic disappointment. The Queen Mother saw qualities in Tony which she believed would 'tame' the rebellious side to Margaret's nature while increasing her self-esteem. She engaged in a benevolent conspiracy which enabled the pair to meet without being keyholed by the press. He arrived several times at Royal Lodge at her invitation, loaded with camera equipment on the pretence of taking royal portraits. Whatever else he may have engaged in at the Lodge, it wasn't taking pictures. Similar 'arrangements' were made at Balmoral and at Sandringham with the Queen a happy and willing 'conspirator'. The object of the clandestine encounters was plainly to head off gossip and allow the couple time to be sure about their relationship. When not being spirited into royal households, the couple used the homes of mutual friends. Billy Wallace let them have the run of his house in South Street, Mayfair. 'I used to go round to Tony's studio in Pimlico' the Princess is quoted as saying, 'but we thought it safer to use other people's houses.'

One trysting place (which might have been Tutankhamen's Tomb by the sensation its discovery caused) was the ground floor of a nondescript house in Rotherhithe, se16 where the couple shared a lavatory with the landlord. (Some time during the romance, with Tony and Margaret elsewhere, the Queen Mother couldn't resist being chauffeured over to have a secret peek at the place.) Just before Christmas 1959, Tony was certain enough to give Margaret an engagement ring, a ruby set in gold and surrounded by diamonds in the shape of a flower. But the couple were asked to defer any announcement. There was another happy event pending. The Queen was expecting her third child. It was decided to wait until after the infant (Andrew) was born. He arrived on 19 February 1960. A week later the Court Circular announced: 'It is with the greatest pleasure that Queen Elizabeth the Queen Mother announces the betrothal of her beloved daughter the Princess Margaret to Mr Anthony Charles Robert Armstrong-Jones, son of Mr R. O. C. Armstrong-Jones QC and the Countess of Rosse, to which union the Queen has gladly given her consent.' For once the Court Circular had hit it on the nail. The Queen Mother certainly had the 'greatest pleasure', and the Queen could not have been 'gladder'. Both must also have been mighty relieved.

Tony and Margaret were married in Westminster Abbey on 6 May 1960. The post-nuptial euphoria evaporated swiftly as MPs argued angrily about the use of the royal yacht *Britannia* for the couple's six-week Caribbean honeymoon. But the Queen Mother, a veteran at handling these attacks, advised Tony to ignore them. Taking up residence at Kensington Palace, the newly created Lord Snowdon laid down the ground rules. He was going to carry on with his job, regardless. Lunching with him there once, I detected signs of a man tailoring his royal connections to his lifestyle, not the other way round. He had highbrow books; lowbrow pop records; pictures and pottery by Snowdon; a packet of anti-smoking pills alongside a carton of cigarettes; his portraits of Stravinsky and J. B. Priestley with a photo of Andy Williams defiantly pinned up by his secretary, Dorothy. Lunch was sandwiches and bottles of Guinness. The conversation was mainly about his work which he refuses, unlike others, to elevate to the level of an art form. He emphasized the demarcation line between his work and Margaret's. He steered clear of her activities as she did of his. 'When I am working I have to be left strictly alone. This is a part of my life I could never give up.' With hindsight, he might have added, 'whatever else has to go'.

No hint then of trouble ahead. Which was just as well for the Queen Mother. Tranquillity is the vital component of her existence. She avoids controversy. And though she will do everything she can for the sick and the maimed, she prefers (according to Dorothy Laird) to be comfortably distanced from them. 'She has an instinctive abhorrence of disease and maiming . . . [but] this dislike has never made her shrink from doing far more than her duty.' She insisted, for instance, on seeing men badly wounded or horribly disfigured in the Second World War just as she had done as a teenager in 1915 for the casualties convalescing at Glamis. However, though sensitive towards other people's injuries, the Queen Mother has always been stoical about her own. The sixties were her bad years for mishaps. She injured her hip stumbling in a paddock. In 1961 at a houseparty at Ascot she fell and cracked a small bone in her foot. (Friends have tried to persuade her not to teeter around on stiletto heels for these occasions. But minor fractures, she feels are a small price to pay for being smartly shod, and walking tall.) The injured foot did not deter her from continuing with the launching of the liner *Northern Star* at Tyneside, 'even if it requires a wheelchair or stretcher party'. It did require a wheelchair, but she sat in it smiling sweetly, her left foot in a surgical boot, the right one in a stilettoed number by the royal cobbler, Edward Rayne. But when someone whispered that the crowds couldn't see her she got out of the chair and hobbled down the ramp. A year later she fell again, this time at Birkhall, breaking the same bone in the same foot. Then she went into the King Edward VII Hospital in 1964 to have her appendix out. Only hours after she was sitting up in bed, cheerful as ever, receiving friends and checking the day's runners with Sir Martin Gilliatt. While she was being operated on, the Duchess of Windsor was having a facial operation a street or two away at the London Clinic. No messages or flowers were exchanged.

Somewhere in between the Queen Mother's setback she celebrated her silver anniversary as Colonel-in-Chief of the Black Watch at a regimental march past in Perth: she flew to Canada for the same regiment's centenary there; she flew to Tunisia, went from Tunis to La Marsa, saw the ruins of

Carthage and the holy city of Kairouan, then stood alone at the Commonwealth war cemeteries at Medjez el Bab and Enfidaville.

There were several commitments in between. Her doctors advised her to take it easy. She advised them not to fret, but compromised by taking a short Caribbean convalescence – visiting Jamaica, Antigua, Tortola, the Virgin Islands, St Kitts and Nevis, Montserrat, Dominica, St Lucia, St Vincent, Grenada, Trinidad and Tobago, and Barbados. She bought a straw hat off a stall and sang a calypso with the local steel band.

She flew back to London to keep in touch with the 312 organizations of which she is either President or Patron. The range is wide: from Master of the Bench of the Middle Temple to the Dachsund Club; from Colonel-in-Chief of eighteen regiments to Lady of the Order of the Garter. She had then, and astonishingly seems to have now, an energy source which ought to be hooked to the national grid. 'I know nobody of her age,' Lady Fermoy said to me last year, 'who can read without glasses, hears everything, has a very light step, a very young voice, and doesn't behave or walk like an elderly person.'

Not bad for a woman born when Queen Victoria was still alive if not kicking. But few would have wagered on her surviving as a robust ninety year old after the emergency abdominal operation she had on 10 December 1966. She had gone into the King Edward VII Hospital for Officers with an overnight bag for a routine check-up. The Queen and the rest of the family fully expected her to be in fine fettle for Christmas, doing her magic and singing at the piano. A huddle of eminent specialists soon disposed of that hope. They ordered an immediate operation to 'relieve a partial obstruction of the abdomen'. This is a serious operation at any time. For a woman of sixty-six it is more hazardous still. But being, to quote a friend, 'as tough as old boots', the operation was a total success. More than two hundred letters a day were delivered to the hospital. Telegrams, flowers, perfume and other gifts were sent by strangers as well as friends. And dozens of boxes of chocolates, the Queen Mother having mentioned her weakness for eating them in bed while reading poetry. (On hearing about her sister-in-law's abdominal operation the Duchess of Windsor is reported to have quipped with exquisite bitchery, 'it must have been all those chocolates!')

The term 'abdominal operation' can cover a variety of distressing conditions. In the absence of precise clinical details some writers have sailed into lurid speculation about the nature of the operation, much to the annoyance of the patient herself. I doubt if this account of the Life and Times of the Queen Mother suffers unduly by not adding to the speculation. However, it *was* a major operation with a slow and painful return to a full recovery. It made her subsequent globe-trotting, climbing those steep steps to airplanes and interminable standing around in the service of the Crown, all the more impressive. Clearly there must have been moments when she could have complained of far more than just, 'my feet are killing me'.

She spent her Christmas and New Year in hospital. Nurses lost count of the cards and the gifts. One afternoon a staff nurse heard a shriek and ran to her room. Her Majesty, watching racing on TV had seen one of her horses win at Sandown Park.

16

Just how serious the Queen Mother's illness had been was evident in the way she looked on leaving the hospital in the New Year, 1967. She was pale and thin, and the weight loss was unmistakable. It had obviously been a more threatening operation than either she, or the doctors were prepared to reveal. It would take more than weeks for her to swing back to normal. But there were always grandchildren on hand to pep up her convalescence, the Snowdons' contribution being Viscount Linley now five, and Sarah Armstrong-Jones, two. Tony and Margaret appeared to be settling into their version of a contented married life: eccentric, volatile, more Kings Road than Constitution Hill. Tony had acquired a couple of hints from Philip, like walking respectfully behind the Princess with his hands clasped behind his back. It was not a role Snowdon would perform without clenched teeth. From my personal knowledge of him, he is not a two-paces-behind kind of individual. The casual good humour is laced with occasional cussedness. He may be a rebel, but rarely without a cause. The documentary films he has made are good indicators: *Don't Count the Candles* highlighting the problems of old age; *Born to be Small* about society's inhuman attitude towards dwarfism; and *Love of a Kind*, ostensibly a comedy about people and their pets, but touching on the loneliness often beneath the surface. His relentless campaigning for more adaptable wheelchairs and facilities for the disabled is well known. Struck down with polio at an early age, disability is not just a word to him.

While all this endeared him further to the Queen Mother, it was bound to distance him from the royal rituals by which Margaret was obliged to earn her keep. His exacting work as a professional photographer with its round-the-world commitments, could never dovetail easily into the meticulous framework of a royal marriage. He must have staked out his territorial claims from the outset. All the essential ingredients existed then for the passion and pyrotechnics which would dominate the style, and the sound-track, of their marriage. By 1967, the gossip writers had their knives out hinting at a rift with Snowdon angrily denying it. As usual, Elizabeth listened but did not lecture. There was no doubt however that she was worried. The Townsend Affair had dragged the Royal Family into the public arena. The Queen Mother, and the Queen, would not have been slow to remind Margaret of it. Bickering in private was one thing. Having the spats sourly chewed over in the gossip columns went down badly with the Palace, worse at Clarence House.

In early June, the Queen Mother had other uneasy thoughts on her mind. The Queen had invited the Duke and Duchess of Windsor to London for the unveiling of a memorial wall plaque to Queen Mary at Marlborough House. This was the first official nod from the Royal Family that Wallis had received in thirty years. It may have been the right gesture but Elizabeth scarcely relished coming face to face with 'that woman'. Thirty years had not softened the enmity. But both protagonists were in no mood to reprise it. When it came to a display of icy decorum neither one could learn anything from the other. But the tension was there as a crowd of five thousand cheered the Queen Mother out of her maroon Rolls-Royce. The stage was set for the confrontation between two mutually-accusing sisters-in-law under the chestnut trees in Pall Mall. Any hostility the Queen Mother may have felt faded at the sight of the Duke and Duchess. Both looked pathetically frail. The Duke, a pouch-eyed, stooping figure, seemed much older than his age, almost seventy-three. The Duchess, nearly seventy, was thin and ashen-faced. Only the faintest echo here of the love-affair that lost a throne. By coincidence, the band of the Goldstream Guards had stopped playing. What followed occurred in total silence. The Queen, unsmiling, walked briskly over to the uncle she had last met fourteen years earlier at Queen Mary's funeral. He bowed. The Duchess curtsied. The Queen Mother joined them. She and David exchanged brief courtesy kisses. Then the two leading women in the drama faced each other with chilled smiles. Her Majesty the Queen Mother was entitled by protocol to receive a curtsey from Wallis. It was pointedly not forth-coming. According to one of her friends, the Duchess com-mented afterwards, 'She stopped people from curtseying to me, why should I curtsey to her?'

True or not, the omission would not have unduly bothered the Queen Mother. She hardly expected any genuflections from Wallis. As the authors of the *The Windsor Story* expressed it, 'In the Duchess's private demonology the Queen Mother was Grand Diabolarch and would remain so.' Elizabeth had no such private demons. She bore more grief than malice. And maybe even pitied this forlorn couple who had drifted aimlessly through the years on the shallow waters of celebrity. The ceremony lasted a little more than five minutes. The Queen Mother was glad to get back to Clarence House.

Later that year, her elder sister Rose, Countess of Granville, died in a Forfar hospital. She was seventy-seven. The Queen Mother was now the last survivor of the Glamis Bowes-Lyons. There was no shortage of volunteers to console her. She and the Queen talk to each other by telephone almost every day. But apart from the immediate family, Earl Mountbatten was her close and affectionate confidant. The empathy between them centred partly on nostalgia. Shared memories of George VI; identical enthusiasm for a thousand years of royal tradition. When the Margaret–Snowdon discord spilled over into the gossip columns both were mightily displeased and closed ranks behind the Queen. 'We would meet very often,' Mountbatten said. 'Sometimes she would come down to Broadlands. Other-wise I would meet her at Buckingham Palace, at Windsor, or Sandringham. We have one enormous common interest and that is we both have great and marvellous memories and affec-tion for the late King. Neither of us ever tire of talking about him, remembering the funny things and laughing about them. We would never be together for very long without reminiscing about him. Though she has never, as I've said, paraded her grief, she feels it and misses him wherever she is or wherever she goes. He was part of a life she cherished more than anything. Not as a former Queen. Simply as a wife.'

Every 6 February, the anniversary of King George VI's death, the Queen Mother has a small private service, usually in the chapel at Royal Lodge in Windsor Great Park. Sir Martin Gilliat, her Private Secretary, has that date permanently ringed in the Queen Mother's diary. 'She would never ever miss a service on that day. It is absolutely sacrosanct. She also treats her wedding anniversary, 26 April, as a special occasion. She receives a wedding bouquet every year by the Worshipful Company of Gardeners. Quite a few messages come in from different parts of the world, mostly from elderly people who remember that that was the day she was a bride.'

But those anniversaries aside, the Queen Mother presents no visible signs of lingering heartache especially to visiting friends. That applies whether she is up at Birkhall fishing for salmon all day in waders. At the Castle of Mey, hiking purposefully ahead, the faint-hearted and the frail keeling over behind her. At Windsor, where once Lord Hailsham reportedly tossed aside his sticks and danced a jig. Or at Clarence House, which is the centre of her diverse and lively activities. Visitors do not need to hear the Exchange Telegraph Racing Tape Machine ticking away, or see a liveried footman taking a racing paper up to Her Majesty's boudoir, to sense that this is no ordinary Royal Household. The Queen Mother loves horses – jumping horses in particular. She also loves jockeys, trainers, grooms, stable-lads, farriers, vets, tipsters, or any of the other colourful characters in or on the fringe of National Hunt racing. Her steeplechasing activities are detailed later, but her successes are evident in the fine collection of silver trophies which gleam behind glass in several antique cabinets. And then there are her dogs. Not the large aristocratic types, but the Welsh corgi with its foxy head and deep chest, short of leg and social graces. The Queen Mother's passion for this tough, no-nonsense breed extends to having Ranger and Dash in her bedroom, sleeping, it's said, in two little beds complete with pillows and blankets. (The source of that vital intelligence was Betty Jones who worked as a domestic at Clarence House for two-and-a-half years. Like the boilerman at Buckingham Palace, she was awe-stricken by the experience. Her secret peek into the royal bedroom also took in the Queen Mother's 'lovely brass bedstead, on either side of it was an enormous clothed stone angel wearing a halo and holding a staff. The maid told me the angels' clothes were washed and starched every three months.')

Guests invited to lunch at Clarence House emerge not just dazzled by the experience, but laughing all the way into their limousines. Lord Callaghan remembered one lunch party where one of the guests laughed so loudly someone said, 'It's obvious this is a Queen Mother function!' What Callaghan remembers most is her 'infectious gaiety and genuine interest in the people she is talking to. She may be, as you say, close to ninety, but I detected little visible evidence of it. She was lively, entertaining, with not the slightest indication of any diminution of her strength, keen wit and remarkable energies. She was as alert and informative as I've always known her to be. What did we talk about? Almost everything, farming, flowers, painting, books, and of course politics.'

Drinks are set up in the long, sunny morning room with its grey walls and ivory woodwork. The Queen Mother's paintings reflect her tastes and the late Lord Clark's sound advice: a Sisley study of the Seine; Piper sketches of Windsor Castle; a rare Monet landscape; a fine Lowry painting of a Lancashire farm; Spy caricatures rising above the wide staircase; and several examples of the late Edward Seago's work, a good friend who gave her a picture almost every year. Crystal chandeliers, and footmen in brass-buttoned blue livery; china with silver edging; dessert plates decorated with painted pheasants; the setting hardly goes with the meat and two veg which the Queen Mother favours over haute cuisine. And if not beef then chicken or lamb will do with maybe ice-cream and a couple of figs afterwards. Guests are never asked to leave. It is all done by instinct. Usually they exit in time for Her Majesty and Sir Martin to check the runners in the three o'clock race. In the summer, Elizabeth might be found sitting in a gilt chair under the trees in the garden reading, anything from Dick Francis, another favourite, to Peter Cheyney or political memoirs. When she has time. Her working day is organized by her Private Secretary, a title which hardly covers all the duties, official and unofficial, that Sir Martin Gilliat attends to in his long, and from what he says, immensely enjoyable stint in Her Majesty's service.

Tall and distinguished-looking, Sir Martin, now in his seventies, had impeccable credentials. Eton, Sandhurst, King's Royal Rifles, then aide to the late Earl Mountbatten, these were Blue Chip qualifications for royal service. What doesn't appear on his cv are his experiences as a prisoner of war in Germany or the three occasions he tried to escape from Colditz. He is a bachelor. This gives him greater freedom to travel with the Queen Mother to faraway places and to the races nearer to home. But also, by all accounts, the Queen Mother likes to have bachelors in what she calls her 'little family'. Sir Ralph Anstruther, the Queen Mother's Treasurer, is also unmarried. So too was Sir Arthur

Penn the former Comptroller at Clarence House. Bachelors are
obviously less tied down and anyway they tend to bring out the
Queen Mother's strong maternal instincts. Or as Cecil Beaton
wrote in his diaries, 'the great mother figure and nannie to us all
. . . who bathes us and wraps us in a counterpane by the
fireside.' That, at any rate, was the effect she had on him. It may
be coincidence, but as Lady Fermoy noted with some amusement, most of the Queen Mother's ladies-in-waiting are
widows. 'I don't say they all are, but they have been very often.
Obviously if you have a home and children it makes the whole
rota (two weeks on, six off) more complicated.'

Sir Martin makes no secret of his admiration, well affection
for the Queen Mother. He has been her Private Secretary for
more than thirty years. To ask, as I did, this very genial
gentleman what he thinks about her did not find him short of the
odd superlative. He was quite prepared to be totally objective as
long as I recognized that 'there's never been a day that I have not
thanked the Almighty for my good fortune'. That theme established, Sir Martin described an average working day that often
did not finish until late in the evening. He admired her ability to
adapt to the changing perceptions of the Royal Family while all
the while remaining in character. 'She has this extraordinary
mystique of being able to remain absolutely herself whatever the
circumstances. When she sets out of an evening with a tiara, say,
to a film première or Covent Garden, no one looks more
splendid than she does. People gasp when they see her going to
Buckingham Palace for a State Banquet. Yet she created the
same excitement when we looked in on a judo session at the
YMCA at Croydon and Wimbledon. Within minutes she had all
the youngsters laughing and crowding around her. He marvelled at her 'strength and her serenity. Goodness knows, she
does not, as happens with people of her age, enjoy all the
changes that have occurred in the last fifteen or so years. But she
is wonderful at adapting herself and saying, "Well, we've got to
buckle down and get stuck in." Every time I go in with my
papers five days a week, three hundred and fifty days a year, it is
a new adventure. The trays filled to brimming every morning,
her reaction to everything we do together, is always interesting
and exciting. She never, never is bored. There are letters from
old soldiers of regiments of which she is Colonel-in-Chief. Or,
as occurred today, from a stretcher-bearer in one of her regiments during the war. He writes to say he has received a present

from the German Embassy here for helping wounded Germans as well as our own men. She registers everything in her mind. Her memory for even small but human things is quite fantastic. I have worked for so many different bosses but there's never been anybody like her.'

Sir Martin was obviously sincere in what he said. But I have too much respect for Her Majesty to leave that pristine portrait un-retouched. Beneath the halo the Queen Mother is as human as anybody else. By which I mean that she can be stubborn, and has a finely honed temper expressed more with a withering look than with words. Those melting, cornflower-blue eyes can freeze an errant flunkey rigid in his buckled shoes. Even Mountbatten, who wouldn't have an unkind or critical word said about her, acknowledged her 'tendency to sulk when something or someone has offended her'. But all below stairs in her several homes will say she is always fair, very considerate when any of the staff have personal problems, and is generous particularly at Christmas.

Film premières find the Queen Mother at her best. Even the most powerful of Hollywood's stars have gone weak-kneed as that smile beneath the tiara hits them face-on. To be able to say something interesting or even intelligible to each of the recipients of her soft-gloved handshake, requires good briefing and much effort. An average royal question rarely rises above the level of 'Are you filming over here now?' But somehow the Queen Mother contrives a one-to-one rapport that no one else in the royal family quite manages to pull off. One or two actors, immobilized by terror, have actually curtsied instead of bowing to the Queen Mother. Shaking hands with Peter Sellers at one première she asked him,

'What are you doing at the moment, Mr Sellers?'

'Standing here, your Majesty,' he replied, straight-faced.

As Lord Callaghan indicated, the Queen Mother's presence is a fair guarantee of un-regal hearty laughter. Basil Boothroyd records a typical example of it following a film show in one Royal Household. 'It was *A Fistful of Dollars*, the first of the so-called spaghetti Westerns. Not that we could hear much of the ear-splitting bombings and shootings, because everybody was laughing too much. He [Prince Philip] and the Queen clutched each other helplessly. We braved it out and returned gasping to the big drawing room. Presently I heard cries of "Bang, bang, you're dead!" and was just missed by a flying ping-pong ball. The three royal ladies (Their Majesties the Queen, the Queen Mother and Princess Anne) armed with the young Prince's pump-guns (this was 1970 remember) had opened fire from a high scrollwork gallery at the end of the room. Prince Charles and some friends countered with a thrown cushion or two.'

Less fun, apparently, was being had by the Snowdons at Kensington Palace. Ten years of marriage had underscored fundamental differences between the two volatile and contrasting characters. Margaret who would say of herself, 'I'm no angel, but I'm no Bo Peep either,' had taken a holiday on her own which re-energized speculation about the marriage. Snowdon, successful and sought-after was too preoccupied with his commissions to bother with the gossip. Renewing innocent friendships – as with Lady Jacqueline Rufus-Isaacs whom he had frequently photographed – was not likely to defuse the situation. The Queen Mother was alarmed, but recognized that if it came to the worst, it was the Queen's problem. She could speak as a mother, which she did, and as a mother-in-law, which Tony welcomed. But if it came to anything more serious, it would be the Queen who would have to take the flak. Attempts to keep the rift from surfacing into headlines became less easy as the strain began to show. Margaret was not the type to smile on demand. She was tense, unhappy, and it showed. Tony looked increasingly grim. The Queen Mother braced herself for another Royal explosion.

On 28 May 1972 the Duke of Windsor died of cancer of the throat. Some months earlier, on hearing that the ex-King was dying, the Queen, Philip, and Charles flew to Paris to see him. Prince Charles handled the occasion with his characteristic mix of good nature and compassion. The Duke knew he had not long to live and requested that when she died Wallis would be buried beside him at Windsor. That wish, offering posthumous recognition, was granted. The day after he died, the Duchess suffered a nervous collapse. She received two telegrams, one from the Queen signed 'Elizabeth R' and one from the Queen Mother, signed simply 'Elizabeth'. This subtle distinction was interpreted as a conciliatory gesture from a sympathetic sister-in-law rather than from a queen. Earl Mountbatten met the heavily sedated duchess at Heathrow Airport. Says Philip Ziegler, 'he found her extremely nervous at having to confront the whole royal family without her husband's support. She was particularly worried about Elizabeth the Queen Mother who, she said, never approved of her. Mountbatten reassured her. "She is so deeply sorry for you in your present grief, your sister-in-law will welcome you with open arms. She remembers what she felt like when *her* husband died."' In the event, the Duchess, disoriented though she was, sensed no hostility from her sister-in-law when they briefly met at the funeral. We know that the Queen Mother took the Duchess's arm. One account adds words to the gesture: 'I know how you feel. I've been through this myself.' It may have been true, or safe guesswork. More relevant is whether that gesture marked a graveside reconciliation. It is difficult to see it as anything else. They were both widows now. Her bitterness must have lost much of its sting over thirty-five years. The target had visibly faded. Not much resemblance now between this pallid, dazed woman and the jaunty socialite who 'had blown in from Baltimore'. The two brothers were at peace. The Queen Mother would have seen little point in disturbing it.

By now, the Queen Mother could see that the marriage between Margaret and Lord Snowdon had become merely an arrangement to protect the children. They were spending more and more time apart. There had been a brief reconciliation which came as a relief to the incumbents of the Palace and Clarence House. But a family holiday with the Aga Khan in Sardinia failed to rejuvenate the relationship. Jacqueline Rufus-Isaacs featured more frequently in the gossip columns, balanced by the emergence of a new name in Margaret's coterie, Roddy Llewellyn. Son of the flamboyant show jumper Lieutenant-Colonel Harry Llewellyn, Roddy bore an uncanny resemblance to Snowdon; similar features, mannerisms and style. Before becoming a research assistant to the College of Heralds he had been a male model in South Africa where his vital statistics were listed as '5 ft 10 in tall, very slim, good teeth, fair hands, can ride a horse, water-ski, drive a car or a motorcycle.' He also wore one earring. Precisely the attractiveness and well-bred eccentricity likely to appeal to the much older, unhappy Princess rebounding from an increasingly doomed marriage. On their first meeting, at Colin Tennant's Scottish estate, she challenged him, 'Explain yourself', her way of disarming an interesting new face. We can assume the young Llewellyn gave the right answers. They met subsequently in London where he was occasionally invited to Margaret's dinner parties at Kensington

Palace. It was a juicy gossip item that was away and running. The Queen Mother, implacably opposed to royal divorces, confronted Margaret who made it plain that her marriage was over. If Margaret expected a green light from her mother, she was sharply disillusioned. The Queen Mother, fond as she was of her younger daughter, was not about to pull another rug from underneath the throne. But when Roddy showed up with Margaret on Mustique, her famous Caribbean bolt-hole, scandal seemed unavoidable. He had now taken over a semi-derelict house with three hundred acres of land in Wiltshire. It became a commune for a cocktail-shake of arty friends and fringe aristocrats, happily living, working, and chewing carrots together. They opened an organic food restaurant in Bath, Somerset, with Roddy delivering his home-grown vegetables in a blue Bedford van. Invited, presumably at Margaret's request, to Royal Lodge, Windsor, Roddy accidentally encountered the Queen Mother in a corridor. He wore nothing but a pair of underpants. The records have him spluttering, 'Frightfully sorry Ma'am. Just looking for nanny to sew a button on this shirt.' The Queen Mother, majestically unfazed, smiled off. But the casual intimacy would have been well noted. More so when Roddy and Margaret showed up again in the Caribbean where pictures of them sunning themselves in swimming gear were published in Germany and eagerly reproduced in Britain. The photos which graphically underscored the defunct marriage, came at the worst time. The Queen and the Queen Mother had had long, sometimes bitter meetings with Margaret, searching for ways to avoid a scandal. The pictures and the gossip from the Caribbean effectively killed all that. Margaret's emotional turmoil had been nothing new. It was evident even before Llewellyn arrived on the scene. There were, according to Ann Morrow, 'tantrums . . . shouting matches; Princess Margaret would throw a handbag across the room and rant and rage until four in the morning.'

The whole affair was more soap opera than scandal. It had a predictable finale. The short statement released from Kensington Palace on Friday, 19 March 1976 was tersely to the point: 'HRH the Princess Margaret, the Countess of Snowdon and the Earl of Snowdon have mutually agreed to live apart. The Princess will carry out her public duties and functions unaccompanied by Lord Snowdon. There are no plans for divorce proceedings.' These would soon come. In the meantime the

Queen Mother, as always, repaired fences. She was ambivalent towards her daughter: sorry that the marriage had failed; angry at all that public self-indulgence. It is clear she absolved Lord Snowdon of much if not all the blame. They get on particularly well together. She admires him tremendously not least for remaining tight-lipped about his private life and the backstage dramas with Margaret. When he comes to lunch with her at Clarence House he invariably enters through a side door. As with Mountbatten, Lord Snowdon hates even the slightest notion that he may be exploiting his royal connections. A skilled professional who knows the way the tabloids work, his vow of silence on all matters royal is chiselled in concrete. But I hope he will not see it as a grave breach of confidence to quote from a post-lunch letter he wrote to me which described his mother-in-law as '. . . this greatest lady of our times whom I have total admiration, respect and love for as I think everyone else in this country has.' He and Princess Margaret may have had some hefty disagreements. But they'd join hands on that unsolicited testimonial to the Queen Mother.

On the other side of the coin, Willie Hamilton, the Scottish MP, in a singularly unpleasant attack on the royal family in New York described the Queen Mother as: 'A charming old age pensioner on £95,000 a year, mostly tax free. Her smile can come on at the touch of a switch. And you would never stop smiling if you had that kind of cash for doing very little.' The fact that the interview coincided with the publication of his anti-royal book *My Queen and I* puts the gibe in a more calculated context. Unimpressed by the Queen Mother's 211 official engagements for one year, 1970, he says in his book, 'she has a life of gaiety, luxury and elegance surrounded by the inevitable retinue of male and female employees or status-loving leeches. She gets through her public relations by pleasing facial exercises or by purposely chatting to "the lads in the back row" and taking a drop of the hard stuff, her native Scotch whisky. Yet behind the matey tipple and the ever-ready smile there lurks the mind of a shrewd business woman.' Willie Hamilton MP, in 1975. Leaving aside the fact that Her Majesty's 'matey tipple' is gin not Scotch, here is the same Mr Hamilton five years later, on the Queen Mother's eightieth birthday. 'My hatchet is buried. My venom dissipated. I am glad to salute a remarkable old lady. Long may she live to be the pride of her family. And may God understand and forgive me if I have been ensnared and corrupted, if only briefly, by this superb Royal trouper.' As usual, the Queen Mother made no response, content to leave the matter between God and Mr Hamilton.

It would never occur to that affable old cynic that the Queen Mother might actually believe in, if not enjoy, those audiences, investitures, and countless other royal appearances. Her most-quoted comment, addressed to her daughters, was 'work is the rent you pay for the room you occupy on earth'. Nothing in the Queen Mother's ninety years suggests that is not what she herself believes. Two jobs she took on gladly: Chancellor of London University (1955–80) because she loved being among young people; and Warden of the Cinque Ports because of the pleasant way the then Prime Minister Jim Callaghan, sold her on the idea. It is no big deal of course. The only perks the un-paid Warden enjoys are the right to any unclaimed wrecks found within the jurisdiction of the ports; a 19-gun salute at sea; any royal fishes caught (though with the responsibility for burying any whales, porpoises and sturgeon washed up along the Cinque Ports coasts). When the question arose of finding a successor to the then Warden, Sir Robert Menzies, the Queen suggested to Callaghan that maybe he might like to take it on. The Labour leader thought this would be a shade presumptuous and suggested the Queen Mother instead. As he explained, 'Remembering how well Her Majesty, then Queen, behaved alongside King George VI during the blitz it seemed entirely appropriate for the post to be offered to the Queen Mother. "Then why don't you come to Balmoral," the Queen suggested, "and ask my mother yourself?" I always enjoyed going to Balmoral particularly since this invariably meant having tea with the Queen Mother. After church on Sunday morning we were having a sherry in the Drawing Room when the Queen said to the Queen Mother, "The Prime Minister has something he wants to say to you. Why don't you both go into the library." There I told her what was on my mind and said I would be very happy if she would become Warden of the Cinque Ports and I was sure everyone in those towns would be very pleased. She paused and then put her hand over her heart. "Oh," she said. "I'm so relieved. I thought you were about to reproach me for something I had said."

'And of course she accepted.'

17

No one, least of all the Queen Mother, would own and race
horses for profit. Leaving aside the fact that there is no quicker
way to separate people from their money, thrift has always been
a dominant virtue with this insistently Scottish lady. Or as the
late Earl Mountbatten delicately put it, 'she is very careful, and
minds her bawbies much more than the English do'. So we have
to seek other explanations for a passion which has lasted for
almost exactly forty years. If the Queen Mother had been born
royal it would be simple. She would merely be following
tradition, the monarchy having hunted, jousted, and lumbered
to war on horses right back to William the Conqueror. Queen
Anne had race horses at York. Queen Victoria disliked the sport
but bred thoroughbred yearlings at Hampton Court producing the famous La Fleche which won the One Thousand
Guineas, the St Leger and the Oaks. Now the Royal Stud is at
Sandringham and Wolferton, managed by the tall, affable
expert, Michael Oswald CVO, who is also the Queen Mother's
racing manager. Other horses are kept with the Marquess of
Townshend at Raynham, Norfolk.

The Strathmores had for years bred and owned horses at
Streatlam Castle, Co. Durham. One of the Queen Mother's
kinsmen, John Bowes, an illegitimate son of a nineteenth-
century Strathmore, won the Derby four times. George VI
inherited and improved on the excellent stud left by his father.
But though as a child she rode a pony – side-saddle of course –
the Queen Mother did not grow up with a strong interest in
bloodstock, or an irresistible urge to go galloping alone across
the limitless Scottish acres. So we can exclude the Queen
Mother from biographer Penelope Mortimer's amusing

diagnosis: 'the mating of those splendid stallions and quivering mares holds a strong attraction for many women, and the pounding of hooves on the track, the straining muscles and flaring nostrils can make many a ladylike heart beat faster and bring a flush to the most discreetly powdered cheek.' It is a delicious idea which probably had Ma'am and Sir Martin falling about at Clarence House. The only thing likely to bring a flush to her 'discreetly powdered cheek' is one of her horses coming in ahead of the field.

The fact is the Queen Mother's racing interests have probably extended her life substantially. Even her own doctors cannot determine what has kept this highly resilient 'royal' going so well and for so long despite two major operations. We know that she never takes drugs preferring homoeopathic medicine if any part of her has the impertinence to ache. Her willpower is basic to it all. She knows she is getting older but refuses to admit to being old. Away from her Scottish homes, the Queen Mother exercises lungs and limbs walking around the stables and the paddocks where her horses are bred and trained. Rainstorms or Force Eight winds don't deter her as she leans into them with her fur-lined coat, umbrella, and chunky boots. She loves the danger and the excitement. She loves the colour, the thump of horses pounding towards the 'jumps', and especially the crowds cheerfully sardined against the rails. She loves to talk horses with the trilby-hatted gentry, the jockeys, and the stable-lads as they do with her. Michael Oswald put it simply: 'She loves racing, racing loves her.' One ecstatic Irish stable-lad chirruped, 'You feel you are in heaven. She takes ten years off ye!' Bookies do not resort to similar adulation. But Frank Keating, a racing expert, was probably on firm ground when he declared, 'If there is a shorter cut to a bloody nose in Tattersalls than to criticize the Queen Mum in any way, I do not know it.'

The love-affair between Her Majesty and this Sport of Kings began casually in 1949. George VI's filly Avila had won the Coronation Stakes at Ascot. Over a celebration dinner at Windsor, the Queen Mother (then Queen) was seated next to Lord Mildmay. A close friend, he had been champion National Hunt jockey for the four previous seasons. The subject naturally turned to horses with Mildmay suggesting that the Queen might like the idea of having her own horse in training over the jumps. She and her daughter Elizabeth went into partnership on a chaser named Monaveen which had the blood if not the good nature of the Derby winner Spion Kop in its veins. A frisky animal, the Irish farmer who owned it hitched it to a fully-loaded milk float to teach him manners. It came fifth in the 1950 Grand National. Manicou was the first horse to race in the Queen Mother's colours, blue, buff stripes, blue sleeves, black cap and gold tassel. These had been the colours of her great-uncle and keen amateur rider, Lord Strathmore. The Queen Mother's trainer Peter Cazalet had been a close friend of the Bowes-Lyons's since she was a child. She often stayed at the Cazalet's estate near Shipbourne in Kent. Manicou won races but eventually displayed a more fruitful talent at stud. Mona-veen had been one of Cazalet's biggest winners but he had a bad fall at Hurst Park, broke a leg and had to be destroyed. It was the first time the Queen Mother had to come to terms with the uneasy reality of National Hunt racing; horses can fall, and may have to die.

Beyond that is the disappointment of seeing your horse gallop ahead of the field towards perhaps the greatest challenge in racing, then fail within sight of the post. This happened when her horse, Devon Loch, ran the 1956 Grand National with jockey Dick Francis in the saddle. It was the sort of story-book ride that Francis could never improve on later as a best-selling fiction writer. Devon Loch took the massive jumps in style slowly working his way up from the back of the field. He passed one horse after another and was lying second at the Canal Turn. Thirty fences behind him, and Devon Loch appeared fresh and still full of jumping. Only a few hundred yards left and the Grand National was his. The Queen Mother, the Queen and Princess Margaret leapt with excitement as they saw the horse take the last fence ahead of ESB and seemed to be fast pulling away from him. It seemed only a formality now before the Queen Mother would achieve the ultimate, leading in the Grand National winner. The disaster that occurred a scant fifty yards from the winning post is part of racing history. For reasons experts still can't fathom, Devon Loch took an odd leap and with his ears still pricked, fell spreadeagled on to his belly. It was, said one spectator, 'sickening to watch'. There was a loud groan from the crowds and few cheers as ESB galloped past the post. All eyes were on the Queen Mother. Whatever she felt was clearly not fully reflected in what she said. 'Well, that's racing,' was her comment. 'Now I think I will go down and talk to the lads.' She consoled them. Some were crying. Later, she gave

Peter Cazalet a silver cigarette box inscribed, 'a memento of that terrible yet glorious day'. And she didn't forget the horse (who ironically, would go on to win other races). 'You dear poor old boy,' she said, patting him on the neck.

But there were many successes. The Rip (son of Manicou) bought by the Queen Mother from the landlord of the Red Cat pub at Wootton Marshes in Norfolk for £400, won thirteen races. In the 1964–5 season she had twenty-seven winners and twenty-four placed horses earning £13,100 in stake money. Ma'as-tu-Vu, Makaldar, Chaou II, Inch Arran – the Cazalet/Queen Mother partnership flourished until his death in 1973. He and his wife had been in her most intimate circle. Cazalet was irreplaceable as a friend. She chose Fulke Walwyn as her new trainer. A friend of Cazalet's, Walwyn had been champion trainer five times. His had been the most successful National Hunt stable since the war. His career as a leading amateur rider from 1929 climaxed by winning the Grand National on Reynoldstown in 1936.

Inevitably, he must have had slight apprehensions at taking over the Queen Mother's horses. Cazalet was bound to be a hard act to follow. He had given the Queen Mother twenty-seven National Hunt winners in one year putting her amongst the top winning owners. But Walwyn, a tall, quiet and much-respected figure in racing, has proved to be as shrewd a judge as his predecessor with a total of a hundred and fifty winners for his royal owner. He trained the talented Tammuz which won the Schweppes Gold Trophy in 1975. A year later, he sent Sunny-boy out to give the Queen Mother her three hundredth winner. And like the Cazalets, he and his equally expert wife Cathy, have become the Queen Mother's friends.

The success of this partnership is evident in the pictures of the winning horses, many of them signed by the Queen Mother, which cover the walls of the Walwyn's sixteenth-century home at Lambourn. As an owner, she has now had a total of 376 winning horses over 'jumps'. She keeps about eight or nine horses in training with Walwyn, among them Sun Rising, The Argonaut, Royal Pavilion, Sunshine Flight and Friary Court. Special Cargo was one of her favourites. He well-earned his keep, winning the Grand Military Cup for three successive years. But the superstar was Game Spirit who won twenty-one races for the Queen Mother. Her affection for him went beyond the successes he notched up. She liked his personality and temperament. According to stable-lads who can read the signs, the feelings were mutual. David Mould, for many years the Queen Mother's jockey, advised his successor on the horse, 'you'll get the same effort from him with a pat as you'd get by showing him the whip'. The Queen Mother agreed with him. She probably recommends the same tactics within the growing family circle.

Everybody liked Game Spirit and the plan was that when his racing days were over he would go to Windsor as a hack for the Queen. But he died suddenly, without warning, at Newbury in 1977. 'It was very upsetting for everyone,' Cathy Walwyn remembered. 'Game Spirit was fifth. We were waiting for the horses to come in but there was no sign of him. Suddenly we saw this crowd. The vet was already there. He said the horse had died instantly (from a massive haemorrhage of the lungs). Luckily Martin Gilliat was there to break the news to the Queen Mother. Eventually we went up to her when everybody had dispersed. She was obviously dreadfully upset. She really loved that horse. But she kept her feelings to herself. As she always does.'

Each Thursday, Sir Martin Gilliat takes the racing papers to the Queen Mother having marked in red any of her horses listed as runners. She then phones her trainer to discuss the prospects of each horse and the opposition facing it. She reads the Form Book, studies the weather, and is as good a tipster as any of the other clairvoyants in the game. She used to wager the odd tenner some years back, placed on her behalf at a betting shop a short canter away from Clarence House. But not now. Her pleasure is to be driven down to Lambourn by car, feet up with a bag of sweets in her hand. At the stables, Cathy Walwyn hands over a bunch of carrots as though they were regimental colours. With a cheery 'See you', off goes the Queen Mother to visit 'her darlings' as she calls them.

Alone with these horses – and her thoughts – in the peaceful Berkshire countryside, the Queen Mother can forget yester-day's ship-launches and tomorrow's handshakes. The ritual carrot-offering keeps her, and the horses happy. Few would begrudge it of both parties. Whenever she wins a classic the Queen Mother throws a party at Clarence House for the jockeys and lads. She takes them around the house, pointing out all her valuable racing trophies. 'We had a cocktail party here once,' Cathy Walwyn recalled, 'for all the jockeys who had ever ridden for her, going back nearly forty years. It was incredible. Most of them had retired and were doing other things. Even we couldn't recognize some of them. But she remembered them all. She went up to them and reminded them where they had ridden for her, and when. What we also find amazing is her extraordinary stamina. She is ten years older than Fulke, but she beats him across the paddock going a million miles an hour in those tiny little high-heeled shoes.' The Queen Mother now keeps about six mares at the Royal Stud. 'She had one very successful brood mare, Queen of the Isle,' said Michael Oswald, 'who bred three horses, Inch Arran, Colonius, and Isle of Man which won fourteen races each. But though she occasionally buys horses, the scale of her racing is, for economic reasons, much smaller than it was. She can no longer spend the kind of money some people pay for young, untrained horses these days – anything from twenty to a hundred thousand pounds. But even on this limited scale she still has fun. She enjoys walking her corgis round the Stud at Sandringham, talking to the men, asking how the mares are doing, watching them come in, and giving each horse a carrot out of the basket. Then off she goes just before dark, the two corgis trotting beside her. Two or three times a year she will go to Raynham where the Head Lady, Mrs Palmer will take her to see the horses. Every one of these gets a carrot. While in Norfolk she will also visit Major Eldred Wilson, an old friend who has looked after her horses for years.'

Racing can be dangerous, accidents to jockeys inevitable. If one of her riders is injured he receives a sympathy letter and gifts, though the largesse falls short of scribbling Elizabeth R on his plaster cast. The Injured Jockey's Fund, created to ensure that no jockey suffers hardship as a result of a bad accident finds the Queen Mother a valuable patron. The well-heeled racing and hunting fraternity know better than to wait to have their arms twisted for a charity this close to the Queen Mother's heart. What the jockeys respect is that if something goes badly wrong in a race through a mistake or bad riding, Her Majesty never utters a word of criticism. 'Win or lose,' says the Walwyns, 'it's all the same to her.'

1981 was the year of Charles and Diana; a year in which a highly sensitive and introverted prince found himself caught in the media wringer. Not even that other Prince of Wales, his phil-andering great-uncle, had faced such a sustained assault of gossip, sarcasm, and sanctimonious lecturing by the popular press. If, during that siege-like courtship, marriage, and honeymoon Charles did not angrily play up in public, it was largely due to Lord Mountbatten and the Queen Mother. Dickie, his 'Honorary grandfather' allowed him to use his beautiful home at Broadlands to avoid the flak and be alone with Diana. The Queen Mother offered similar clandestine hospitality at Birkhall, throwing in as a bonus, good Scottish wisdom. She could see that her grandson was in a no-win situation. If all he did was play polo, race fast cars, jape around with Spike Milligan between the Palace rituals, then to the gossip writers, he was just another free-loader of the monarchy. If he rejected that image, spoke his mind on serious matters concerning the environment and the hideous City architecture, then he was a royal upstart burbling way out of his depth. This Catch-22 dilemma accounted for much of Charles's moodiness and occasional outbursts of anger. His education decided by a committee at Windsor Castle, he must have felt manipulated from the beginning. Out of uniform, he entered into the ribbon-scissoring business with strong misgivings. Deep inside his troubled soul is the conviction that there ought to be more to life than this. Film stars whimper on about intrusion and 'life in a goldfish bowl'. But it is largely bogus, most of them relishing in private what they allegedly despise in public. Charles detests publicity. He did so long before his over-publicized friendship with the distinguished traveller and Jungian philosopher, Sir Laurens van der Post. Briefed by Mountbatten and the Queen Mother on the life and times of the Duke of Windsor, Charles was determined never to be seen as another trend-setting play-boy prince. That other Prince of Wales had made public noises about the unemployed and the poor, returning hastily to sip a rejuvenating cocktail with another man's wife at the Ritz. Charles – and both the Queen and the Queen Mother admire him for it – has a genuinely compassionate nature. He wonders, with his father's short-circuited irritation, why in a prosperous democracy the poor and the homeless have to sleep in cardboard boxes on the Embankment. He isn't afraid to tell British architects of the grievous bodily harm committed against the City skyline. And every time he speaks out, grannie at Clarence House is delighted with him. Nothing she likes better than seeing him draw blood where it matters. He has become the surrogate voice of the monarchy which is forbidden to go anywhere near the deep end of politics. The Queen Mother is proud of the social conscience which has prompted Charles to put his intelligence and charisma behind some admirable causes: his Prince's Trust aimed at helping disadvantaged youngsters to help themselves; the Prince's Young Business Trust which gives expert guidance to young people on how to make a start; his much-praised Prince of Wales Summer School in Civil Architecture backed by an enthusiastic team of architects and art historians; and now the threat of the 'Greenhouse Effect'.

If the danger of 'monstrous carbuncles' (his words) defiling Britain's skylines has receded, Charles can take much of the credit. Maybe Charles has been too clever, too outspoken for those who believe that royals should be seen but not heard. Too bad. Until such time as a crown is put on his head effectively silencing him, he intends to say his piece. His conscience, he says, is always needling him. Which scarcely deserved Jean Rook's complaint in the London *Daily Express*, 'I'm weary of watching the man born to be our modern monarch wandering around Scotland like Landseer's stag with a wounded frown on his face.' The said 'wounded frown' was a reaction against precisely that form of tabloid whingeing. His love-affair and the Di-hysteria that ensued, did not help. In the turbulent run up to the altar, every publication lurched into trembling prose, their cameras homing in on his fiancée's demure downward glance under soft lashes, and her creamy white shoulders at first-nights. And when not obsessed by the frocks she wore, the length of her skirt and depth of her neckline, they switched to Charles's visible bald patch and hesitant royal-speak. It can be no coincidence that a cushion on his drawing-room couch has a picture of a frog complaining, 'It's no fun being a Prince'.

The 'fun' Prince Charles might crave has nothing to do with self-indulgence. There has never been a 'Charles-and-Di Set'. He gets more fun sheep-shearing or potato-planting than emulating the effete night-prowling of the former Prince of Wales. Inevitably, the media, active as ever prospecting the royal landscape, drove Charles and Diana into taking evasive action. Here, Mountbatten and the Queen Mother happily entered the conspiracy. Broadlands, with its vast acreage, peace and isolation, allowed the celebrated sweethearts some tactful privacy. And when Mountbatten's 'trysting place' was otherwise engaged, the Queen Mother offered Birkhall which is big enough for young lovers never to encounter accidentally the Lady of the

House. Not that the excursions up there could be undertaken easily. Reporters and photographers were on permanent vigil outside Diana's London home. To dodge them, she would saunter out with a small overnight case, get into her Metro and drive away ostensibly for a long weekend somewhere. Instead she parked nearby and in another car was spirited up to Scotland. Once there, the Queen Mother discreetly distancing herself, Diana and Charles were as close as they would ever get to royal tranquillity. Then, in her eighty-first year, this wise and devoted grannie could speak to them in a way that parents probably cannot. Charles's respect and affection for the Queen Mother goes deep. She had been a second mother to him in his childhood years when the Queen and Philip were on long official duties abroad. That bond has become even stronger over the years. Grandsons tend to go overboard in praise of their grand-mothers. But it is the measure of Charles's integrity that nobody doubted for a second the sincerity in these words:* 'Ever since I can remember my grandmother has been the most wonderful example of fun, laughter, warmth, infinite security and above all else, exquisite taste in so many things. . . .'

The Queen Mother's feelings towards Charles go beyond grandmotherly pride and affection. She believes he will one day make a fine King, and one likely to go way beyond royalty's ice-cool neutrality towards Number Ten Downing Street. Not long after ascending to the throne, George VI laid down strict ground rules for the way the King (or Queen) business should be run. It would surprise no one if over the years our highly capable monarch has quietly deleted some of the more fossilized rituals. Prince Charles, as King, will probably get rid of the rest. The Queen and Prince Philip, like the Queen Mother, have backed him all the way. But Lord Mountbatten was an early champion. His assessment of Charles, made fourteen years ago when the Prince, twenty-eight, was still in the Navy, suggests that the former Viceroy and First Sea Lord was no mean judge of character: 'This boy, I'm very fond of him indeed. I have the highest regard for him. He has the same dedication the Queen has. And the same ability. I watched him one day on the bridge of the *Bonnington*. Let me tell you he was completely in com-mand. He gave his orders, never raised his voice, but he was

---

* Godfrey Talbot, *Country Life Book of Queen Elizabeth the Queen Mother*, 1978.

obviously in complete control. The Chief Petty Officers asked me if I'd go down to their mess. I went down alone and sat with them. I asked them what they thought of the ship. They couldn't have been more enthusiastic. "It's a hell of a great ship!" they said. I said, "Tell me, do you like having the Prince of Wales as your captain?" "Do we like it! We love it." "What about defaulters and so on?" "We have no defaulters," they said. "But you must have a few leave-breakers?" "Yes, we have a few of those. But they don't pull the wool over Prince Charles's eyes. If a chap breaks leave he knows he's for it. But we don't have many – they're just terrified they might be drafted to another ship!"'

Mountbatten forecast, correctly, that once out of the Navy, Charles would slowly be eased into arcane duties of royalty. 'Though the Queen is not consciously grooming him for his eventual role, she would not discourage his interest. If he asked to see the dispatch boxes she would certainly let him see them. Prince Philip does not ask to see them because he is concerned that no one should think that he is trying to pry into politics. He wants that to be absolutely understood so that he can feel free, independently, to criticize as an individual without it appearing that it is based on inside knowledge. On the other hand Charles is now bound to enlarge his scope, meet ministers, and enter affairs of state.'

Though Mountbatten was totally sold on Charles as a future king, he passed on the question of who might make a suitable queen. His advice, spoken with the wisdom of an old campaigner, was that the Prince should sow as many wild oats as possible before making his choice. By all accounts, Charles dutifully carried out the former Sea Lord's orders. But sowing is one thing, reaping is another. Charles's blueprint for a happy marriage demanded the underpinning of a strong friendship. He wanted someone physically attractive but with a good mind to go with it. Mountbatten sympathized with his great-nephew who couldn't sow his wild oats for the photographers and reporters on twenty-four hour stake-outs. He fell in and out of love with a variety of girls, none of whom could be regarded as a serious contender. He and actress Susan George were, as they say in gossip-column parlance, a brief 'twosome', which just as quickly faded. 'I'll make you this prophecy,' Mountbatten said, 'when he finds someone he wants to marry he will not ever see her in public. He will not be seen with her in centres of social and court gossip. He's got one enormous plus. He is such an essentially charming young man who has a wonderful character and who will make a wonderful husband. The girl he finds will marry him for his own sake, and put up with having to be Queen!' (Always the tactician, Mountbatten tried to steer Charles towards his granddaughter Amanda Knatchbull, subtly fixing it so they spent a holiday together at the Knatchbull home in the Caribbean. (They came back sun-tanned but cheerfully at arms' length.)

The Queen Mother could have told her friend Dickie that he was wasting his time. She and her Lady-in-Waiting Ruth Fermoy were a couple of gleeful matchmakers plotting behind the scenes. Their game plan was to match Charles with Lady Fermoy's beauty of a granddaughter, Diana Spencer. Conveniently born within strolling distance of the Queen's home at Sandringham, she had briefly met Charles years earlier. In fact it was her elder sister Sarah who had once been Charles's girlfriend. But she was never in love with him and broke the house rules by confessing as much to a reporter. ('I wouldn't marry anyone I didn't love whether it was the dustman or the King of England.') Which was just as well since Charles, on taking a closer look at the younger sister, realized love had been lingering on his doorstep all the time. And exactly as Lord Mountbatten had prophesied, he went into some well-organized, covert wooing, using decoy girlfriends and a variety of aliases and secret locations. Finally he raised the subject of marriage to Diana and received encouraging responses from the blushing nineteen year old. So far so blissful. But there was a hiatus while Charles consulted his inner-self trekking alone in the Himalayas. He emerged from this forty-eight hours of soul-searching 'calm and confident' according to those around him. He had made up his mind. But as Lord Mountbatten predicted, he told no one when he returned to London. Not even the Queen. But finally, at Windsor he informed his mother and Prince Philip that he had made up his mind. Would Mama have Diana up to Sandringham for the New Year? Request granted. The Queen was delighted. Philip was glad that the dithering was over. The Queen Mother was ecstatic, picturing in her mind the breathtaking bride Diana would make. And did. The wedding, the most stunning media event of the century, featured the first royal kiss on that historic balcony, the innovation being demanded by the roaring multitude, (700 million others watched it around the globe).

221

'Di-dology', the tabloids' gruesome label, had reached its mind-boggling apogee.

Tragically, Mountbatten did not see his great-nephew marry. His absence from St Paul's added poignancy to the enormous grief and sense of loss Charles suffered on the day of the assassination. It left a gaping hole in his life. He had lost a friend, advisor, confidant, and stand-in grandfather. Mountbatten would have relished the occasion. And when, less than a year later, William was born taking care of the succession, he would have regarded his mission as complete. It was unfortunate perhaps that Charles and Diana were stuck with the label 'fairy-tale lovers'. Whatever fantasies Diana spun in her imagination, reality slowly began to erode them. Long after, when the pressure was on and the media spoke openly of a rift between the royal couple, it would have been helpful for Charles to have had Mountbatten to call on. But if the Broadlands' counselling service had ceased, there was always that dependable shoulder at Clarence House.

The Queen Mother's infinite capacity for taking pain – other people's – did not alter the fact that she was alarmed by all the stories. Margaret's emotional gear-crashing had been an embarrassment, but no blood was spilt. She was not, after all, in the reckoning as far as the throne was concerned. But Charles was different. Everything he did, or said, had to be seen in the context of his eventual role as king. On matters of royal boat-rocking, the Queen Mother always has her ear close to the ground. And if not her ear, then selected courtiers do the listening for her. She would have been disturbed at what she heard. First there were tangible signs that Diana, with the blithe enthusiasm of her earlier calling – kindergarten teacher – was re-styling the prince more to her taste. Sharper clothes, a blow-dry hair style, boxer shorts, all of which, Charles himself conceded, made him feel, as well as look, much younger. This zesty rejuvenation tipped him towards 'natural' foods and holistic medicine, with a bower in which he could meditate among his plants. All harmless and respectable activities for a sensitive, introspective soul. According to Anthony Holden's biography of the prince, Philip wondered if his son was becoming a bit of a crank. 'Ruthlessly down to earth, he [Philip] never had much time for matters of the spirit, and now worried that married life with Diana was turning his eldest son "soft". The word "wimp" was even heard on Prince Philip's lips. . . .'

All of which would have been as painful to the Queen Mother as it was to Charles himself. She believed that all of Charles's so-called eccentricities, indicated strength not weakness. When the second child, Harry, was born the rumours of a rift slackened off. But the ingredients for discord were always there. The more his 'Action Man' persona brought him – and his causes – valuable public attention, he couldn't help noticing that wherever he appeared, the crowds looked over his shoulder for Diana. But she was becoming manifestly disenchanted with the royal rituals. There were arguments. One of these, reportedly, was over Diana's alleged unwillingness to attend the annual Festival of Remembrance at London's Albert Hall. She had not been feeling well. The heated dialogue that was said to have ensued centred on royal duty before private inclinations. It was what Charles, his mother, his grandmother were stuck with. Diana dried her tears and got to the Albert Hall five minutes after the Queen, no small infringement of the 'rules'.

It is certain that the Queen Mother, exercising her prerogatives as a grandmother, did her best to cool things down. The echoes of the Margaret–Snowdon affair became uncomfortably persistent. But Diana was equally concerned to exercise her prerogatives as an independent female and as a wife. And was royally mauled by the Press as a result. The dreamy, Dresden-china image had gone. In its place, a more confident, determined princess rehearsing perhaps for her role as Queen. The Queen Mother must be glad that the couple have managed – as of 1990 – to keep any disagreements private. But she more than anyone else, would have noticed that they had spent more and more time apart doing 'their own thing'; Charles, an unrepentant anti-feminist, Diana restless and much younger, fighting to shake off the royal halter. Both still fond of each other, but struggling to reconcile their age difference, different friends, different life-styles and preoccupations. Current indicators suggest that problems or not, they are managing to make the marriage work successfully if not ecstatically. They certainly seemed happy enough together in Indonesia where Diana looked ravishing, Charles's smiling glances at her reflecting considerable pride of ownership. With that problem no longer on the boil, a more vital matter to the Queen was Charles's increasingly high profile on controversial issues. One could hear voices in the Palace 'Mafia' muttering, 'this feller is becoming a bit of a problem'. His stinging attacks on Britain's architects in

November last year, had one of his critics comparing his views to those of Hitler and the Nazis in the 1930s. (Charles had suggested that the new British Library building resembled an academy for the training of secret police.) Having the views of her son, the future King, being compared to those of the Nazis, would have left the Queen singularly unamused. But it was part of a pattern. Charles flexing his muscles: sending out clear signals of the kind of king he intends to be – signals bound to induce shivers among the backwoodsmen of the monarchy. The mutual respect and affection between the Queen and Charles does not alter the fact that he heralds a new-style monarchy; a king who might just escape from the gilded cage and speak out against the injustices of his time. But any suggestion of a change in the style and operation of the family is bound to make some people nervous, not least the Queen and the Queen Mother. The hot-line between Buckingham Palace and Clarence House must have buzzed more urgently as Charles cheerfully continued to cattle-prod the more sensitive parts of the Establishment.

18

1984 . . . and though there might have been a touch of Orwell around at the time, the Queen Mother sailed on in her own serenely olde worlde style. There had been a minor panic at Buckingham Palace when a fishbone stuck in her throat requiring surgery under general anaesthetic. 'For a split second a whole choked nation held the breath for which the Queen Mum was fighting . . .' (*Daily Express*) summed up the media prose of the day. In March she unveiled a memorial stone to her old friend, the late Sir Noel Coward, in Westminster Abbey. It was her kind of occasion. She smiled approvingly as Sir Richard Attenborough paid tribute to 'a playwright, actor, composer, lyricist, cabaret artist, author, painter, director, screenwriter, essayist, novelist, diarist, journalist, producer and impresario.' But when they played those nostalgic melodies, 'Someday I'll Find You', 'I'll See You Again' and 'London Pride' tears came. Memories of happy years with Bertie. Outside the Abbey she would probably have sung the choruses. Apart from the fishbone incident the Queen Mother was in great shape for a woman in her eighty-fifth year. She had gone into the King Edward VII Hospital for Officers for a three-day check and emerged beaming at the doctors' advice, 'Carry On Ma'am'. Which was just as well with twenty-two official engagements already pencilled in for the autumn.

The last lingering bitterness in her life appeared to be fading with the now semi-comatose Duchess of Windsor in Paris. The Queen Mother had sent a conciliatory message. But on a short visit to England – to check on her eventual burial place alongside the late Duke – the Duchess appeared not to have made any reciprocal gestures. But in the early months of 1986 it no longer mattered. Senile, and suffering from acute arteriosclerosis, she died on 24 April. Apart from the auction of her jewellery, all controversy concerning the Duchess of Windsor seemed to have been buried at last. Certainly the Queen Mother had kept a stern silence on all questions relating to the Abdication. When Ludovic Kennedy went to Clarence House to discuss a television film on the life of the Queen Mother, she told him firmly that it must on no account touch on the Abdication. He replied that to ignore that episode was akin to talking about the Second World War without mentioning Churchill. Her Majesty charmingly dug her high heels in: no reference to the Abdication. The project was abandoned. But any notion the Queen Mother may have had that the Feud had ended with the Duchess's death was blown apart by an extraordinary article in the June 1986 edition of the American magazine, *Vanity Fair*.

It was written by one of Wallis's closest friends, the attractive socialite Aline, Countess Romanones. It followed a visit to the Windsor's home on the Bois de Boulogne in Paris shortly after the Duke died. The reported conversation between the Countess and the Duchess revealed the extent of Wallis's obsessive hatred, and not merely of the Queen Mother. Describing the Queen's brief call on her dying uncle in Paris, the Duchess, according to Countess Romanones, commented: 'She was not at all warm to his wife of thirty-five years. But then I shouldn't complain. She was just as cold to him. Her expression was hard when she entered the room.' The words were in character. But I doubt their inference. It is difficult to imagine the Queen – or anyone else – having anything but pity for this frail, dying man. The Duchess switched her attack to the Duke of Edinburgh who, she implied, was no kinder than the others. 'Not he, or anyone else, offered me any solicitude or sympathy whatsoever.' The Duchess unsheathed her claws for the Queen Mother: 'We called her "Cookie" because she looked like a pudding dolled up. My dear! How she was dressed! It looked as if she had just opened some old trunk and pulled out a few rags and draped them on herself. And that eternal bag hanging on her arm.' It was a sour echo of an episode which the Queen Mother had hoped was dead and buried. Its resurrection in bitchy 'girls' talk' was hardly worth answering. The Queen Mother probably decided it was bad enough to be forgiven.

Hating controversy, she was equally concerned when a proposed trip on Concorde was attacked in the House of Commons by the Labour MEP, Bob Cryer. Ignoring the fact that British Airways had offered the trip to the Queen Mother as an eighty-fifth birthday gift, the MP railed: 'The cost of this exercise must run into several thousand pounds. Both the Concorde and the Royal Yacht *Britannia* provided at the taxpayers' expense, could well be extended to a wider range of pensioners so that they too could enjoy the benefits of the taxpayers' investment.' The House yawned, deciding perhaps that hard-up pensioners were not exactly clamouring to go supersonic. Tory MP Anthony Beaumont-Dark hit back, 'If he [Cryer] lives as long as the Queen Mother and does 10 per cent as much to help this country I will be the first to praise him. But I think it highly unlikely.'

The eighty-five-year-old great-grandmother flew through the sound barrier and decided it was the only way to travel. Everything about her, her brisk, head-up stride, the extraordinary ability to go on for hours, seemed indestructible. But now and again there is a hint that the Queen Mother isn't as fit as she claims. When Councillor William Payne, then Mayor of Southwark, told her he was an arthritic she confided that she too suffered severe pain because of arthritis in her right hand. She mentioned it out of sympathy for him. But she would rather no one knew about it or about her bouts of intense sadness which she once described as being 'engulfed by great black clouds of unhappiness and misery'. These centred on her painfully premature widowhood, which her lady-in-waiting at the time said, 'knocked her sideways'. This isolating grief dismayed the Queen, and also her friend Winston Churchill. Uninvited, he flew up to Balmoral and persuaded her that there was a life after Bertie and that the country needed her. She was grateful to him but the pain persisted. Friends suggested at the time that she might derive some comfort from spiritualism. (This was nothing new to royalty. Queen Victoria was said to have kept contact with her dear departed Albert through her ghillie, John Brown, who doubled as an amateur medium. According to Gordon Adam, son-in-law to the famous spiritualist Lillian Bailey, all records of sittings were ordered to be destroyed.)

Lillian Bailey's credits were impressive. Her clientele included several public figures. The Queen Mother, then clutching at straws, decided to seek her help. Arrangements for the sessions were understandably clandestine. Her personal life had always been a closed book. Spiritualism was bound to be its most closely guarded chapter. The phone call to Lillian Bailey apparently came as a total surprise. She was requested to go to an address in Kensington. There, so the record shows, she was blindfolded and taken to another house. When the blindfold was removed she looked around and saw the Queen Mother, the Queen, Princess Alexandra, the Duchess of Kent and Prince Philip. A fly on the wall could have dined out on the occasion, Philip's expression during the proceedings being well worth a second glance. This session was followed by several private ones with the Queen Mother alone. They clearly helped. Much of the Queen Mother's serenity of mind returned. Now and again, the Queen Mother makes a sentimental journey to the woods around St Paul's Walden Bury to the spot where the late George VI proposed. And no doubt she smiles at the memory. She had kept the pleading Duke on the end of a string for far too long before she finally, in those woods, put him out of his misery.

It is highly unlikely that the Queen Mother these days is 'engulfed by great black clouds of unhappiness and misery'. She is a contented eighty-nine year old, happy with her work, her horses, and the occasional fun-and-games at seasonal parties. But the Queen Mother's most effective anti-depressant is her grandson Prince Charles supported by an army of subsidiary siblings and their broods yammering to catch grannie's eye. But as recent events have demonstrated, that tranquillity, like the best soap operas, is fairly regularly shattered.

In the spring of 1987 the Queen Mother's pristine public image received an uncomfortable jolt. Two Bowes-Lyon nieces few had ever heard of, were suddenly thrust into the limelight. Until then, little if anything had been known about Katherine and Nerissa Bowes-Lyon. They were handicapped and in a mental hospital. For reasons never fully explained, both nieces had been listed in *Burke's Peerage* as having died, Nerissa in 1940 and Katherine in 1961. In fact, Nerissa died four years ago. Katherine, now sixty-three, remains in the Royal Earlswood Hospital, Redhill, Surrey, and has been there for nearly fifty years. The Queen Mother had never concealed the fact that there were skeletons in the Bowes-Lyon cupboard. But the emergence of two 'forgotten nieces' both incarcerated in a mental hospital, one to be buried in a plain grave, was clearly an embarrassment to her. Headlines like 'Skeleton in Royal Cupboard' could not have made comfortable reading in the Clarence House drawing room. It was their mother, Fenella Bowes-Lyon, who unaccountably reported the two sisters as dead in

1962. There were dark hints that the early indication of the two unfortunate children's mental problems so embarrassed the family, details of their birth were muffled before they were quietly admitted to the hospital.

Fenella was the wife of the Queen Mother's brother, John Herbert Bowes-Lyon who died in 1930. Nerissa and Katherine were their third and fifth daughters. As children, they attended, for two years, a special school in Hemel Hempstead, Hertfordshire. There they received regular visits from members of the Bowes-Lyon family including the Queen Mother. But some time during the Second World War they were committed. For years the Queen Mother and other relatives thought the nieces had died. Lord Litchfield, a nephew of the two stricken sisters thought so too, and reportedly gave that as his reason for not mentioning them in his autobiography. That belief persisted until 1982. It was then that the League of Friends at the Royal Earlswood Hospital discovered that the two women they were buying Christmas and birthday presents for, had relatives while other patients had none. The fact that those relatives included the Queen Mother made the good-hearted women of the League wonder if Her Majesty knew of the existence of her nieces; and whether, under the circumstances, it was entirely appropriate for them to receive charitable gifts in this way. They wrote in those terms to the Queen Mother and received an immediate and generous response from Clarence House. It was obvious, most convincingly to the League, that the Queen Mother hadn't the slightest notion then that her two nieces were alive. No bulletins are issued when members of the Royal Family go mildly into shock, but it is a safe guess that the Queen Mother must have been considerably shaken. 'Almost by return,' declared Mrs Maude Steuart, vice-chairman of the hospital's League of Friends, 'we received a cheque to buy presents with a promise that if we needed anything more we were to let her know. The money was ample. The patients had a mental age of three or four. They were not mentally capable. They certainly had no idea they were related to the Royal Family.'

There was one final, perhaps conscience-stricken gesture. Nerissa's grave at Redhill Cemetery, Surrey, pitiably identified with plastic tags, 'M11125 . . . Bowes-Lyon' received a suitably engraved headstone. But the Bowes-Lyon cupboard could not yet be closed. Three more fringe relatives – cousins of the two sisters – were revealed as having been admitted to the same hospital. All three were as well cared for as the others and equally unaware of their tenuous relationship to royalty. But this proliferation of case histories induced a reaction in at least one member of Mencap, the society for the mentally handicapped. Mr George Parker, a non-voting member of the society whose patron is the Queen Mother moved to have Her Majesty replaced, citing the case of the two nieces. The suggestion was instantly, and angrily, thrown out. An incorrect entry in *Burke's Peerage* was scarcely an excuse for depriving Mencap and the many for whom it cares, of its most effective fund-raiser. If the Queen Mother was offended by the move to have her replaced, she showed no sign of it. Her tactics are to ride out all storms, batten down the hatches and send out no distress signals. That strategy applies most forcibly when royal marriages strike a reef as in the case of the marriage of Princess Anne and Mark Phillips. How long, she and the Queen must have wondered, before that relationship splintered apart.

19

It would be highly beneficial to the shelf life of the monarchy if the Queen Mother would live to see this century out, to become the first one-hundred-year-old British royal. This would realize one of Her Majesty's livelier ambitions, to receive that congratulatory telegram from the Queen – or Charles as the case may be. But there is a more crucial advantage in having the Queen Mother around for just as long as she can walk, smile and wave. The monarchy needs her. She is more than just a power behind the Throne. She is a trusted model to up-and-coming royals, and a useful stabilizer when members of the family occasionally drift into rough seas. She is also the heartbeat of an ageing institution which until recently was treated like the family silver, to be brought out only on special occasions. The situation has changed, Charles and the Princess Royal spearheading a not insignificant Palace revolution. Nevertheless, the fact that the Royal Family has stayed all of a piece owes much to the Queen Mother. Like the sweeping beam of Eddystone Lighthouse, she signals safety and security, warning racier craft like Diana and Fergie, not to sail too close to the wind. Over recent years she has watched the Royal Family's attempt to appear more human, a subtle campaign aimed at showing that real people, not plummy-voiced stereotypes, exist in their several palaces around the capital. Prince Charles, who needed no encouragement, has given interviews, albeit hand-picked, with no visible damage to him, or the Crown. Informal pictures of the Queen letting her guard if not her hair down, have been shown on TV without the viewers feeling they've been peeping through the keyhole. Even the Palace press officers, normally as tight-lipped as the KGB, now practise upper-class *glasnost*

(which effectively, means they are far more open about nothing in particular).

The Queen Mother, had she been asked, might have quietly warned the Palace gurus that a love-affair with the media is one thing; attempting to seduce it is another. After all, royalty can hardly show its 'human face' while the tabloids focus on Fergie's rear. From the day Prince Philip urged industrialists to 'pull their fingers out' the royal family has moved away from the platitude business. That arid 'My husband and I' syndrome has been lampooned into oblivion, with Anne's 'Naff Off!' becoming an acceptable royal expletive under duress. (Acceptable, that is, to everyone except the sweetly uncompromising great-grannie at Clarence House.) This outburst against crass intrusions by pressmen revealed Princess Anne as the least manageable thoroughbred in the royal stable. She had, in fact, been kicking against the doors for years. Born into a similar, second-string situation to Charles as Margaret had been to the Queen, Anne grew up determined – in today's jargon – 'to buck the system'. Unlike Charles, virtually sentenced without the option, she could distance herself from it, and did so with a vengeance. With or without the Queen's approval – we will never know – she made a unilateral declaration of independence. Watching her at Charles's investiture as Prince of Wales, she seemed remote. She would say later: 'I have always accepted being second in everything from quite an early age. You start off life at the back of the line; you don't think anybody's paying much attention to you; then much later that public attention is on you too.' Charles can take it or leave it. Diana, dressed by the best, luxuriates in it. The chirpy Duchess of York, the Sloane Rangers' Patron Saint, devours it. (The media currently update Fergie's hip measurements as regularly as the Dow Jones average.)

But Princess Anne loathes the soap-opera side of royalty with a passion.

Moody, independent and outspoken in her early adult years, she won no medals for charm. Her sullen expression, which frowned its way into newspapers around the world, was not restricted to jumping events. She became – for a time – the princess the media were delighted to hate. Courtship and then marriage to Captain Mark Phillips somewhat softened her image. She made an arresting bride. With a little ingenuity by a French make-up artist, her oval, Modigliani-style features looked almost paintable. It seemed like a promising match too.

The Queen Mother liked Mark Phillips, though in her canon, anybody who rides horses over jumps receives automatic endorsement. It was the Queen Mother who observed that if their particulars had been separately run through a computer dating service they would have been selected as an ideal pairing. Mark's father, Peter William Garside Phillips MC, had been in mining and farming, before becoming a purchasing director for Walls. The fact that a princess was marrying the son of a man with his eye on the quality of sausages, was a refreshing contrast from the usual monarchical matchmaking. It was certainly in line with Anne's pleb's-eye view of life. Asked by the *Observer*'s Kenneth Harris in 1980 which commoner she would most like to change places with, there was no hesitation. 'A long-distance lorry driver,' she said. (An analyst might read into that choice an unconscious yearning to escape into hard-driven anonymity, four-letter words and chips with everything.)

Mark Phillips had no preferred incarnation. He loved horses and the Army, period. That life-style would have to remain untouched whatever happened. He would take no title which was in line with Anne's determination that any children they might have should be brought up as commoners. Peter was born in November 1977, Zara in May 1981. (The Queen Mother's frilly-pink attitude to maternity must have been jolted by Anne's heavily quoted comment, 'Pregnancy is a bore. It is the occupational hazard of being a wife.') However, bore or not, there were two more grandchildren for the Queen and Prince Philip; another two great-grandchildren for the Queen Mother; but no noticeable bliss in the lives of Anne and Mark. It was becoming ominously clear that they had a greater passion for horses than they had for each other. There were long and significant separations. In recent years they had been apart for six months or more. On their fifteenth wedding anniversary Anne was at Windsor, Captain Phillips 17,000 miles away in Australia. There were inevitable rumours which finally exploded into stories of stolen letters which were said to have been written to Anne by Commander Tim Laurence, the Queen's former equerry. There was no point in the Queen or the Queen Mother playing honest broker between the two. The marriage was over, bar the cold deliberations by lawyers and accountants. The terse official announcement might have been penned with embalming fluid. 'Her Royal Highness the Princess Royal and Captain Mark Phillips have decided to separate on terms agreed between them. There are no plans for divorce proceedings.'

The cool announcement perfectly reflected the rigor mortis in the marriage. Mark who had parlayed his riding skill into lucrative commercial tie-ups barely paused in mid-gallop. While if Anne, now Princess Royal, shed any tears, they were for the thousands of sick and starving infants she saw in the gruelling mileage she has covered on behalf of the Save the Children Fund. Its Honorary President since 1970 she has helped heft its funds from three to more than fifty million pounds. Commuting between London and Africa, she has bunked down in tents and camel-dung huts with field workers who began to see this royal patron in an entirely different perspective. In headscarf, open-necked shirt and safari boots, Anne proved that royal connections counted for nothing unless there was an obvious commitment behind the extended handshake. She was genuinely moved by what she saw. It was once fashionable for troubled celebrities like the Beatles to seek meaning to their lives from some Himalayan sage, returning just as confused as when they left. Princess Anne sought no high-priced mystic to discover her role in life. She found it among the starving in the drought-ridden wastelands of the Third World. Taking her cue from Prince Charles, instead of fighting it she exploited her royal status and hereditary privilege for all it was worth – to others. All the major international agencies in the famine areas have considerable admiration for this no-nonsense princess. While she toiled with associates dreaming up schemes to squeeze out more money for the Save the Children Fund, her not-so-fragile sister-in-law Diana was shaking hands with lepers in Indonesia. Some cynics had a field day, scorning the gesture as a piece of royal tokenism. They had reacted in the same way when she pointedly clasped hands with Aids victims. They somehow couldn't square this stoic display with her coy, but misleading, fashion-plate image. She will surprise them yet. The directors of the Leper Hospital had no doubts at all about the value of that much-publicized royal handshake. They declared publicly that Diana, precisely because she was the princess and a future Queen, had in one spontaneous gesture done much to dispel the instinctive terror of contact with lepers.

Back home at Buckingham Palace and Clarence House, the two old campaigners in the royalty business, smiled their approval. The Queen must have been delighted by the caring and responsive image this new generation of royals were presenting. But neither she, nor the Queen Mother were prepared for the headlines on Sunday, 12 November, when the good young Duke of York threw his coronet into the ring too. 'Andrew's Pay Up Shock,' bellowed the *Mail on Sunday*; with the sub-heading, 'Prince joins fight over "unjust" pensions for the war widows.' This intervention ('defying the Royal vow of silence', the paper noted) was over the disparity between the pensions received by war widows whose husbands died before 1973 (a minimum of £2,946) and those widowed after 1973 (at least £6,491). Andrew, a Falklands veteran, launching the 1989 Poppy Appeal, used the occasion to confront Social Security Under-Secretary Lord Henley. He called the discrepancy in the pensions unjust. His sharp comments, as intended, reverberated along Whitehall and into Downing Street. The message was loud and clear; another 'royal' was determined to be seen *and* heard. His intervention, backed by all-party pressure in Parliament, finally forced a £40-a-week increase for the hard-pressed widows.

1989, then, was the year that the heirs to the Throne stepped out of their Constitutional captivity and marched to the barricades: Charles on social divisions and the global ecology; Anne on Third World deprivation; Diana on the victims of ostracizing illnesses; the Duke of York on the treatment of war widows. Clearly, royalty's solemn vow of silence on political matters was visibly falling apart. What this signals surely, is that Charles will never be a back-seat monarch. He will not be, as Willie Hamilton MP sarcastically commented, 'A fresh young monarch to go soft over. Just a multi-millionaire with a middle-aged spread.' On the contrary. He will exercise his Constitutional 'right to know' making life tiresome if not hell for whoever may be at Number 10 Downing Street at the time. He will, if he has his way, disprove this accusation by Edgar Wilson in *The Myth of the Monarchy* that '. . . the monarchy does not help to solve any of the more serious problems of our society.' If that were true, Charles will have to be dragged shrieking to the Throne. Apart from Philip and the Queen, who have encouraged him unstintingly, Charles identifies the late Earl Mountbatten and the Queen Mother as the two most significant influences in his life.

Charles will certainly remember as a much younger prince, the note of caution from his late great-uncle about Edward VIII:

'Remember the other Prince of Wales. Don't think that because you have become some kind of pop idol of royalty the public will always support you. They will only do so as long as you do your duty.' The Queen Mother concerned herself with less solemn advice. With her sound Scottish common sense, she taught him how to handle emotional problems. The tutoring came easily to her. She would have loved to have had a son. Denied that, Charles was a more than adequate substitute. Helping him and Diana to come to terms with the fact that their private lives had been sunk without trace, was crucial. She understands his frustration, trying to contain a bursting social conscience inside the royal restraint. Like Princess Anne, Charles finds the millstone of hereditary privilege too heavy for comfort. He does not find it easy, as the son of the richest woman in the world, to enjoy life while half a mile away from the Palace, derelicts and the young homeless sleep in cardboard boxes. 'If anything, he cares too much,' mused one of his friends. 'He is probably a much better royal than the nation deserves.'

Precisely what Britain deserves may be hard to define, particularly now, with royalty more centre-stage than ever before. Is it a luxury item way past its sell-by date – or is there still a strong argument for another thousand years of British royalty? To the late Earl Mountbatten at least, the question did not arise. His case for the Monarchy and his particular references to the Queen Mother and the Queen are unique in their candour. Rarely has one member of the royal family spoken so intimately about another. Affectionate and partial of course. But Mountbatten's sincerity discounts any notion of special pleading. 'What I think about the Queen is simply this: I've known her since she was a small child; I've watched her grow up. I've never known her say an unkind or unpleasant thing. When she criticizes she does it justly. I've never known her to be deflected from her one ideal, which is the country and the family. She is extremely intelligent without being a blue-stocking. On the death of the King she was very hard-pressed and overworked from the outset. Endless audiences, endless appearances, particularly at the beginning of her reign. Prince Philip was determined to keep out of it. He wasn't going to be thought to be putting his finger in the pie.

'In my view, the Queen, over the years, has become by far the most competent and professional head of state in the world. What does that mean? It means reading carefully all the cabinet papers, not just those she has to approve. It means reading all the telegrams that come in from all over the world. She has to keep right up to date. Newspapers? She reads the bloody lot! She has a table with every paper on it you can think of. When any member of the family talks about a story the Queen always seems to have read it. She knows as much as the Prime Minister of the day about what is going on in the world.

'But she has this great advantage. Instead of being burdened with a party political outlook on how to handle things, she thinks for the nation and gives the answer for Britain. She enjoyed dealing with Harold Wilson. She likes Jim Callaghan very much. Of course she has had many Prime Ministers to deal with. It is absolutely certain – and I can testify to this – that she is as sociable, friendly and delighted to deal with Labour ministers as she is with Conservative ministers. They go for walks. She talks with them about everything under the sun. She probes. She questions. She wants to know! Believe me, she is committed entirely to the British people. And that is the way she is perceived abroad. I know this as I have been on a number of state visits with her.

'People criticize the expense of the Royal Yacht *Britannia*. But the British have always had a Royal yacht manned by the navy. They get more sea experience in fact than any of the other officers in the regular service. The Queen arrives, no matter where it is, and brings not just a ship but part of the Court of St James, part of Buckingham Palace with her. She comes in, this beautiful ship with its escort, and thousands of little yachts, and it is a tremendous and majestic way of arriving. The world leaders she invites on board, never, never forget it. The Queen is not a good sailor. She is occasionally seasick. So she would never travel on the royal yacht for pleasure. To her it is a duty like everything else.'

Lord Mountbatten then switched tack. 'The strength of the Monarchy,' he insisted, 'is in its total separation from executive power. And as such it is completely honourable and incorruptible. Watergate,' he suggested, 'could never have happened in Britain. Nobody in America was fully aware of it at the time in America because Richard Nixon was both Head of State and the Chief Executive. But the Queen, as a kind of watchdog for the British people, could have asked, would have demanded to know, "what is going on?"

'Now let us look at her family life. It is really quite simple: she dotes on Philip and he is obviously very fond of her. There is no competition between them. Two people, a husband and wife, doing their own work. Now what is their relationship like? It is absolutely marvellous. She has never looked at another man nor he at another woman. But there is no question about it – he is the boss in his own house. There is absolutely no argument about that. He runs the estates at Balmoral and Sandringham. They might occasionally argue the toss like any other couple. But he is the head of the family domestically. And that is the secret of the success of it. They have their time together like any other happy family.

'Now look at the Queen's life. It is very frugal and simple. She shares her mother's cautious rejection of needless extravagance. The royal style is usually one of largesse. But the Queen has inherited from the Queen Mother a respect for thrift. She likes dressing very, very simply. Boots and breeches or tweeds, and light cotton dresses. When people say that she is dressed in dowdy clothes and old style, that is good. Why should she go around looking like Marlene Dietrich? She eats almost nothing. I never know how she maintains her strength.'

'Does she *enjoy* being Queen?' Mountbatten pondered the question and laughed. 'That is an interesting one. Would you ask God if he enjoyed being God? Look, there are many things she finds tiring, tiresome and boring. There are many things she finds exciting and thrilling. I don't think she ever considers it. She is, in a sense, stuck with it. The least-known aspect of the Queen is her athletic achievements. She is one of the finest riders I have ever met. She is absolutely marvellous on a horse. She looks beautiful. Although I can say she is fearless, I think she might sometimes be just as afraid as anybody else at times, but she never shows it and the horse never senses it. If she had not been the Queen, just Lady Elizabeth Bowes-Lyon for example, and had gone into riding she would have been every bit as good, perhaps even better, than Princess Anne. She is first class at improving a horse that is difficult.' Reflecting further, Mountbatten's voice softened, repeating an earlier comment, 'pure gold right through.'

The Queen Mother, of course, totally identifies with the Mountbatten thesis on the importance of the Monarchy. Only the very few have any notion of where she stands politically. I asked three former Prime Ministers, the Lords Home, Callaghan, and Wilson for clues beyond the standard, 'wise counsel and great source of strength to the monarchy'. All three smiled knowing smiles, drew up the drawbridge and changed the subject. I doubt if she holds strong political views. But as with Prince Charles, injustice sometimes touches a nerve. When residents of York's Brackenhill Home for the Elderly were threatened with eviction she inquired politely what their future plans were for the building. And won a reprieve. She personally intervened when a gravel-digging firm submitted a planning application to dig 1.65 million tons of gravel at the famous Burnham Beeches, Buckinghamshire. In March last year, she moved behind the scenes to help save the British Theatre Association Library. Admittedly none of these gestures by the Queen Mother were particularly momentous. But she did the best she could given that protocol ties one hand behind her back. All letters written in genuine anguish, such as a complaint against a stiff-necked local authority, or a glaring case of injustice involving pensioners and old soldiers, are shown to her and usually result in a courteous inquiry, on Clarence House notepaper, of the relevant department. These gentle approaches have at least as much clout as an MP's question in the House.

The Queen, as the Sovereign, has less room for manoeuvre. Her political impartiality is chiselled in the concrete of the Constitution. But she has no objection to Charles acting, in a sense, as her surrogate conscience. Both he and Diana have acquired the Queen Mother's flair for personalizing the ritual walkabout; the ability to fix on one pair of eyes in the crowd instead of looking absently over heads at nowhere in particular. All the princesses and duchesses currently on the Palace rota still watch the Queen Mother in action and envy the sure touch, the control, behind the most disarming smile in the dynasty. They marvel at her energy, and the way she whirls here and there by helicopter as casually as others whistle up a taxi. When a Wessex she was flying in had to make an emergency landing, the RAF officer's concern for his eighty-nine-year-old royal passenger was met with a chirping, 'never mind, it's a nice day for it'. Likewise the waiter at a Mansion House banquet who dropped a sardine in her lap. 'I promise not to say anything,' whispered Her Majesty to the terrified servant, 'only if you will bring me another one.' Typical, I would guess, of the kind of person who signs her letters 'Yours affec' and never missed an episode of *Steptoe and Son*.

It is no minor art for the people who wear crowns, putting the less privileged at their ease. A guest arriving nearly half an hour late for a private dinner to the Queen Mother had his trembling apology interrupted with, 'Don't worry. At last I've been able to watch the whole of *Dad's Army* before dinner.' And if Charles insists that his grandmother is strong on wit as well as wisdom, the following may confirm it. Scene: lunch for two in the library of Clarence House. 'I wonder,' the Queen asked her mother, 'if I might have a glass of wine?' 'Is that wise?' Her Majesty inquired solemnly of her daughter. 'You know you have to reign all afternoon.'

This pixilated humour springs from her totally sanguine view of life – and death. She knows that the BBC and ITV have worked out plans for the day she dies, ITN's secret project being code-named Open Ender. The BBC would not discuss its own plans, explaining primly, 'it might be considered bad taste to discuss it'. Well yes. But Ma'am knows all about it, having taken a lively interest in the event from the day troops held a secret dawn rehearsal on the London streets. Always the perfectionist, she has scrutinized the plans for her funeral with the same interest she shows for her engagements of the day. She has even earmarked the kind of candles she'd like used. Always flawlessly alive, she wants her Lying-in-State to be just as impeccable. And beautiful. The late Cecil Beaton would have brought just the right touch.

But as of March 1990, the Queen Mother was far more concerned with life than with death. There was too much to do and in any event, she was only eighty-nine. Earlier, when most great-grandmothers would settle for a high-backed chair, a footstool and their memories, this irrepressible Dowager Queen was careening over distant landscapes: Northern Ireland, Italy, France, Canada, West Germany, Berlin to visit the British Military Hospital, Belgium for a reprise of the Battle of Waterloo; then back again for the tour of duty at home. Well, say some, she doesn't have to do it. Perhaps not. But she does not go to these places uninvited. The Irish Guards expect their Colonel-in-Chief to put in an appearance on St Patrick's day. She felt she owed a similar duty to the Black Watch in Montreal at their 125th anniversary. Anyway the Canadians love her and she likes going there. And as it happens, the Black Watch is the Bowes-Lyon regiment, as their Roll of Honour shows.

Nobody nudging her ninetieth birthday, would undertake all this either without a pistol to her head or a stubborn belief that she must continue to earn her keep. That still begs the question:

where does she get her energy? To one of her friends, the secret is: 'Willpower. She simply will not admit she is old.' To Michael Oswald, her friend as well as racing guru, the secret lies in her attitude of mind. 'To start with, she surrounds herself with people of all generations, from teenagers to people in their eighties. In that sense, she is ageless. Fundamentally she likes people, and if you like the human race as she does, it's an easy, downhill run all the way. If she has a weakness at all it is for rascals. She doesn't mind rogues at all, as long as they're amusing. But essentially it is her attitude to life which makes her so remarkable. She has a simple rule: you must not dwell on or discuss old age, retirement, or death. Obviously these things happen. She hopes that you will get better, and is sorry if you don't and drop off the perch. But she never makes a fuss when she has a knock or a sore throat and expects others to be the same.' (The Queen Mother's belief in homoeopathic medicine is total. If she suffers an occasional bruise, she relies on Arnica ointment derived from the yellow flowers of a semi-arctic plant. It doesn't bother her at all to hear it is also used on her horses.) Michael Oswald thought it significant that the Queen Mother never uses a walking stick, refusing to have one on the basis that if you haven't got one you can't use it. 'Nobody in her entourage,' he said, 'ever really retires. They may actually stop functioning officially, but somewhere she sees to it that they are not lost in the shuffle. As for the Queen Mother she is determined to go on and on. If it is her ambition to reach a hundred I see no reason at all why she shouldn't make it.'

But ninety years is good to be going on with. As she sits in her private sitting room at Clarence House, she is entitled to feel a sense of 'mission accomplished'. The 'family business' as she calls it, has survived a formidable number of image-fracturing blips of which Major Ronald Ferguson's reported peccadilloes were the most spectacular. By contrast, her daughter, Queen for thirty-seven years, hasn't stumbled at a single fence. The Duke of Edinburgh, doing good deeds while cracking bad jokes, has sired some fine heirs and remains master of his house. Princess Margaret, once the Royal Family's *enfant terrible*, has settled for a more muted life as a royal maverick. Sixty in August, she has outgrown her predilection for odd-balls and old-Etonian pranksters, sadly reconciled, perhaps, to a life alone. Apart from the glass of whisky and the defiant cigarette at the end of a slim holder, there is none of the old wilfulness and danger which made her royalty's fatal attraction of the sixties. Today, living in no particular discomfort at Kensington Palace, she is an energetic and dedicated fund-raiser on behalf of the NSPCC, the Sunshine Home for Blind Babies and several other organizations concerned with the problems of child abuse and deprivation. She may have been unfortunate as the 'second child' in the royal line up; badly treated in the Townsend Affair, and unlucky in her subsequent marriage. But her mother, her sister the Queen, and the children are abundant compensation. Her affection for them is evident in the densely populated photo-display on her baby-grand piano. Princess Anne, despite the breakdown of her marriage, has helped Africa's starving, giving royal patronage an infinitely more human dimension. Diana touched the 'untouchable' in the Far East; Andrew pleaded for war widows back home.

Meanwhile, Fergie has chortled competently on to the royal merry-go-round, pausing only for breath and pregnancy. If occasionally she indulges in a quip too far, a glance into those cool blue eyes at Clarence House provides an instant corrective. And now Prince Edward shows encouraging signs of an independent mind behind the milk-fed image. All in all, the Queen Mother is entitled to look back over her life with some pride and few regrets. She could claim – even if others dissent – that the Royal Family is giving value for money. The argument that the Monarchy is an expensive anachronism in this modern age, will not go away. But in the end, it is the way that royalty is perceived that matters. It does not exist for the benefit of television and newspapers, though the tabloids have found the Royal Family a 'nice little earner' over the years. Whenever circulation sags, intimate tales about selected members of the Royal Family are a guaranteed sales booster.

The critics of the monarchy assert that it perpetuates class division. But this division depended upon myths which have largely been blown away. The Queen may cause backs to stiffen a bit, but the rest of the royal family inspire more fun than awe. All that royalty perpetuates is itself. The cynics may sneer at Princess Diana's bedside compassion in hospitals at home and abroad. But the Indonesian lepers and the Aids victims in England must have felt a shade less isolated at having this royal comforter clasp their hands. When the Princess Royal rails against incompetence costing African babies their lives, she is more than just a visiting 'royal'. True there has been an inevitable change of style. The old ritual tokenism of 'gracing an occasion' simply by being there, is increasingly short on magic. The new young royals recognize that the 'Ooh-Ah!' syndrome alone will not guarantee the monarchy an easy ride into the twenty-first century. They have added a social conscience to the regalia of modern royalty and look all the better for it. The muscle comes from Buckingham Palace; the heartbeat from Clarence House.

Once, when the Queen was being driven to some State ceremony, a friend overheard a woman in the crowd mutter to her Cockney companion. 'Richest woman in the world!'

'Well I don't envy her nothing,' snorted the other. 'Except . . .' she paused, 'her mum.'

'Work,' the Queen Mother said many years ago, 'is the price you pay for the place you occupy on earth.' As she flies to some far-flung Army base; stands for an excruciating hour or two at a fund-raising ceremony; writes a sympathetic letter to a suffering war widow, or quietly gives grandmotherly advice to the man who will be King, the Queen Mother continues to pay her dues. And has done so, good humouredly and with unerring grace for more than sixty years. She has forced Time, and official historians, to kick their heels while she blithely flitters on and on, willing herself into the year 2000 and beyond. History will judge her generously. For by any fair criteria, she is the lady of the century. And a mighty hard act to follow.

London, March 1990.

Bibliography

Airlie, Mabell, Countess of, *Thatched with Gold*, 1962
Asquith, Lady Cynthia, *Diaries 1915–18* London, 1968
Beaton, Cecil, *Self Portrait with Friends, Selected Diaries*, London, 1979
Birmingham, Stephen, *Duchess*, London, 1981
Boothroyd, Basil, *Philip*, London, 1971
Byran, J. and Murphy, Charles C. V., *The Windsor Story*, London, 1979
Cameron, James, *The Best of Cameron*, London, 1981
Campbell, Judith, *Royal Horses*, 1983
Castellani, Aldo, *Microbes, Men and Monarchs*, London, 1963
Cathcart, Helen, *The Queen Mother Herself*, London, 1979
Channon, Sir Henry, *Diaries*, edited by Robert Rhodes James, London, 1967
Churchill, Winston S., *The Gathering Storm*, London, 1948
Cooper, Diana, *The Light of Common Day*, London, 1959
Crawford, Marion, *The Little Princesses*, London, 1950, New York, 1950
Clynes, J. R., *Memoirs*, London, 1937
Davison, J. C. G., *Memoirs and Papers 1910–37*, edited by Robert Rhodes James, London, 1969
Day, James Wentworth, *The Queen Mother's Family Story*, London, 1967
Dempster, Nigel, *Princess Margaret*, London, 1981
Donaldson, Frances, *Edward VIII*, London, 1974; *King George VI and Queen Elizabeth*, London, 1977
Duncan, Andrew, *The Reality of the Monarchy*
Edwards, Ann, *Matriarch*, London, 1984
Frischauer, Willi, *Margaret: Princess Without a Cause*, London, 1977

Gilbert, Martin, *Finest Hour: Winston Churchill, 1939–41*, London, 1983

Glendinning, Victoria, *Edith Sitwell: A Unicorn Among Lions*, Oxford, 1983

Hardinge, Helen, *Loyal to Three Kings*, London, 1967

Holden, Anthony, *Charles, Prince of Wales*, London, 1979

Johnston, Sir Eric, St, *One Policeman's Story*, London, 1978

Judd, Dennis, *King George VI*, London, 1982

Junor, Penny, *Charles*, London, 1987

Lacey, Robert, *Majesty*, London, 1977

Laird, Dorothy, *Queen Elizabeth the Queen Mother*, London, 1966

Lockhart, Sir Robert Bruce, *Diaries*, London, 1973

Longford, Elizabeth, *The Queen Mother*, London, 1981

Middlemas, Keith and Barnes, John, *Baldwin: A Biography*, London, 1969

Morrow, Ann, *The Queen Mother*, London, 1984

Nicolson, Harold, *Diaries and Letters, 1930–39*, London, 1967

Parker, John, *The Princess Royal*, London, 1989

Pope-Hennessy, James, *Queen Mary*, London, 1959

Roosevelt, Eleanor, *Autobiography*, New York, 1961

Rose, Kenneth, *King George V*, London, 1983

Secrest, Meryle, *Kenneth Clark*, London, 1984

Sencourt, Robert, *The Reign of Edward VIII*, London, 1962

Sitwell, Osbert, *Queen Mary and Others*, London, 1974

Stuart, James, Viscount Stuart of Findhorn, *Within the Fringe*, London, 1967

Talbot, Godfrey, *Country Life Book of Queen Elizabeth the Queen Mother*, London, 1978

Taylor, A. J. P., *English History 1914–45*, London, 1965

Thornton, Michael, *Royal Feud*, London, 1985

Townsend, Peter, *Time and Chance*, London, 1978

Vanderbilt, Gloria and Furness, Thelma, *Double Exposure*, London, 1959

West, Rebecca, *1900*, London, 1982

Wheeler-Bennett, Sir John, *King George VI*, London, 1958

Windsor, The Duchess of, *The Heart Has Its Reasons*, London, 1956

Ziegler, Philip, *Mountbatten*, London

Index